ENTREPRENEURIAL ALLIANCES

ENTREPRENEURIAL ALLIANCES

Jeffrey J. Reuer

Krannert School of Management
Purdue University

Africa Ariño

IESE Business School
University of Navarra

Paul M. Olk

Daniels College of Business
University of Denver

Prentice Hall

Boston Columbus Indianapolis New York San Francisco Upper Saddle River
Amsterdam Cape Town Dubai London Madrid Milan Munich Paris Montreal Toronto
Delhi Mexico City São Paulo Sydney Hong Kong Seoul Singapore Taipei Tokyo

Editorial Director: *Sally Yagan*
Editor in Chief: *Eric Svendsen*
Acquisitions Editor: *Kim Norbuta*
Product Development Manager: *Ashley Santora*
Editorial Project Manager: *Claudia Fernandes*
Editorial Assistant: *Meg O'Rourke*
Director of Marketing: *Patrice Lumumba Jones*
Marketing Manager: *Nikki Ayana Jones*
Marketing Assistant: *Ian Gold*
Senior Managing Editor: *Judy Leale*

Production Project Manager: *Debbie Ryan*
Project Manager: *Susan Hannahs*
Senior Art Director: *Jayne Conte*
Cover Designer: *Karen Salzbach*
Full-Service Project Manager: *Aparna Yellai,*
PreMediaGlobal
Composition: *PreMediaGlobal*
Text and Cover Printer/Bindery:
Courier/Stoughton
Text Font: *10/12 TimesTen Roman*

Credits and acknowledgments borrowed from other sources and reproduced, with permission, in this textbook appear on appropriate page within text.

Library of Congress Cataloging-in-Publication Data

Reuer, J. J. (Jeffrey J.)
  Entrepreneurial alliances / Jeffrey J. Reuer, Africa Ariño, Paul M. Olk. — 1st ed.
    p. cm.
  Includes bibliographical references and index.
  ISBN-13: 978-0-13-615636-9 (alk. paper)
  ISBN-10: 0-13-615636-3 (alk. paper)
  1. Strategic alliances (Business) 2. Entrepreneurship. I. Ariño, Africa. II. Olk, Paul M.
III. Title.
  HD69.S8R48 2011
  658'.044—dc22

                                                                            2010019286

10 9 8 7 6 5 4 3 2 1

Prentice Hall
is an imprint of

www.pearsonhighered.com

ISBN 10:   0-13-615636-3
ISBN 13: 978-0-13-615636-9

To Larissa, John, and Paul
—JJR

To Angel and Araceli
—AA

To Lynn, Emily, and Ella
—PMO

BRIEF CONTENTS

CONTENTS

PREFACE

The last decade has witnessed a change in how many entrepreneurs organize. Where earlier small companies may have been likely to try to go it alone in creating a market or in offering a product or service, increasingly they have turned to setting up alliances with other organizations. Many entrepreneurs are motivated to form an alliance because it may help their start-up company leverage its scarce resources and increase the likelihood for economic success. Further, in many industries alliances have become part of the standard business practice and start-ups cannot survive without them.

While the practice has blossomed, the knowledge of how best to form and manage these alliances has not kept pace. Many entrepreneurs do not have any experience in managing alliances. Those that do have likely discovered that there is no single model for when to use or how to structure an alliance. Alliances may take one of a variety of different forms and an entrepreneurial company may find itself partnering with a range of companies, including a small company, a large company, overseas organizations, or even a competitor. Consequently many entrepreneurs find themselves considering using, or even involved in, an alliance without a strong understanding of the best way to proceed. Similarly, courses in entrepreneurship and books dedicated to helping entrepreneurs may talk about the importance of partnering but often do not provide specific advice on when and how to develop an alliance. Moreover, the books dedicated to alliances tend to be oriented to the needs of larger or more established organizations. The purpose of our book is to fill this important gap.

OBJECTIVES

There are two primary objectives to our book. The first is to help entrepreneurs prepare for, create, and manage alliances. Our experiences with talking to entrepreneurs about their use of alliances suggest that many are not very skilled at alliance management, and in many cases entrepreneurs are not even aware of the many challenges they will face. This has led to poor-performing alliances and in some cases, the demise of the company. To help entrepreneurs prepare for and overcome some of the common problems associated with alliances, we discuss challenges they will likely face and recommendations for how to address them and increase their odds of success. We believe that, with some careful planning and preparation, most entrepreneurs can become better at managing alliances.

The second objective of our book is to address alliance management through the lens of an entrepreneur. Many books and articles offering advice on how to manage alliances discuss them from the perspective of large companies, often large multinationals or other organizations having more resources to dedicate to their alliances. Many entrepreneurs trying to apply these recommendations will not find them to be very useful. In this book we modify existing frameworks and introduce new ones that will help entrepreneurs become more effective at alliance management.

ORGANIZATION

We take a lifecycle approach to understanding entrepreneurial alliances. After laying out the scope of our discussion in Chapter 1, in Chapter 2 we turn to the issue of when and why an entrepreneurial firm would want to enter into an alliance, and why use an alliance versus a different structure, such as an acquisition. This is followed in Chapter 3 by addressing the next issue in the formation process: Now that a firm wants to engage in an alliance, what type of arrangement should it pursue? Chapter 4 continues along the activities in the formation sequence by focusing on how to search for and select an appropriate partner. After selecting a partner, companies then turn to alliance negotiations, which is the topic of Chapter 5. Chapter 6 deals with the various conflicts entrepreneurial companies will likely face after the alliance is formed, including when to dissolve the alliance. Having completed the lifecycle of an alliance, Chapter 7 expands upon this framework by focusing initially on some of the unique challenges of forming an alliance with more than two partners and then discussing how an entrepreneurial company can become better at managing a portfolio of alliances. This is followed by Chapter 8, in which we examine how an entrepreneurial company can improve how it manages alliances and develop a stronger alliance capability. Our book concludes with a discussion in Chapter 9 of how entrepreneurial companies can evaluate the performance of not only a single alliance but all of their alliances in their expanding portfolios.

UNIQUE FEATURES

There are several unique features in our book that we hope entrepreneurs, students, and instructors will find useful.

LIFECYCLE APPROACH

As was just described, we take a lifecycle approach to the topic. This not only helps entrepreneurs with no alliance experience have a roadmap for what issues they can expect to face along the way as they form and manage one, but it also helps those who are in the middle of an alliance, or who have some experience, focus their attention on the next issues that deserve focus and attention.

BALANCE OF ECONOMIC AND BEHAVIORAL PERSPECTIVES

Alliances are a mix of economic and behavioral considerations. For most companies, there is a clear economic rationale behind the decision to enter into an alliance. Without obtaining these benefits, the company may question the wisdom of entering the alliance. Yet to achieve these benefits, companies need to pay attention to the behavioral side of alliances. Such issues as communication, trust, shared decision-making, and conflict management are often overlooked in purely economic treatments of alliances but are necessary to make alliances successful. Our approach recognizes that for a company to have an effective alliance it needs to attend to both of these issues at the same time. For these reasons, we discuss critical structural and process dimensions of alliance management throughout this book.

CURRENT DISCUSSIONS OF ALLIANCE MANAGEMENT TOPICS

Our discussion of entrepreneurial alliances incorporates some of the most recent conceptual developments in the management of alliances. Such topics as when to use an alliance instead of alternative approaches, which types of conflict will develop between partners and how to overcome them, and how to evaluate the performance of a portfolio of alliances are just a few of the topics that are discussed in depth in this book that readers are unlikely to find in other books.

INSIGHTS FOR BOTH ENTREPRENEURS AND ALLIANCE MANAGERS

By focusing on the intersection between entrepreneurship and alliances, we offer recommendations that are valuable for both entrepreneurs as well as managers who oversee alliances in larger or more established firms. For entrepreneurs we fill an important gap in the entrepreneurship literature. We discuss a topic that is increasingly critical to a start-up company's chances of success but about which there is limited information. For alliance managers in larger firms, we not only provide insights that can be used in approaching entrepreneurial companies about forming alliances but also address some topics of general importance that can help in managing alliances in other domains.

BROAD RANGE OF EXAMPLES

In presenting our frameworks, tools, and concepts, we therefore provide a wide variety of examples. The entrepreneurial alliances discussed come not only from diverse industries, including service and manufacturing, but also from different countries and include multinational alliances. We hope the range of experiences we present helps illustrate best alliance practices to managers, students, and instructors.

SUPPLEMENTS

Supplements are available for adopting instructors to download at www. pearsonhighered.com/irc. The website also includes detailed descriptions of the supplements. Registration is simple and gives the instructor immediate access to new titles and new editions. Pearson's dedicated technical support team is ready to help instructors with the media supplements that accompany this text. The instructor should visit http://247.pearsoned.com/ for answers to frequently asked questions and for toll-free user support phone numbers. Supplements include:

- Instructor's Manual
- PowerPoint Slides

COMPANION WEBSITE

A useful companion website, www.pearsonhighered.com/entrepreneurship, offers free access to teaching resources for all books in the Prentice Hall Entrepreneurship Series including additional activities, links to latest research, sample entrepreneurship curriculum and syllabi, teaching tips, and Web resource links.

COURSESMART TEXTBOOKS ONLINE

An exciting new choice for students trying to economize. As an alternative to purchasing the print textbook, students can subscribe to the same content online and save up to 50% off the suggested list price of the print text. With a CourseSmart eTextbook, students can search the text, make notes online, print out reading assignments that incorporate lecture notes, and bookmark important passages for later review. For additional information on this option visit www.coursesmart.com.

ACKNOWLEDGMENTS

This book would not have been possible without our own collaborations with other researchers and organizations over the past two decades. We would also like to express our thanks to Duane Ireland and Mike Morris, the series coeditors, for the valuable feedback and guidance they have provided us. We also gratefully acknowledge the financial support received from the Spanish Ministerio de Ciencia e Innovación (grant SEJ2007-67463 and Acción Complementaria ECO2009-06490-E/ECON).

ABOUT THE AUTHORS

Jeffrey J. Reuer is the Blake Family Endowed Chair in Strategic Management and Governance at the Krannert School of Management at Purdue University, where he is also the area coordinator. Before joining Purdue, he was the Boyd W. Harris, Jr. Distinguished Scholar and professor of Strategic Management at the Kenan-Flagler Business School, University of North Carolina. He was the first recipient of the Strategic Management Society's Emerging Scholar Award for research, education, and related academic activities. He has also taught in executive education programs at Harvard Business School, Duke University, INSEAD, and the Indian School of Business. He is a recipient of the Excellence in Teaching Award from the Fuqua School of Business, Duke University, for the best core course in the weekend executive MBA program. His research on alliances, acquisitions, and initial public offerings has appeared in a number of scholarly journals, including the *Academy of Management Journal*, *Strategic Management Journal*, *Organization Science*, *Journal of International Business Studies*, *Strategic Organization*, *Strategic Entrepreneurship Journal*, *Journal of Management*, *Journal of Management Studies*, *Research Policy*, *Journal of Business Venturing*, *Journal of Economic Behavior and Organization*, and *Managerial and Decision Economics*. He has presented papers at more than fifty universities throughout the world. The results of his work have also appeared as practice-oriented articles and research briefings in the *Harvard Business Review*, *MIT Sloan Management Review*, *Financial Times*, *Journal of Applied Corporate Finance*, and *Long Range Planning*. His books are titled *Strategic Alliances: Theory and Evidence* (Oxford), *Handbook of Strategic Alliances* (Sage), *Strategic Alliances: Governance and Contracts* (Palgrave Macmillan), and *Real Options Theory* (Elsevier). Professor Reuer serves as an associate editor for the *Strategic Management Journal* and as a consulting editor for the *Journal of International Business Studies*. He also serves or has served on the editorial boards of the *Academy of Management Review*, *Academy of Management Journal*, *Organization Science*, *Strategic Organization*, *Journal of Management*, *Journal of Management Studies*, and *Journal of Business Venturing*. He is a recipient of the Outstanding Editorial Board Member Award from the *Strategic Management Journal* and the Best Reviewer Award from the *Journal of International Business Studies* as well as the *Journal of Management Studies*. He was a program chair of the Strategic Management Society's international conference in Washington, DC and is currently the assistant program chair of the Business Policy and Strategy

Division of the Academy of the Management. He has also been active in the profession by serving on that organization's executive committee and research committee, leading developmental workshops, and consortia for faculty and doctoral students, and by organizing several conferences in the United States and Europe.

Africa Ariño is Professor of Strategic Management and Director of the Ph.D. Program at IESE Business School at University of Navarra (Spain). She has also taught in Executive Education programs at Helsinki University of Technology (Finland), IAE, Universidad Austral (Argentina), Nile University (Egypt), Universitat de Barcelona (Spain), and Vlerick School, University of Gent (Belgium). Her research on alliance structures and processes has been published in a number of scholarly journals, including the *Strategic Management Journal*, *Organization Science*, *Journal of International Business Studies*, *Journal of Management*, *Journal of Management Studies*, *Journal of Business Venturing*, *Managerial and Decision Economics*, *Group & Organization Management*, *European Management Review*, *Organization Studies*, and *International Studies of Management and Organization*. She received the Sara and George McCune Award for the best paper published in *Group & Organization Management* during 2001 and twice the Excellence in Research Award from the IESE Alumni Association. She has presented her research at numerous universities in seven different countries. She has published her work as well in journals of a managerial orientation such as *California Management Review*, *The Academy of Management Executive*, and *European Management Journal*, and has given numerous talks to executive audiences. Her books are titled *Strategic Alliances: Governance and Contracts* (Palgrave Macmillan) and *Creating Value through International Strategy* (Palgrave Macmillan). She serves as an associate editor of the *Global Strategy Journal* and the *European Management Review*, and serves or has served on the editorial boards of *Strategic Management Journal*, *Journal of Management*, *Journal of Management Studies*, *Journal of Strategic Management Education*, *Journal of International Business Studies*, and *Group & Organization Management*. She has organized three international conferences at IESE Business School that focused on strategic alliances and international strategy, has served in the organization committee of several meetings of the Strategic Management Society, and has been a member of the Scientific Committee of the European Academy of Management meetings. She has served in the Executive Committee of the Business Policy and Strategy Division of the Academy of the Management. She has lead or participated in various consortia for faculty and doctoral students. She has participated in various consulting projects related to strategic alliances, strategic plan formulation, and design and implementation of governance bodies. She serves the community as a director of Asociación Cultural Pineda, a school in an underprivileged area in Barcelona, and as a founder and promoter of Foro Mujer de Empresa, a developmental environment for women in business.

Paul Olk is professor of Management and the Director of Academic Research and Accreditation at the Daniels College of Business of the University of Denver. His research on strategic alliances and networks has appeared in several books and in a number of scholarly journals, including *Organization Science, Strategic Management Journal, European Management Journal*, the *Journal of Personality and Social Psychology*, the *Journal of Applied Social Psychology*, and the *Journal of High Technology Management Research*. Additional work has appeared or will appear in the *Academy of Management Learning and Education*, the *Journal of Management Inquiry and Human Resource Management*. His alliance research has also been published in leading practice-oriented journals like the *California Management Review, MIT Sloan Management Review*, and *Case Research Journal*. He is the editor of the forthcoming book *Strategy Process Research* (Edward Elgar Publishing) and serves or has served on the editorial review boards of *Organization Science, IEEE Transactions on Engineering Management, Group and Organization Management*, and *Journal of Management Inquiry*. The recipient of multiple teaching awards, he has taught in several executive education programs and has consulted to small and large companies and to projects sponsored by U.S. federal government agencies. His strategic alliance research has been funded by the National Science Foundation, The Alliance Edge (Queen's University), and the Center for Innovation Management Studies (Lehigh University) as well as numerous university sources. Professor Olk is the current program chair of the Technology and Innovation Management Division of the Academy of Management, and previously served on the Executive Committee of the Knowledge and Innovation Management Division of the Strategic Management Society. He is a past organizer of two Organization Science Winter Conferences and has held numerous committee member positions for other professional associations. He has also served his profession by organizing numerous conferences, panels, sessions, and colloquia on a range of management research and teaching topics.

INTRODUCTION TO ENTREPRENEURIAL ALLIANCES

"The greatest change . . . in the way business is being conducted may be the accelerating growth of relationships based not on ownership but on partnership . . . semi-formal alliances of all sorts."

"The entrepreneur always searches for change, responds to it, and exploits it as an opportunity."

—PETER DRUCKER

INTRODUCTION

Alliances, or collaborative relationships between organizations, have clearly altered the business landscape in the last two decades. The business press routinely uses terms such as *coopetition*, *ecosystems*, *network organizations*, and *open innovation*, and related concepts. Alliances indeed play central roles in new models of competition, innovation, and organization. In a 2007 survey of management practices, Bain & Company reports that alliances are one of the most widely used current tools (68%).[1] Though firms' alliance usage rates vary across different regions of the world, with new alliance formations currently more numerous in North America and Europe and less so in Latin America, there is no doubt that the total number of alliances has exploded across countries and sectors. Many firms share in the conviction that you can't go it alone in today's business environment. Thousands of new relationships are formed each year (see Figure 1.1),[2] and the Bain study just noted reports that the alliance usage rate by small firms (66%) is now nearly as high as for medium-sized (71%) or large organizations (72%).[3]

FIGURE 1.1 Cumulative Alliance Formations

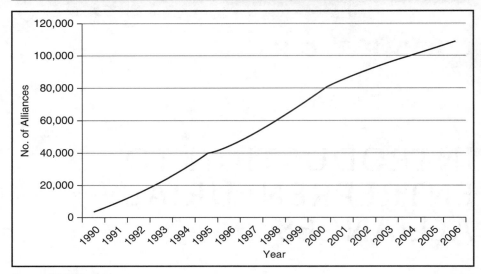

Source: SDC Database

What is equally clear is that alliances have generally not lived up to firms' expectations. As alliances have come to represent a substantial percentage of some firms' revenues and profits (i.e., 20–50%), their failure rates appear to be just as considerable. Defining what is meant by collaborative success or failure in general is difficult, however. For instance, termination of alliances is sometimes taken as an indicator of alliance failure, but this need not be the case since one or more partners might have satisfied its initial objectives and brought the collaborative agreement to a conclusion. Nevertheless, numerous studies have shown that between 30 and 70% of all alliances fail.[4] In one well-known case, Alza, an entrepreneurial firm based in California and specializing in advanced drug delivery systems, signed a research agreement and sold an equity stake to Ciba-Geigy (now Novartis) in order to develop controlled-release drugs. The alliance experienced difficulties as it became clear that the involvement of downstream functions such as manufacturing and marketing was needed for technology applications. The absence of joint teams and inter-faces also made cooperation between the two firms difficult, owing in part to their very different sizes, structures, and cultures. The partners eventually experienced delays in bringing new products to market, problems with their working relationships, and suspicions about each others' motives.[5] Alliances fail for many different reasons related to the way they are designed as well as managed over time (see Table 1.1). Subsequent chapters will consider ways by which firms can govern and manage collaborative agreements more effectively.

TABLE 1.1 Illustrative Reasons Why Alliances Fail

1. **Environment of the Alliance**
   - Shifts in technologies
   - Changes in product demand or customer needs
2. **Partners' Strategies**
   - Shifting of strategic priorities during the course of the alliance
   - Optimistic expectations or divergent strategic interests
   - Poor connection between firm strategy and partner selection
3. **Alliance Governance**
   - Form of alliance misaligns with alliance purpose
   - Mismatch between contract and business logic
   - Inadequate control or insufficient flexibility
4. **Managerial Capabilities and Commitments**
   - Top management's lack of attention to the collaboration
   - Clashes and lack of connectivity between the cultures
   - Ambiguous career paths for managers
   - Inadequate metrics
5. **Collaborative Processes**
   - Failure to adapt
   - Poor implementation
   - Lack of communication and trust
   - Inadequate coordination and conflict resolution processes

OPPORTUNITIES AND RISKS FOR ENTREPRENEURIAL FIRMS

While alliances have proven difficult to manage for many organizations, they can be particularly challenging for entrepreneurial firms for several reasons. Entrepreneurial firms often suffer from a "liability of newness," which stems from their lack of resources, legitimacy, and access to external markets and relationships. On the one hand, this liability of newness makes alliances very useful to entrepreneurial firms, as alliances allow the firms to leverage other organizations' resources and capabilities. On the other hand, the liability of newness can also make it difficult for entrepreneurial firms to manage alliances effectively. For instance, entrepreneurial firms' lack of legitimacy and access to external markets and relationships can make it difficult for them to attract the best possible partners. Moreover, once agreements are signed, entrepreneurial firms can find it challenging to make alliances work, owing to their lack of administrative capabilities. For example, whereas an established firm with scores of alliances and deep financial pockets might have a wealth of experience to draw upon, well-developed knowledge management tools for alliance investment and execution, or even an in-house function dedicated to alliance management, such resources and investments might be nonexistent, infeasible to make, or not sensible for entrepreneurial firms. It can also be the case that an entrepreneurial firm can be at a disadvantageous bargaining position in an alliance. This situation can arise, for instance, when an entrepreneurial firm joins a "constellation," or group of allied firms, that is dominated by an established incumbent in an industry.[6] Entrepreneurial firms therefore face a fundamental paradox: Alliances can be very attractive to pursue new opportunities or solve particular problems, but alliances will also be particularly challenging for entrepreneurial firms to manage successfully.

KEY QUESTIONS AND CHALLENGES POSED BY ALLIANCES

Alliance war stories, failure rate statistics, and the opportunities and risks associated with alliances raise a number of fundamental questions for entrepreneurial firms evaluating whether alliances can enhance their survival prospects and can help them carry out their strategies:

- When should they use alliances rather than alternative investments? Or avoid them?
- How should alliances be designed and structured? How can alliances be governed appropriately to achieve collaborative objectives?
- How can firms navigate complex alliance processes more effectively (e.g., partner selection, negotiations, and relationship management)?
- How can firms best manage their involvement in extended networks?
- What are the organizational and managerial requirements of effective alliance implementation (e.g., capabilities, teamwork, etc.)?
- How can partners gauge the performance of their alliances and make improvements?

Alliances therefore pose many questions and challenges for firms. Table 1.2 distills these and other questions into three core challenges that firms must meet in order to get the most out of alliances, and the table also provides some subsidiary challenges for illustrative purposes. First, firms must understand when and how to invest in alliances and set up appropriate governance structures. We refer to these challenges collectively as the *alliance investment challenge*, which captures the deal-making requirements firms face in setting up the alliance's governance structure prior to the execution of the collaborative agreement.

TABLE 1.2 Key Challenges Presented by Alliances		
The Alliance Investment Challenge	*The Alliance Implementation Challenge*	*The Alliance Institutionalization Challenge*
• Choosing between an alliance and other forms of investment	• Managing cultural differences in alliances	• Building alliance capabilities
• Choosing between different types of alliances	• Building trust among partners	• Learning from own and others' experiences
• Designing alliances	• Adapting alliances over time	• Developing organizational and managerial competence

Firms must meet the "alliance implementation challenge," which comprises all of the tasks and processes involved in actual collaboration between firms. If the alliance investment challenge captures the content of collaborative agreements, *alliance investment challenge* refers to the processes that actually ungird the search for collaborators, selection of a partner, execution of the alliance agreement, building of relationships, and the processes that take place when firms work together and subsequently adapt or terminate their collaboration. One well-known example of this challenge is the need to address cultural differences between partners, be they differences in national culture or organizational culture. Other illustrations include developing trust between partners and adapting relationships to changes that are either internal or external to the collaboration.

Finally, *alliance institutionalization challenge* refers to all of the new capabilities partners will need to possess if they are to get the most out of their alliances. These capabilities might be accumulated through prior experience with alliances, might be developed through more formal means (e.g., structure and staffing), or might be sourced from external experts. Whereas the previous two challenges are specific to individual deals, this challenge is more of a firm-wide concern as to how to cultivate alliance management capabilities. Various chapters of this book will take up each of these three challenges. In this chapter, first, we turn to some fundamental definitional issues, and then conclude by introducing steps entrepreneurial firms can take to prepare for alliances, by summarizing key success factors and by offering an overview of the remainder of the book.

FORMAL DEFINITIONS OF COLLABORATIVE AGREEMENTS

ALLIANCES

In seminars or workshops when entrepreneurs or other business executives are asked to define the term *alliance*, several phrases are frequently mentioned: *partnership*, *marriage*, *dating*, *working together to achieve common goals*, *contracts with other companies*, and so on. They quickly realize that there are many different ways to define the term *alliance*, and that they hold various conceptions of what such collaborative agreements are, or are not. For instance, some entrepreneurs define alliances based on their objectives and state that partners need to have common goals; others submit that partners' goals need to be complementary rather than exactly the same (e.g., accessing technology versus accessing markets). Others who define alliances based on their governance structure, or legal organization, enter debates as to whether joint ventures, mergers, or other arrangements should, or should not, be considered alliances. For example, some argue that once equity ownership is involved, as in the case of a joint venture, an alliance does not exist, whereas others view mergers as a type of business relationship between firms and hence call them alliances.

In order to address these issues in a useful way at the outset, alliances need to be defined in such a way that they are distinguished from other types of investments while also recognizing the diversity of interorganizational relationships that might be considered alliances. These relationships might serve many different purposes (e.g., exploring new markets, accessing others' resources, gaining scale, and so on) and might represent many organizational forms (e.g., equity joint ventures, research contracts, production agreements, etc.). In addition, more important than the precise definition of alliances per se is arriving at an operational definition that allows for better understanding of how to tackle the three key alliance challenges just mentioned.

For our purposes, alliances can be defined as:

> agreements between independent organizations who work together under an incomplete contract.[7]

Several elements of this definition are worth elaborating:

PARTNERS TO AN ALLIANCE REMAIN INDEPENDENT ORGANIZATIONS

This aspect of the definition necessarily rules out mergers and acquisitions. As we shall see in a subsequent chapter, it is useful to exclude mergers and acquisitions from our definition of alliances because a critical investment decision that high growth firms must make concerns when to invest in an alliance rather than an acquisition. In the same way, entrepreneurial firms might also consider selling a firm or obtaining other firms' resources through an alliance. Whereas the combined entity in the case of an acquisition has a chain of authority that is typical of the hierarchy inside all companies, alliances are more difficult to control since two or more organizations exert partial influence over alliances' operations. We will discuss a variety of other differences in the characteristics of alliances and acquisitions that help decision-makers know when to go with one form of investment or the other, whether the decision-maker is on the buy side of the deal or the sell side of the transaction.

While full mergers and acquisitions are excluded from our definition of alliances, a variety of other types of business relationships involving equity ownership are not, since these investment structures still preserve the essential independence of firms:

- A minority equity partnership involves one firm taking a small ownership position in another firm. For instance, in early 2007, GS AgriFuels Corporation, a manufacturer and wholesaler of fuels from agricultural products, purchased a 14% equity stake in Sustainable Systems Inc., a provider of research and development services for renewable energy and bio-based products.
- Corporate venture capital (CVC) also involves a firm taking a minority equity stake in another firm, though typically the investee is a start-up company and other unique contractual safeguards and rights accompany

such agreements that are typical of venture capital (e.g., rights of first refusal, liquidation preferences, convertible securities, etc.). Immediately following the bursting of the dot-com bubble, corporate funds invested in start-ups fell by roughly 80% in a one-year period, but some firms such as Microsoft, Merck, Qualcomm, and Millenium Pharmaceuticals continued to invest significantly in such deals during this time period.[8] CVC might be distinguished from *corporate venturing*, which often refers to corporate funding of projects that are outside of the firm's core business and are given operational autonomy, yet are still legally part of the organization and so might be termed *internal new ventures*.

- An equity joint venture exists when partner firms share ownership in a distinct business entity. In 2006, Syntroleum Corporation of Tulsa, Oklahoma, and Bluewater Energy Services B.V., Hoofddorp, the Netherlands, each of which had fewer than four hundred employees, joined forces to provide oil production and exploration services in the Netherlands. Parties to a joint venture might own their business on a 50/50 basis, as Syntroleum and Bluewater did, or one firm might have more ownership than the other partner. For example, in 2006 Micron Technology Inc. and Photronics Inc. announced a joint venture to manufacture and develop photomasks for leading-edge and next-generation semiconductors; Micron was to have a 50.01% equity stake in the joint venture, and Photronics was to hold a 49.99% interest.

PARTNERS TO AN ALLIANCE RELY ON AN INCOMPLETE CONTRACT

The phrase *incomplete contract* comes from the economics of law and indicates that parties cannot specify all terms in advance. In the examples just provided, firms might even use relatively open-ended contracts to govern their joint venture relationships, but the presence of shared ownership and joint control helps to align their incentives and enables them to coordinate activities. Often the scope of alliances will broaden during the course of the collaboration; alliances can progress in unpredictable ways; and it is difficult, if not impossible, to anticipate how the industry or partners themselves will evolve. Given firms' inabilities to identify all potential contingencies, as well as appropriate responses to them, in the uncertain environments in which collaborative agreements are formed, alliance contracts are invariably incomplete. In fact, many alliance contracts incorporate terms such as *reasonable* or *best efforts*, contain legally unenforceable items relating to the business plan, and describe internal dispute resolution procedures and allow for arbitration.[9] For this reason, they are sometimes labeled "relational" contracts rather than "classical" contracts. By contrast, other discrete transactions occurring in various markets (e.g., cash for bread exchanges at the supermarket, sourcing contracts, etc.) need not involve such flexibility. In classical contracts, the subject is described in as much detail as possible, and court enforcement is the preferred means of settling disputes. Different types of alliances have elements of both the relational and classical contracting perspectives in varying degrees, but a common feature of collaborative agreements is their inherent incompleteness and reliance on internal adaptation as well as relational norms (e.g., trust) to facilitate coordination.

PARTNERS TO AN ALLIANCE WORK TOGETHER

In other words, alliance partners make some specific investments in a relationship and share risks and rewards. As a consequence, alliances are not like market transactions in which it is inexpensive if not costless to switch exchange parties. Some alliances will involve a fixed ending date, whereas others will be open-ended, but in either case the important point is that firms are working together and investing in a relationship.

Figure 1.2 depicts the value chains, or the distinct operating and support activities of two companies, Partner 1 and Partner 2. Several possible alliances are illustrated by lines connecting these firms' value chain activities. In some alliances, sometimes termed *horizontal collaborative agreements*, firms combine forces in the same value chain, or functional, activity. For instance, the solid lines suggest a potential alliance that brings together the two firms' marketing and sales organizations, as well as a potential alliance that pools together the firms' production activities, which is illustrated by a recent joint venture involving Warner Music and Seoul Records called WS Entertainment, to manufacture CDs together in South Korea. As another concrete example of a horizontal alliance, a number of years ago fourteen computer and semiconductor firms formed the Microelectronics and Computer Technology Corporation to develop advanced technologies for software and computers.

Vertical collaborative agreements, by contrast, have one firm contributing one value chain activity, and the partner contributing another value chain activity. One of the dashed lines indicates that Partner 1 might provide production expertise and Partner 2 could offer its marketing skills, for instance. Alternatively, Partner 1 might offer design skills or some other technological

FIGURE 1.2 Horizontal and Vertical Alliances

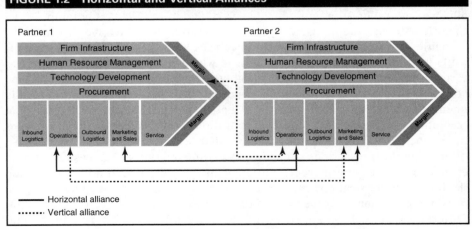

— Horizontal alliance
········· Vertical alliance

capabilities while Partner 2 agrees to manufacture a product based in part on these inputs. As another example of a vertical alliance, WWP Group LLC and LiveWorld entered into a joint venture to offer online marketing and social networking services in the United Kingdom. WWP Group was responsible for the development of marketing strategies and branding, and LiveWorld was to contribute its online technical expertise.

Naturally, alliances will vary in scope from narrow (i.e., single functional area) to broad (i.e., multiple functional areas), as well as in the overlap in partners' contributions to the collaboration. This suggests that in many alliances partners will contribute some common and some unique value chain activities to the agreements, and such alliances blend the features of the horizontal and vertical agreements just noted. Even in situations in which partners come from very different industries, or collaborators are using alliances to enter brand new markets, partners make specific investments in their relationships with one another and therefore become interdependent to some degree.

ALLIANCES AS HYBRID ORGANIZATIONS

The fact that alliance partners work closely together under an incomplete contract while remaining independent legal organizations explains why bargaining, goal conflicts, and many other management challenges are part and parcel of collaborative agreements, particularly if alliances occur in uncertain environments and between firms having different resources and cultures. Alliances are often collectively referred to as *hybrid organizations*, and this description is apt: They blend features of organizations and markets, cooperation and competition, flexibility and commitment, trust and formal contracts, and so on. Figure 1.3 provides examples of the many different types of alliances that firms use to pursue new opportunities and to carry out their strategies. As the figure demonstrates, alliances are hybrid organizations as they involve less integration than mergers (as collaborators remain legally independent organizations), but they also represent higher levels of integration than arm's-length market transactions (as collaborators become interdependent). The types of alliances appearing in this diagram are not meant to be exhaustive, but illustrative of the rich array of collaborative agreements that exist between firms and that qualify as hybrid organizations.

ENTREPRENEURIAL ALLIANCES

While the previous discussion clarifies what an alliance is, in what sense are some alliances "entrepreneurial"?

Entrepreneurship has been defined in many different ways, often with a focus on the individual entrepreneur. Some authors have recently noted that the domain of the entrepreneurship field can be demarcated more broadly as the study of "how, by whom, and with what effects opportunities to create future goods and services are discovered, evaluated, and exploited."[10] This definition would highlight the sources of opportunities; the processes of discovery, evaluation, and exploitation of opportunities; as well as the individuals involved in these

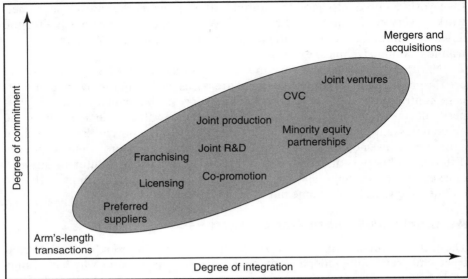

FIGURE 1.3 Alliances as Hybrid Organizations

processes as key to entrepreneurship. It also raises three sets of related questions that serve to define the boundaries of entrepreneurship:

1. Why, when, and how do these opportunities come into existence?
2. Why, when, and how do some people (and not others) exploit these opportunities?
3. Why, when, and how are different "modes of action" used in this process?

Alliances intersect with these aspects of entrepreneurship in several important ways.

ALLIANCES AS SOURCES OF ENTREPRENEURIAL OPPORTUNITIES

First, alliances themselves can be seen as sources of entrepreneurial opportunities that are well defined at the outset. We will discuss the many benefits that alliances can provide firms, but they include accelerated growth, expansion into new geographic markets, exploration of new technologies and other resources, and even creation of new markets, and these benefits are partly associated with the partner a firm teams up with. Often firms stumble upon lucrative prospects to form partnerships in a serendipitous fashion, but in other cases partners are pursued in a more deliberate manner. The search for partners involves some cost, whether due to the use of intermediaries or due to the opportunity costs associated with the time involved. Given these costs, the limited attention of decision-makers, and the unique information held by different individuals, decision-makers will recognize different opportunities to form partnerships. For example, for the reasons just noted, decision-makers might naturally be more likely to focus upon opportunities that are geographically proximate or closely connected to their prior experiences. Under this perspective, the partnership itself is viewed as an opportunity, which is well defined at the outset of the collaborative agreement (e.g., access to a new market, resource, etc.).

ALLIANCES TO DISCOVER OR CREATE OPPORTUNITIES

Second, alliances can be seen as a means of discovering or creating completely new opportunities that are not well known prior to the formation of the collaboration. Under this perspective, the alliance is an organizational arrangement that provides the complementary resources and processes used to discover or create brand new opportunities. In other words, firms may enter into a collaboration prior to understanding clearly what kinds of opportunities exist, and these opportunities emerge during the course of implementing the partnership. Many alliances are used to access or internalize a partner's knowledge, which might be specified from the start, but in other partnerships new technological or market knowledge will be generated during the course of the collaboration. For example, in some research collaborations, partners' patenting activities surge even after an alliance has been dissolved.[11] Alliances often evolve in unanticipated directions and generate new, unexpected opportunities for partners. One well-known example concerns Xerox's long-standing joint venture with Fuji Photo Film, which evolved from a relatively simple marketing relationship to distribute Xerox copiers in Japan into a major R&D engine and source of innovative new products for Xerox.

ALLIANCES AS VEHICLES TO EXPLOIT OPPORTUNITIES

Third, alliances are one of several "modes of action" by which individuals or firms exploit the opportunities they recognize or create. Entrepreneurial activity commonly occurs through de novo start-ups, but there are other ways by which opportunities are exploited (e.g., within an existing organization, in spinoffs, via the sale of opportunities to other organizations, and even acquisitions).[12] The important point is that each of these arrangements involves costs as well as benefits, so they need to be understood in comparative terms, and decision-makers need to consider their relative benefits and costs. For example, pursuit of entrepreneurial opportunities within existing organizations affords greater coordination with complementary resources, and the slack financial resources of such firms can be valuable if it would be difficult for entrepreneurs to obtain financing in an independent venture. By contrast, entrepreneurship via de novo startups can be preferable when innovations are autonomous, or do not require extensive coordination with other, related innovations.[13] Traditionally, "markets" and "hierarchies" have been seen as the two primary means by which opportunities are exploited. Because alliances are hybrids, they are intermediate organizational forms that blend the merits and demerits of other modes of action, as noted earlier. This observation suggests that an important aspect of investing in entrepreneurial alliances is understanding when alliances, or other, modes of action, are most appropriate for the pursuit of opportunities, a topic we will return to in Chapter 2. Figure 1.4 summarizes how alliances fit within the entrepreneurship process.

FIGURE 1.4 Alliances Within the Entrepreneurship Process

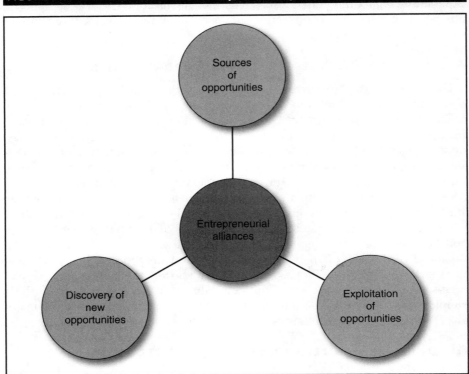

These three observations also suggest one potential definition of entrepreneurial alliances:

> agreements between independent organizations who work together under an incomplete contract to access, discover, or exploit opportunities for future goods and services.

While this definition offers a functional conceptualization of entrepreneurial alliances that considers how entrepreneurial processes work within collaborative agreements, alliances can also be used more broadly to support the entrepreneurial process in parent firms. Therefore, entrepreneurial alliances can also be defined simply as collaborative agreements entered into by one or more entrepreneurial firms. This definition naturally raises the question of what an entrepreneurial firm is. The entrepreneurship field has used a variety of qualitative or more concrete indicators to identify entrepreneurial firms and discriminate them from others. These indicators include factors such as firm size or age, growth rate, the presence of the firm's founder, growth orientation, innovativeness, risk preferences, and so on.[14] For instance, some use a firm size cutoff of five hundred employees or fewer to distinguish small firms from other firms.[15] Others use an eight-year cutoff for firm age to differentiate new ventures from established organizations, and the age of firms has been associated with risk-taking propensity.[16] Others have used more restrictive (i.e., six-year) or lenient (i.e., twelve-year) cutoffs to identify new ventures.

Alliances can be useful to implement the strategies and support the operations of small firms, new ventures, or other types of entrepreneurial firms. Because of this, and because alliances are used to discover, create, and exploit opportunities with the ultimate objective of obtaining competitive advantages for firms, individual alliances will often have important strategic as well as entrepreneurial aspects to them. As a consequence, rather than drawing a clear line between strategic alliances and entrepreneurial alliances, we would suggest that many alliances could be classified as both. In any event, irrespective of these definitional issues, entrepreneurship and strategic considerations need to be integrated in alliance dealmaking and implementation. At a fundamental level, both entrepreneurship and strategic management address how firms create change and exploit opportunities arising from market failures. Furthermore, firms need to prioritize those opportunities that are likely to lead to longer-lasting advantages, and the creation of wealth ultimately hinges upon both opportunity-seeking (e.g., entrepreneurship) as well as advantage-seeking (e.g., strategic management) activities.[17]

DELIVERING ON ALLIANCE BENEFITS

Alliances offer many internal and external benefits to entrepreneurial firms and can support the entrepreneurship process in a variety of important ways. Fundamentally, alliances allow firms to tap into new skills and resources, whether offering new ventures downstream expertise in production or marketing or supporting more established firms' corporate entrepreneurship activities to enhance their innovation and renewal initiatives. They can also aid entrepreneurial firms by addressing their liability of newness and financial constraints, both of which can otherwise have an important negative impact on these firms' survival odds and prosperity. Externally, alliances can help firms create new businesses and market space, accelerate their growth in markets, and facilitate rapid internationalization. They can also help firms manage competitive, technological, and other uncertainties by joining forces with other firms or teaming up with a dominant incumbent. These rationales for alliances are by no means exhaustive and will be discussed in much more detail in Chapter 2, which discusses economic foundations of alliances. However, these rationales capture some of the most interesting and important benefits that alliances can bring to firms and these benefits are particularly germane to the entrepreneurship process and to entrepreneurial firms.

Yet we also know from statistics on failure rates that many firms are not obtaining the promises that alliances hold out for them. In broad terms, this is because firms are all too often not meeting the three alliance challenges presented earlier. Firms do not meet the "alliance investment challenge" when they make inappropriate alliance investment or governance decisions. For instance, firms encounter two types of risks: investing in alliances when some other investment vehicle would have made more sense, or rejecting alliances in favor of other "modes of action" when collaborative agreements would have been best. As a second

FIGURE 1.5 The Alliance Life Cycle

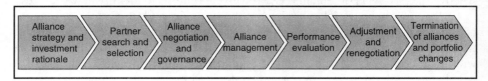

illustration, when alliances are set up, firms can encounter two analogous types of risk when putting governance mechanisms in place. On the one hand, a firm might use a simple alliance structure and open-ended contract for a very complicated business opportunity involving multiple tasks and having high coordination needs. In other cases, firms might burden alliances with excessive governance safeguards for simple transactions or deals that might call for greater flexibility.

Second, firms often do not meet the "alliance implementation challenge" when the collaborative agreement is not executed appropriately. The lack of trust, poor communication, cultural differences, lack of adaptation, and inadequate coordination or conflict resolution processes are all examples of problems that can crop up during the implementation of collaborative agreements. The key tasks associated with alliance implementation are depicted in Figure 1.5, which arrays these processes in a sequence known as the alliance life cycle. Often alliances do not involve or require every single stage, and firms might revisit earlier stages rather than proceeding in such an orderly, linear fashion. However, this model reflects an ordering that is characteristic of many collaborative agreements and summarizes some of the key processes that firms must implement well for alliances to be effective. Each of the chapters of this book will cover some of the most important aspects of managing the different stages of the alliance life cycle.

Finally, firms sometimes do not meet the "alliance institutionalization challenge" if they don't possess adequate alliance capabilities or tools to implement their collaborative agreements. This is particularly problematic for new ventures which, compared to more established firms, are lacking in alliance experience, well-developed knowledge management tools for alliance investment and execution, and staff that can be dedicated to alliance management. Moreover, many firms are simply not prepared to conduct alliances given the strategies they are pursuing, they way they are organized, or their managerial abilities.[18]

Preparing for Partnerships

Table 1.3 raises a number of illustrative questions that entrepreneurs or executives might ask themselves to determine if they are prepared to form partnerships with other organizations. For example, on a strategic level, it is difficult to use alliances if the firm's strategy is not clear in the first place, or if it is unclear precisely why the firm will be using alliances to carry out their strategies. These broader considerations also need to be translated into concrete partner selection criteria. The firm might also learn about alliance possibilities as well as effective practices by monitoring potential partners and by benchmarking the collaborative activities of rivals.

TABLE 1.3 Preparing for Partnerships

1. Strategic Issues
- Does the firm have a clear vision and strategy?
- Does the firm understand where to form alliances, and where not to?
- Are partner selection criteria clear?
- Are potential partners being monitored?
- Are the alliance activities of rivals being benchmarked?

2. Organizational Issues
- Does the firm have a culture of cooperation?
- Is there strong teamwork in the firm?
- Does communication flow freely?
- Is responsibility decentralized in the firm?

3. Managerial Issues
- Are employees comfortable in situations requiring responsibility without control?
- Do employees work well with others from different cultural backgrounds?
- Do employees possess general management skills?
- Do top managers display commitment to new initiatives?

On an organizational level, firms will be ill-suited to developing alliance relationships if there isn't already effective teamwork, trust, and communication within the firms as these problems tend to magnify across organizational boundaries. Firms that operate in a centralized, bureaucratic, or command-and-control mode will find alliances particularly challenging. Finally, on a managerial level, alliances present unique challenges to employees who will be involved in collaborative agreements. For instance, partnerships require employees to be comfortable and effective in situations requiring responsibility without control. Alliance managers also need to possess strong general management abilities and be able to work well with other individuals or firms with very different national or organizational cultures.

KEY SUCCESS FACTORS

We have related some of the key problems raised by alliances to the three broad challenges firms face in crafting and executing collaborative strategy (i.e., the alliance investment challenge, implementation challenge, and institutionalization challenge), as well as to the hierarchy of strategic, organizational, and managerial issues that need to be attended to, if possible before alliances are formed. Consulting firms have also provided surveys to identify some of the more common reasons why alliances fail in order to help firms increase their odds of success. For example, in a survey of 593 CEOs, *Dataquest* reported that the number one reason alliances fail is that partners' expectations were too optimistic (73% of CEOs). Over half the respondents indicated that alliances failed because of changes in the environment (56%) or poor communication (54%). The next most common reasons for alliance failure were: lack of common benefits (49%), strong cultural differences (44%), weak leadership (43%), and slow results (42%). The CEOs also indicated the key success factors in managing alliances, the top five

TABLE 1.4 Key Alliance Success Factors
1. Develop a clear strategic purpose for the alliance.
2. Choose partners with complementary capabilities and compatible goals.
3. Choose the right alliance structure.
4. Negotiate a thorough, yet flexible, contract.
5. Enhance incentives to cooperate and minimize conflicts.
6. Improve trust, communication, and teamwork.
7. Develop and implement performance metrics.
8. Plan for evolution and termination.

being selection of partner (75%), management support (73%), clear definition of roles (49%), communication between partners (48%), and clear definition of goals (44%). As another example of a consulting survey, Accenture has found the following to be the most important reasons why alliances fail: a shift in partner or partners' strategic direction (87%), diminishment of top management's attention (83%), champions moving on (81%), lack of career path or staff shortage (62%), clash of corporate cultures (62%), and disagreements over the distribution of returns (50%). McKinsey has flagged "seven alliance sins"—unclear objectives, lack of a detailed business plan, decision gridlock, aligning with a weak or competitive partner, unmanaged cultural clash, failure to learn or protect core capabilities, and failure to plan for evolution.[19] These missteps and the work noted earlier form the basis of some of the most critical success factors for alliances (see Table 1.4), which also cover many of the stages in the alliance life cycle presented earlier.

WHERE WE GO FROM HERE

Subsequent chapters tackle these interesting and important challenges raised by alliances, and the remainder of the book is organized as follows: In Chapters 2 and 3, we take up some of the economic foundations of alliances that are fundamental to the alliance investment challenge. Chapter 2 discusses in greater depth the economic rationales for forming alliances and takes up the question of when firms should pursue alliances relative to other investment vehicles. This chapter discusses some of the conditions under which alliances will be more efficient than other types of investment. Chapter 3 continues with this theme by examining the design of alternative types of alliances and considers the alternative ways that firms can govern their collaborative agreements, giving particular attention to the alliance contract.

Chapters 4 to 6 take up some of the most important dimensions of the alliance implementation challenge by focusing on how firms can manage specific alliance processes more effectively. In Chapter 4, we discuss partner search and selection. This chapter examines some of the challenges associated with finding partners, alternative ways of searching for partners, and selection criteria for choosing an alliance partner. Chapter 5 discusses alliance negotiation, covering the challenges firms encounter in conducting negotiations and how particular negotiation approaches can improve the outcomes of the negotiations process.

In Chapter 6 we turn to the execution of alliances and discuss how firms can overcome collaborate challenges, build good relationships, and manage the post-formation dynamics of alliances (e.g., contractual renegotiation or termination). Chapters 7 to 9 examine some of the more complicated aspects of alliance management. Chapter 7 shifts attention away from dyads, or traditional two-partner alliances, in order to consider issues that arise in more complex deals such as multi-party alliances and in managing alliance portfolios. Chapter 8 is devoted to how entrepreneurial companies can develop their alliance capability to become better at managing alliances. Finally, Chapter 9 concludes with a discussion of performance management in order to consider how firms can know whether or not their collaborations are on track. This chapter presents some of the metrics that firms can use to assess their alliances, covers some of the nonfinancial aspects of alliance performance, and presents a methodology for selecting and developing the appropriate measures to evaluate an alliance.

Key Terms

- strategic alliances
- entrepreneurial alliances
- relational contracts
- horizontal and vertical alliances
- alliance life cycle

End of Chapter Questions

1. Why have alliances become so prevalent? How have the types of collaborations changed over time?
2. How do alliances differ from other types of relationships such as customer relationships or supplier relationships?
3. What are the main costs, or drawbacks, of collaborative agreements?
4. What are some of the unique challenges entrepreneurial firms face in forming strategic alliances?
5. If you were to enter into an alliance, what would be the main causes of failure as well as the key success factors that you would be most sensitive to? Which ones would you believe you need to work on as an individual entrepreneur or manager?

References

1. For the full survey, see http://www.bain.com/management_tools/home.asp.
2. Spekman, R. E., & Isabella, L. A. 2000. *Alliance competence.* New York: John Wiley and Sons; Ireland, R. D., Hitt, M. A., & Vaidyanath, D. 2002. Alliance management as a source of competitive advantage. *Journal of Management*, 28: 413–446.
3. See also Dollinger, M. J., & Golden, P. A. 1992. Interorganizational and collective strategies in small firms: Environmental effects and performance. *Journal of Management*, 18: 695–716. Golden, P. A., & Dollinger, M. 1993. Cooperative alliances and competitive strategies in small manufacturing firms. *Entrepreneurship Theory and Practice*, 17: 43–56; Marino, L., Strandholm, K., Steensma, H. K., & Weaver, K. M. 2002. The moderating effect of national culture on the relationship between entrepreneurial

orientation and strategic alliance portfolio extensiveness. *Entrepreneurship Theory and Practice*, 26: 145–160; Steensma, H. K., Marino, L., Weaver, K. M., & Dickson, P. H. 2000. The influence of national culture on the formation of technology alliances by entrepreneurial firms. *Academy of Management Journal*, 43: 951–973. Zacharakis, A. L. 1998. Entrepreneurial entry into foreign markets: A transaction cost perspective. *Entrepreneurship Theory and Practice*, 21: 23–39.

4. Bamford, J. D., Gomes-Casseres, B., & Robinson, M. S. 2003. *Mastering alliance strategy*. New York: John Wiley and Sons.

5. Doz, Y. L. 1996. The evolution of cooperation in strategic alliances: Initial conditions or learning processes? *Strategic Management Journal*, 17: 55–83.

6. Gomes-Casseres, B. 1997. Alliance strategies of small firms. *Small Business Economics*, 9: 33–44.

7. See Bamford, J. D., Gomes-Casseres, B., & Robinson, M. S. 2003. Op. cit., for a similar definition.

8. Chesbrough, H. W. 2002. Making sense of corporate venture capital. *Harvard Business Review*, 80: 90–99.

9. Hagedoorn, J., & Hesen, G. 2007. Contract law and the governance of inter-firm technology partnerships: An analysis of different modes of partnering and their contractual implications. *Journal of Management Studies*, 44: 342–366.

10. Shane, S., & Venkataraman, S. 2000. The promise of entrepreneurship as a field of research. *Academy of Management Review*, 25: 217–226.

11. Branstetter, L., & Sakakibara, M. 2002. When do research consortia work well and why? Evidence from Japanese panel data. *American Economic Review*, 92: 143–159.

12. See, for instance, Zahra, S. A., Ireland, R. D., & Hitt, M. A. 2000. International expansion by new venture firms: International diversity, mode of market entry, technological learning, and performance. *Academy of Management Journal*, 43: 925–950.

13. See, for example, Cohen, W., & Levin, R. 1989. Empirical studies of innovation and market structure. In R. Schmalensee & R. Willig (Eds.), *Handbook of industrial organization*: 1060–1107. New York: North-Holland; Teece, D. 1986. Profiting from technological innovation: Implications for integration, collaboration, licensing, and public policy. *Research Policy*, 15: 286–305; New York: Elsevier. Shane, S., & Venkataraman, S. 2000. The promise of entrepreneurship as a field of research. *Academy of Management Review*, 25: 217–226.

14. Autio, E., Sapienza, H. J., & Almeida, J. G. 2001. Effects of age at entry, knowledge intensity, and imitability on international growth. *Academy of Management Journal*, 43: 909–924.

15. Acs, Z., & Audretsch, D. 1988. Innovation in large and small firms: An empirical analysis. *American Economic Review*, 78: 678–690.

16. Begley, T. 1995. Using founder status, age of firm, and company growth rate as the basis for distinguishing entrepreneurs from managers of smaller businesses. *Journal of Business Venturing,* 10: 249–263; McDougall, P. P. & Oviatt, B. M. 1996. New venture internationalization, strategic change, and performance: A follow-up study. *Journal of Business Venturing*, 11: 23–40.

17. Ireland, R. D., Hitt, M. A., & Sirmon, D. G. 2003. A model of strategic entrepreneurship: The construct and its dimensions. *Journal of Management*, 29: 963–989.

18. See also Doz, Y. L., & Hamel, G. 1998. *Alliance advantage*. Boston, MA: Harvard Business School Press.

19. Ernst, D. 2003. Envisioning collaboration. In J. D. Bamford, B. Gomes-Casseres, & M. S. Robinson (Eds.), *Mastering alliance strategy*. New York: John Wiley and Sons.

CHAPTER 2

MOTIVES FOR ENTREPRENEURIAL ALLIANCES

INTRODUCTION

Entrepreneurial alliances have proliferated in recent years because they enable firms to access resources and new markets to accelerate profitable growth. For example, the biotechnology firm Invitron had an equity partnership with the agricultural firm Monsanto and as a consequence was able to go public when it was less than three years old. It has been estimated that the effect of the Monsanto alliance was a 91% increase in Invitron's market value.[1] The advantages that alliances can bring to entrepreneurial firms are many, and recent texts have recognized over a dozen benefits that firms might attain by engaging in collaborative agreements.[2] In this chapter, we will cover the economic foundations of entrepreneurial alliances in order to understand some of the most important motives that entrepreneurs have in mind when considering the formation of alliances.

When entrepreneurs are asked to enumerate the reasons why their firms might take on a partner, they often list reasons such as the following: (1) to improve their survival chances, (2) to obtain critical resources, (3) to tap into others' financial capital, (4) to create new businesses, (5) to accelerate growth in certain product markets, (6) to achieve rapid internationalization, and (7) to cope with various uncertainties. Each of these rationales for entrepreneurial alliances will be explored in this chapter, and Chapter 8 will also emphasize how firms learn from partners as well as learn how to manage alliances themselves more effectively.

Of course, firms might use alternative investment vehicles to realize such objectives. For example, if a firm wants access to resources that complement their own and achieve growth, an acquisition is also possible, and entrepreneurial firms have recently become more involved in the acquisition market.[3] In addition, entrepreneurial firms routinely find themselves on the sell side of acquisition transactions, so the question arises as to whether it is better to obtain resources by selling the firm to another company versus forming an alliance with them. There are also other means by which firms can directly obtain financial capital. Alliance investments should therefore be made after conducting a thorough analysis of alternative ways of accomplishing the entrepreneur's primary objectives. We will illustrate this point by considering alliances as an alternative to an acquisition, and we will consider entrepreneurial firms on both the buy and sell sides of such transactions. First we examine the key objectives that lead firms to consider forming an alliance.

MOTIVES FOR FORMING ENTREPRENEURIAL ALLIANCES

The confluence of several trends in the business environment has contributed to the rise in entrepreneurial alliances as the economy undergoes important transitions. Globalization has created new market opportunities to sell products and services to international customers, yet pressures to internationalize quickly can also seriously strain a firm's resources and administrative capacity, particularly if the firm seeks to do everything on its own. Technological changes also present new opportunities to work collaboratively with other firms and achieve more out of the firm's scarce resources. The possibility of developing dominant technological standards in some industries encourages firms to move quickly to obtain a first-mover advantage, and alliances can be used as a way to develop technological standards. Deregulation and industry convergence create new opportunities for collaborative agreements to expand into new markets, build scale, and bring together the needed resources. Hypercompetition has eroded the half-life of valuable resources and market positions and therefore places a premium on speed. These and other developments have contributed to a complex set of requirements for organizations to be more specialized yet coordinated, committed while flexible, and so on. Alliances can play an important role in responding to these conflicting needs and challenges.

There are many different rationales for why firms enter into strategic alliances, and we have already touched upon some of them in Chapter 1. Our goal is not to offer an exhaustive list of collaborative motives, but to highlight several of the most interesting and important objectives of partnering firms and to give attention to those motives that are especially germane to the entrepreneurship process and to entrepreneurial firms (see Table 2.1).

TABLE 2.1 Illustrative Drivers and Objectives of Entrepreneurial Alliances	
Environmental Trends	*Alliance Objectives*
• Globalization	• Overcoming the liability of newness
• Technological changes	• Tapping into new skills and resources
• Deregulation	• Accessing financial resources/substitutes
• Industry convergence	• Creating new businesses and market space
• Hypercompetition	• Accelerating growth in markets
• Deintegration of value chains	• Achieving rapid internationalization
	• Managing risk

OVERCOMING THE LIABILITY OF NEWNESS

New ventures face many obstacles that must be overcome to survive and prosper in the marketplace. Often they lack relationships, or have an undeveloped set of relationships, with key stakeholders such as investors, suppliers, employees, and customers. Such stakeholders might view the new venture with natural skepticism because of the short time the firm has had to develop a track record or reputation. New ventures also often lack important experiences that accumulate with time, whether in marketing, production, or other administrative tasks tied to the execution of the new venture's business model. For many new ventures, particularly those in high-tech domains, their key resources are intangible in nature, such as a new technology, whose efficacy and market prospects might be highly uncertain and difficult for investors and other resource providers to evaluate. Compounding these problems, many new ventures might not have the financial wherewithal to make necessary investments or withstand technological or commercial setbacks. Together these problems exacerbate new ventures' risk of failure and contribute to their liability of newness.[4] The liability of newness can be seen as the root problem new ventures need to address in order to survive and prosper, and alliances can be one important tool for addressing this problem.

Alliances can begin to counter firms' liability of newness in at least two different ways, directly and indirectly. First, alliances can help address a new venture's resource shortfalls by teaming up with a larger or more established firm. Biotechnology firms, for instance, routinely partner with other firms to obtain access to production or other expertise during clinical trials and commercialization. A new venture might also team up with a more established partner to distribute the new venture's product. In effect, the new venture not only gains access to the established firm's expertise and relationships in particular marketing channels, but it "bonds" itself to this firm, or borrows its good reputation, while the legitimacy of the new venture might otherwise still be in question.

Second, relationships with reputable partners can also have beneficial effects on the new venture's ability to secure resources from other sources as well. In this way, alliances can bring important indirect benefits to firms. Because new ventures are difficult to evaluate, they can find it challenging to obtain the resources they need from investors or other firms. Alliances with reputable partners can have the effect of "endorsing" the new venture, or providing a signal to other potential exchange partners that the new venture is of high quality. Evidence exists, for instance, that new ventures partnering with prominent organizations are able to undertake an initial public offering (IPO) sooner and raise greater proceeds compared to other new ventures, yet this effect declines as new ventures age and the liability of newness recedes.[5] Alliances can therefore have an important impact on the new venture's ability to obtain funds or other resources from other organizations on attractive terms. This suggests that partnerships with other organizations can both directly as well as indirectly help reduce entrepreneurial firms' liability of newness.

TAPPING INTO NEW SKILLS AND RESOURCES

At the root of many other motives to form alliances is the rationale of getting access to new skills and resources. Environmental trends such as globalization, technological developments, industry convergence, and so on suggest that skills and resources will be distributed widely across firms, even across industries and countries. Entrepreneurial alliances can therefore be useful as a way of tapping into these resources and capabilities that other organizations possess. This can benefit new ventures and more established organizations alike during the entrepreneurial process.

Alliances by New Ventures to Access Resources and Capabilities

Founders and others in new ventures will often have particular competencies and other strengths, but the success of entrepreneurial initiatives will often ultimately hinge upon management's ability to assemble a whole range of complementary resources that are needed to implement the firm's business plan. Semiconductor start-ups, for instance, are more likely to rely upon alliances in emergent or highly competitive markets, or when attempting pioneering technological strategies, because new ventures' resource needs and vulnerability are especially great under these conditions.[6] In other instances, very specific resource gaps can be filled by hiring a few key personnel or through internal development of the needed competencies or resources. Internal development is inefficient, however, when another firm has the needed expertise and resources, and such expertise and resources are time-consuming for the new venture to replicate yet inexpensive for another organization to share.[7] In the language of economists, such expertise or resources have a "public goods" quality to them. For instance, a distribution system can have a low marginal cost because, once it is set up, the cost of using it for a related product is negligible. Alliance partners can also provide country-specific expertise or other resources that would be time-consuming for the new venture to develop itself, yet other organizations can offer at low cost. Thus, alliances can be an important way for entrepreneurs to get access to complementary resources in a timely and cost-efficient fashion.

Alliances as a Part of Corporate Entrepreneurship Activities

Alliances can be useful not only for new ventures to access important resources and skills, but they can also be an important part of corporate entrepreneurship activities in established organizations. *Corporate entrepreneurship* refers to the processes by which established firms innovate, renew themselves, and develop new businesses.[8] Innovation is one of the core activities of corporate entrepreneurship, and R&D alliances have long been recognized as important sources of innovation. Some of the earliest perspectives on alliances and innovation suggested that alliances designed to outsource certain R&D activities might substitute for internal R&D efforts, but more recently such alliances have been portrayed as an important complement to firms' internal R&D initiatives. In particular, firms have adopted more open models of innovation that rely on alliances and external knowledge to enhance their corporate entrepreneurship activities. For instance, Procter and Gamble has replaced its "invent it ourselves" approach to innovation to a "connect and develop" model that includes collaborations with various entrepreneurial firms to increase its R&D productivity and discover new growth opportunities.[9]

As another example of how alliances can be used for purposes of corporate renewal, Intel Corp. took a minority equity stake in Xircom, Inc. with the aim of developing advanced mobile business computing products. One of Intel's market objectives in entering into this alliance was to obtain better growth prospects outside of its maturing computer chip business. As Intel's growth in its core business slowed further, it acquired additional equity ownership in Xircom in order to boost its wireless offerings. By forming alliances in new domains to access external knowledge, established firms are able to enhance their entrepreneurial activities and can renew their strategies and growth prospects.

ACCESSING FINANCIAL RESOURCES OR SUBSTITUTES

Although firms of all types enter into alliances to obtain various sorts of resources, entrepreneurial ventures can find alliances attractive to access financial resources in particular, or as substitutes for needed financial resources. This raises the question of why entrepreneurial firms seek such relationships rather than pursue other sources of external finance, including stock offerings, debt, venture capital, angel investors, and so on that other firms routinely tap into.

The answer to this question finds its roots in the failures that exist in financial markets, which entrepreneurial firms often experience. If we were to assume hypothetically that financial markets are perfect and entrepreneurs are entirely rational, entrepreneurs would make investment decisions solely based upon the marginal profitability, or net present value (NPV), of their potential projects. However, financial markets are imperfect because external capital providers (e.g., banks, equity investors, etc.) often do not have adequate information on entrepreneurs, their businesses, and their future prospects. While entrepreneurs could conceivably provide this information, two difficulties arise in practice.

First, the entrepreneur does not want to disclose information that is sensitive, or could be used by a potential competitor to imitate his or her business model. Second, the entrepreneur desires funds on the best possible terms and therefore has a natural incentive to disclose positive information on his or her abilities and prospects as well as withhold negative information. This implies that information is asymmetric, and that external investors might not know as much about the entrepreneurs' resources, capabilities, and future prospects. Moreover, even if an entrepreneur is committed to being forthcoming with external investors, he or she can face a credibility problem when disclosing information due to these incentives. When these problems cannot be resolved, external investors face the risk of funding ventures that wind up being inferior, and the entrepreneur's cost of external finance can be much higher than its cost of using internal funds. The venture can then become "liquidity constrained," or cannot pursue certain projects in the absence of internal funds.[10]

Addressing this problem can therefore be critically important for the growth and even survival of entrepreneurial firms. Studies of start-ups note that founders are often left to finance early-stage ventures primarily out of the own savings, and that entrepreneurs are limited to a capital stock of roughly one and one-half times their wealth.[11] Other research has concluded that new ventures with better financial resources are more likely to survive, grow faster, and perform better.[12] Addressing the problem of liquidity constraints can enable firms to invest, how and when they need, in order to pursue the opportunities they have discovered or created.

While no one action is likely to address this problem completely, alliances might be a useful part of the solution in three ways. First, as discussed earlier, alliances enable firms to access resources and capabilities of other organizations rather than requiring entrepreneurial firms to develop all of these resources and capabilities internally. As such, the entrepreneurial firm's partner makes what might be thought of as a "payment in kind" by contributing access to distribution channels, production expertise, or some other resource for the contributions the entrepreneurial firm makes. The partner's resources in effect substitute for financial resources since the alliance partner provides the resources that the entrepreneur would have needed to finance. By obtaining access to resources and capabilities in this fashion, the entrepreneurial firm addresses the problem of either bearing the high costs of external finance or not making needed investments when internal funds are lacking.

Second, alliance partners themselves can provide financial resources for projects in which the new venture is engaged. For example, Eli Lilly and Company has sought to become the alliance partner of choice in the pharmaceutical industry and has engaged in a host of alliances. Many of these collaborative agreements involve Lilly taking an equity stake in other firms with products at very early stages of development (i.e., preclinical, animal trials) and lacking financial resources to support their R&D programs. Of course, access to financial resources via alliances also comes at a significant cost for the entrepreneurial firm. In an alliance between Lilly and Repligen, Lilly had control over all aspects of marketing and could conduct extensive reviews of new products under development, though Repligen had substantial control over the lead product. In a more extreme example, in a partnership between Alza and Ciba-Geigy, Alza was experiencing a financial crisis and ceded almost all of the control rights to Ciba-Geigy when the partnership was formed. For instance, Ciba had a supermajority on the board that oversaw research projects as well as eight out of the eleven seats on Alza's board, the right to license and produce Alza's current and future products, and the right to block future alliances that Alza might pursue.[13] When facing liquidity constraints, entrepreneurial firms clearly pay when teaming up with alliance partners to counter this challenge.

Finally, even if alliance partners do not provide funds directly, they can ease liquidity constraints in a more indirect fashion. When an entrepreneur engages in an alliance with an established organization with a good reputation, this can send a powerful signal to external investors that the firm is of high quality, even if its resources and prospects remain difficult for external investors to appraise.

CREATING NEW BUSINESSES AND MARKET SPACE

In all of the examples just noted, alliances can have an important impact on the entrepreneurial firm's resources and capabilities, whether by enhancing a new venture's legitimacy and helping it to address its liability of newness, or helping an entrepreneurial firm access needed resources and capabilities, or addressing its liquidity constraints. While these and other motives for alliances are internally focused, the rationales for alliances can also be expressed in terms of external, market objectives. These external objectives can be seen as opposite sides of the same coin of trying to enhance the entrepreneurial firm's survival odds and prosperity, as they often go hand in hand with objectives such as shoring up the firm's resources and capabilities. One such example is some firms' usage of alliances to create new businesses and market space.

Alliances can be useful in creating innovative businesses because they can connect firms that operate in different industries or have different customer bases. Alliances therefore help entrepreneurial firms as well as established companies create new market space and attempt to offer buyers a new set of utilities over existing offerings. As one potential example, out of IBM's informal, unpaid alliance with the Mayo Clinic to research genomics grew opportunities in bioinformatics to search large-scale databases containing data on millions of patients, without compromising patients' privacy, giving IBM an opening into the $1.4 trillion healthcare business.[14] Partnerships are also emerging between energy firms, biotechnology companies, and agricultural firms to develop and market biobutanols and other advanced biofuels.

ACCELERATING GROWTH IN MARKETS

Once new businesses are created, alliances can also be useful to accelerate firms' growth trajectories. As one notable example, alliances have been used by Starbucks to leverage its brand in many different ways.[15] Many of their partners have allowed for expansion into particular geographic markets (e.g, Alsea in Mexico, Shinsegne in Korea, Rustan in the Philippines, etc.). Other alliances are with corporate partners such as Westin Hotels and Resorts to provide new marketing channels. Starbucks has also formed alliances with partners to pursue new products and marketing opportunities (e.g., with Pepsi for bottled coffee drinks).

Even in the years surrounding Starbucks' IPO in 1992, partnerships were important to the firm's business model and expansion plans. Prior to going public, Starbucks obtained the Horizon Air account; introduced a coffee sampler with CARE, the international relief and development organization; and began a relationship with Host Marriott Services (HMS) for airport kiosks and in-hotel coffee cafes. While these partnerships are now well known, Starbucks initiated some of them when it had fewer than sixty stores. Right after Starbucks completed its IPO, it initiated partnerships with other retail-format partners, including Barnes and Noble for coffee stores within bookshops. Within three years after its IPO, Starbucks had been awarded accounts with Sheraton Hotels (now part of Starwood) and United Airlines; formed an alliance with Chapters Inc., a Canadian bookstore chain; partnered with Dreyer's to introduce super-premium coffee ice cream; and entered into a joint venture with Sazaby Inc. to open coffee stores in Japan. At this time its total number of stores stood at roughly seven hundred. Ten years later, its footprint stood at more than twelve thousand stores, and Starbucks reported how it was using alliances to form new record labels (i.e., with Concord Music Group), to distribute Ethos Water (i.e., with Pepsi), and to partner with Brazilian retailers (i.e., Cafés Sereia do Brasil Participações S.A.). Although we don't know exactly what Starbucks' growth trajectory would have been like without these partnerships, alliances have played an important role in its expansion plans over the years.

ACHIEVING RAPID INTERNATIONALIZATION

A special case of the motive just discussed is some entrepreneurial firms' usage of alliances to internationalize rapidly. In years past, firms were portrayed as internationalizing in a slow, evolutionary manner.[16] According to this perspective, a firm first undergoes a period of domestic maturation during which its products, processes, financial assets, and so on are developed. Subsequently the firm expands overseas in a gradual manner, first expanding into countries presenting less uncertainty due to different cultures and institutions, and then incrementally expanding into progressively more uncertain countries as the firm's overseas experience accumulates.

More recently, a phenomenon of "born globals" has been noted, which denotes firms internationalizing from their inception rather than waiting to go overseas and following an incremental approach to growth. While some of the environmental trends noted earlier have likely contributed to a rising number of global start-ups, entrepreneurs do have discretion in deciding whether or not it is

TABLE 2.2 Questions Determining Start-ups' Pace of Globalization

1. Are the necessary human resources overseas?
2. Is foreign financing more readily available or attractive?
3. Do customers require the firm to be international?
4. Will international competitors respond quickly to the start-up?
5. Are worldwide sales needed for the venture's survival and profitability?
6. Will inertia make internationalization more difficult in the future?

sensible for their firm to internationalize at once or approach internationalization in a more evolutionary manner. Table 2.2 summarizes six questions that can be used to determine if a start-up should globalize in such a rapid manner.[17] Answers of yes to these questions suggest a greater need for the start-up to internationalize rapidly.

These questions also suggest a number of requirements for global start-ups to be successful: a global vision, internationally experienced managers, strong international networks, a unique intangible asset (e.g., brand or technology) to preempt a market, continuous innovations for product or service extensions, and worldwide coordination.[18] This is a tall order for entrepreneurs, and alliances can be useful to begin to address these challenges. For example, OptimaNumerics, a new venture formed in the United Kingdom in 2002, has an Asia Pacific sales office in Singapore, and R&D collaborations with organizations such as Ames Laboratory, Joint Supercomputer Center, and universities as well as many hardware/software partners and resellers such as SGI, Dolphin, McIntyre Computing Group, HP, and Quadrics to develop and sell software for scientific and technical computing solutions. As another illustration, Techmar Jones International Industries (TJII) of Atlanta had international sales and technology transfer rights to water treatment systems, and they quickly built up a network of international partnerships to market the product internationally, garnering sales revenues from Japan, Korea, Saudi Arabia, Germany, and Belgium.

Naturally, firms can use alliances to address both the "liability of newness" and the "liability of foreignness" encountered in overseas markets that can be fraught with risk. For instance, in the TJII example just cited, the firm later experienced difficulties setting up a manufacturing joint venture in the Middle East, which caused the firm to scale back its operations and even put the firm's future in question. As a second example, Bidland Systems, a seventy-five-employee firm in San Diego, had developed software for online auctions and was seeking a joint venture with Telefonica for Spanish-speaking markets outside the United States. Bidland later sued Telefonica, alleging that Telefonica promised the firm a joint venture to access Bidlands' technology and marketing strategy and then used this intellectual property (IP) to launch its own auction site, Katalyx.com. The case was settled over four years later for an undisclosed sum.[19]

MANAGING RISK

The motives just noted suggest a proactive stance toward the use of alliances to develop new businesses, accelerate growth, and internationalize rapidly. Firms also enter into alliances with an eye toward mitigating the effects of competitive or other uncertainties facing the entrepreneurial firm. For instance, the integration of markets in Europe has witnessed a rise in alliances between firms, in part to respond to new threats from competitors in other markets as well as to pursue new opportunities in those markets. European regulators have also encouraged such collaborations, known as European Economic Interest Groupings (EEIGs). As another example, three independent game developers—Altar Games, Bohemia Interactive Studio, and Black Element Software—formed the Independent Developers Association (IDEA Games) in order to address the dominance of the strongest publishing houses and provide independent software developers resources and support for bringing new games to market. As an alternative to joining forces with other small firms or new ventures, entrepreneurial firms might join multipartner alliances or coalitions with dominant incumbents in order to increase their survival odds in industries in which significant technological uncertainty exists. Such partnerships have been evident, for example, in emerging industries involving the development of technological standards.[20] Firms appear to trade off entering large-scale coalitions that are more likely to be successful with entering those that contain close rivals or otherwise reduce the share of benefits the firm will attain from joining the coalition. Years ago Sun, MIPS, and other firms were developing competing RISC architectures for workstations, and each of these firms orchestrated its own set of allied semiconductor firms, systems integrators, product suppliers, licensees, and other organizations.[21] More recently, the Wi-Fi alliance had over two hundred firms and competed with other technologies such as HomeRF, Bluetooth, and HiperLAN before the IEEE 802.11 standard supported by the Wi-Fi alliance became the de facto industry standard.[22] Chapter 8 will discuss some of the unique management challenges presented by multiparty alliances and alliance portfolios.

CHANGES IN THE CHARACTER OF ALLIANCES

While all of the motives discussed earlier apply to alliances today, there has also been a shift in the nature of collaborative agreements that is also related to the types of motives firms bring to collaborative agreements and to their management challenges (see Table 2.3). Historically, the preponderance of alliances was formed by large and diversified multinational firms, who used equity joint ventures to enter into a developing country. Often such investments were outside the firms' core business, which also made the investments more peripheral to the firm. These joint ventures were often the result of the host country government's restrictions on foreign direct investment, which precluded the establishment of wholly owned subsidiaries through acquisitions or organic growth. Technology transfer was commonly unilateral, from the multinational corporation to the host

TABLE 2.3 Conventional versus Contemporary Alliances	
Characteristics of Conventional Alliances	*Characteristics of Contemporary Alliances*
• International joint ventures into developing countries • Responses to government restrictions • Unilateral technology transfers • Local market access objectives • Commodity industries	• Coopetition (collaboration between rivals) • Networks • Multiproject deals • Multiparty alliances • Bilateral technology flows • Global market aspirations • Sectoral diversity

country, and the multinational firm's primary objective was to access the local market on a stand-alone basis. Joint ventures were particularly widespread in commodity industries.[23]

Today, however, alliances are often formed between direct competitors and therefore involve a complex blending of cooperation and competition. Knowledge development rather than market access is often a primary goal of partners, and knowledge flows both ways between parties. Deal structures are often quite complex, with multiparty and multiproject alliances being commonplace, firms are entering alliances as part of larger constellations in high-tech industries, and networks of alliances are becoming pervasive as the number of alliances has grown. Collaborators from a diverse set of industries are active in forming alliances, and they often enter into alliances with global, rather than local, market objectives in mind. In short, while alliances have been around for a very long time, it is fair to say that they have become more central to firms' strategies and operations, they involve greater competition and learning, and they are more complex.

THE NEED FOR COMPARATIVE ANALYSES OF ALLIANCES

While any of the rationales discussed in this chapter might prompt firms to consider forming alliances, this is not to suggest that alliances are the only, or even the preferred, way to obtain these benefits. This suggests that entrepreneurs investing in alliances need to understand not only what benefits alliances might offer their firms but also when alliances are appropriate compared to other alternatives such as organic growth and internal development of resources on the one hand and acquisitions on the other. As we will argue next, entrepreneurs and firms need to avoid making one of two types of errors: (1) using alliances when other alternatives might be better, and (2) failing to select alliances when they are to be the preferred mode of expansion. Thus, when an entrepreneur considers an alliance to obtain access to resources, exploit economies of scale, expand overseas, and so forth, a critical follow-on question needs to be asked:

> Why should the firm use an alliance rather than some other alternative for this business opportunity?

In other words, why should the entrepreneur seek out a partnership rather than getting access to complementary resources through an acquisition or by pursuing the opportunity by itself? Generally speaking, it will be time-consuming to assemble and develop other resources and capabilities through internal development and organic expansion, compared to using an alliance and accessing the resources and capabilities other companies have already developed. However, the firm can quickly obtain these resources either through an alliance or through an acquisition, and in fact new ventures have recently been more active in pursuing acquisitions.[24] Thus, these alternatives need to be compared rather than making a go/no-go decision for either one of them in isolation. We will therefore focus on when firms should use alliances versus acquisitions, and the considerations that guide this decision are distilled in Figure 2.1.

INFEASIBILITY

For many entrepreneurial firms, it is simply not feasible to consider purchasing another firm, particularly if the firm is just getting started or is subject to the liquidity constraints described earlier. What is financially feasible for a more established entrepreneurial firm hinges in part upon the slack financial resources it does have as well as conditions in the financial markets. When markets for IPOs are hot, for instance, an entrepreneurial firm can go public and obtain funds to engage in an acquisition program, rather than pursuing alliances while the firm is still privately held and lacks financial capital.[25] Some firms have also found it valuable to team up with private equity firms to be able to acquire larger firms than they otherwise could on their own. Blackstone, for instance, is a major private equity firm, and roughly a fourth of their commitments involved acquisitions that were conducted in partnership with operating companies.[26] For example, some Chinese firms eager to expand into new markets but who lack expertise to execute mergers and acquisitions (M&A) transactions have teamed up with private equity firms to expand overseas.[27]

INFLEXIBILITY

Another reason why acquisitions are often not pursued by entrepreneurs and other organizations is that they are not flexible. In other words, they can involve a rather large investment in a target firm under significant uncertainty. By contrast, alliances can help firms enhance their flexibility because alliances can involve smaller investments and enable firms to terminate them at low cost in the future. Such flexibility can be especially valuable under conditions of technological or market uncertainty.[28]

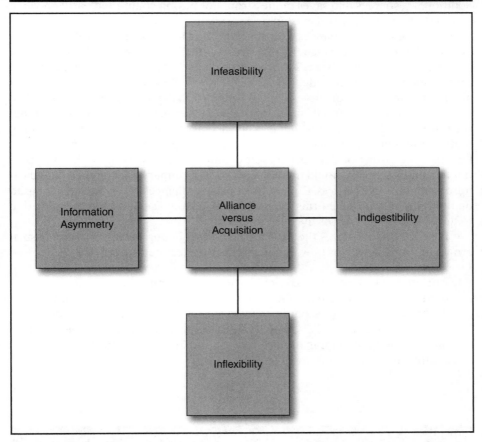

FIGURE 2.1 Drivers of Alliance Versus Acquisition Choices

An interesting analogy exists between investments in alliances and investments in financial options. In the latter case, an investor holding on to a financial call option has the right, but not the obligation, to make a certain investment decision (e.g., purchase the underlying stock) in the future. This option, or right, enables the investor to take advantage of upside opportunities that might emerge (e.g., a rising stock price) and also limit his or her downside losses (e.g., the investor is not compelled to buy the stock if it declines in value). In a similar way, investments in so-called real options, including "growth options" like alliances, enable the firm to position itself in order to capitalize on emerging opportunities in uncertain markets. If a certain technology or customer demand turns out to be more favorable than expected, the entrepreneur can devote additional resources to the technology or market.[29] However, if the technology or market does not develop so favorably, the entrepreneur is not obliged to commit additional resources and saves money from not having committed early on when substantial uncertainty still existed.

Under this view, alliances can therefore be useful as they enable entrepreneurs and other firms to stage their commitments. This perspective therefore challenges other views of alliances that view them as "marriages," or organizational arrangements meant for life. Some might view the duration and stability of alliances as indicators of success, and termination as an indication of failure. The "options" view, by contrast, suggests that alliances are valuable as transitional organizational arrangements that can be used as stepping stones when investing in uncertain markets. As a consequence, firms can gain by terminating alliances by either increasing or decreasing their commitments to certain business opportunities, and longevity should not be taken to be a primary goal or even an indicator of collaborative success. Rather, like options, alliances are to be judged based on their ability to reduce firms' downside risk as well as enhance their value due to the upside opportunities they present to firms.[30]

Figure 2.2 summarizes the processes involved in purchasing or creating such growth options as well as how to manage these investments over time.

1. Entrepreneurs first need to decide whether to commit to a technology or market or seek more flexibility. Both approaches can have merit under different circumstances. For instance, a strategy of "get big fast" to lock in customers and gain a first-mover advantage might be valuable when rivals might preempt emerging opportunities, but in other cases there is value in waiting and being more flexible.

FIGURE 2.2 Processes Underlying Investments in Options

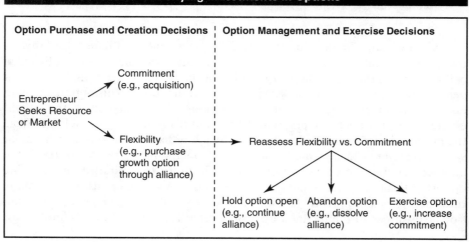

2. During subsequent processes, entrepreneurs make decisions whether to retain the option and the flexibility it affords by continuing on with a collaborative agreement, whether to abandon the option (e.g., dissolve the alliance), or whether to exercise the option and increase commitments to the technology or market based on the market signals that are forthcoming. This implies a need to revisit the initial logic for the alliance, judge changing internal needs or market realities, and be disciplined about terminating alliances and expanding commitments based on external market signals.

Even if the entrepreneurial firm is not interested in staging commitments in this manner, it needs to be concerned about the motives of its partner. For instance, an entrepreneurial firm might consider a particular collaborative agreement as a long-term solution to one of its needs, such as access to a distribution network or source of supply. However, it can run into difficulties if its partner sees the alliance as an option, or stepping stone, to access a technology or new market. Once the partner has acquired the necessary technological, market, or other resources it needs, it might not see much value in continuing an alliance with an entrepreneurial firm.

Entrepreneurial firms might also consider using an alliance prior to a sale, rather than prior to an acquisition. In the former case, the entrepreneurial firm is effectively granting another firm the option to expand its commitment, and the entrepreneurial firm needs to recognize that this option can be very valuable when it negotiates its collaborative agreements. For instance, many entrepreneurial firms partner with Cisco prior to selling their firms to this company.[31] Entrepreneurial firms can therefore use alliances to sequentially sell their companies to other organizations, and it is important that they value the options they are granting other organizations correctly since traditional valuation methods (e.g., analysis of discounted cash flows) often underestimate the value of such opportunities.[32]

INDIGESTIBILITY

Another reason why entrepreneurial firms might prefer to invest in a strategic alliance is to avoid the integration challenges and costs that acquisitions can involve during the merging of companies. *Indigestibility* refers to the problems that acquiring firms encounter when attempting to integrate certain target companies that are difficult to merge.

There are two main sources of indigestibility problems.[33] First, it can be costly to integrate firms' structures when the target is large in size compared to the acquirer, which can often be the case for more developed entrepreneurial firms considering an acquisition of another organization. Second, it can be costly to integrate a target firm that has a national or organizational culture that is quite different from the other firm. Given that entrepreneurial firms are often growing fast and their routines and structures are less determined than more established firms, they can encounter problems during the process of integrating organizational cultures, particularly if a bidder would impose its practices and policies on the entrepreneurial target firm. Alliances can be useful to avoid the problems of structural and cultural integration because they do not require the firms to integrate structures and cultures and they preserve the resources and functional policies of the target firm.

INFORMATION ASYMMETRY

Finally, an organization might choose to form an alliance with a target firm rather than conduct an acquisition when it is difficult to evaluate the assets of the target firm. Information asymmetries will exist, for instance, when the target firm operates in a different industry or possesses intangible assets that are difficult to appraise. In such cases, the buyer will only fully understand the value of the assets after an acquisition has been completed, despite the firm's efforts at due diligence to evaluate the target prior to an acquisition. There are at least three problems presented by asymmetric information: (1) Buyers face a risk of overpayment, sometimes called "adverse selection"; (2) sellers receive discounted offer prices; and (3) some otherwise attractive acquisitions might not happen because parties cannot come to agreement on price or other terms.

Alliances can be helpful prior to an acquisition transaction under these circumstances for several reasons. To begin with, the buyer is able to gain first-hand experience with the desired assets, and the alliance facilitates information sharing.[34] If this information sharing and learning convince the buyer that the assets are of high quality, the buyer can proceed with an acquisition with lower overpayment risk. For these reasons, research has found that the stock market responds favorably when firms create alliances when faced with the problems presented by asymmetric information.[35] As in the previous discussion, alliances can be very useful either prior to engaging in an acquisition or prior to selling a business, in order to resolve the problems presented by asymmetric information (e.g., overpayment risk for buyers and reduced offer prices for sellers).

Conclusion

This chapter has considered seven of the most important economic reasons, or investment rationales, that entrepreneurial firms might consider when evaluating alliances. Collaborative agreements are useful to entrepreneurial firms seeking to:

1. Overcome the liability of newness
2. Tap into new skills and resources
3. Access financial resources or substitutes
4. Create new businesses and market space
5. Accelerate growth in markets
6. Achieve rapid internationalization
7. Manage risk

Because alliances and other alternatives (e.g., organic growth through internal development of resources, inorganic growth through acquisition, etc.) have overlapping benefits, this chapter has also emphasized the need to compare alliances with alternatives rather than just making a go/no-go decisions for a particular collaborative opportunity. To illustrate this point, we have noted that firms often have similar growth objectives in forming alliances or engaging in acquisitions. It is also the case that motives for both types of deals are similar—economies of scale, access to complementary resources, synergies, and so on. Comparative analysis of alliances therefore raises the analytical hurdle and highlights new criteria for pursuing an alliance. For instance, an entrepreneurial firm might need to engage in an alliance rather than an acquisition if it is liquidity constrained. For firms with sufficient resources, alliances might still emerge as the best option if an acquisition provides insufficient flexibility to deal with uncertainties, if an acquisition would involve high integration costs due to structural or cultural integration difficulties, or if an acquisition would lead to overpayment risk given information asymmetries. We have also noted that alliances can not only be useful to help firms expand sequentially, or as a precursor to acquisition, but they can also be useful prior to completing a sale.

In Chapter 3, we will examine alternative types of alliances that firms might implement, once a decision to enter into some form of alliance has been made. We will also get into the details of how entrepreneurial alliances might design their collaborative agreements depending upon their motives for collaboration.

Key Terms

- liability of newness
- liquidity constraints
- liability of foreignness
- real options
- information asymmetry

End of Chapter Questions

1. What is the liability of newness, and how do alliances help address this challenge facing entrepreneurial firms?
2. Why are alliances useful for firms that are liquidity constrained?
3. What are the benefits and drawbacks of joining a constellation of firms seeking to advance a technological standard?
4. What firms should seek to internationalize quickly, and how can alliances help address the liability of foreignness?
5. How are alliances like financial options, and how are they unlike such options?
6. When should entrepreneurial firms engage in alliances prior to exiting through M&A?

References

1. Stuart, T. E., Hoang, H., & Hybels, R. C. 1999. Interorganizational endorsements and the performance of entrepreneurial ventures. *Administrative Science Quarterly*, 44: 315–349.
2. See, for instance, Hitt, M. A., Ireland, R. D., & Hoskisson, R. E. 2001. *Strategic management: Competitiveness and globalization*. Cincinnati, OH: South-Western College Publishing.
3. Zahra, S. A., Ireland, R. D., & Hitt, M. A. 2000. International expansion by new venture firms: International diversity, mode of market entry, technological learning, and performance. *Academy of Management Journal*, 43: 925–950.
4. See, for instance, Stinchcombe, A. 1965. Social structure and organizations. In J. G. March (Ed.), *Handbook of organizations*: 142–193; Hannan, M. T., & Freeman, J. 1984. Structural inertia and organizational change. *American Journal of Sociology*, 49: 149–164.
5. Stuart, T. E., Hoang, H., & Hybels, R. C. 1999. Interorganizational endorsements and the performance of entrepreneurial ventures. *Administrative Science Quarterly*, 44: 315–349.
6. Eisenhardt, K. M., & Schoonhoven, C. B. 1996. Resource-based view of strategic alliance formation: Strategic and social effects in entrepreneurial firms. *Organization Science*, 7: 136–150.
7. Hennart, J.-F. 1988. A transaction cost theory of equity joint ventures. *Strategic Management Journal*, 9: 361–374.
8. Guth, W. D., & Ginsberg, A. 1990. Guest editors' introduction: Corporate entrepreneurship. *Strategic Management Journal*, 11: 5–15. Zahra, S. 1995; Corporate entrepreneurship and company performance: The case of management leveraged buyouts. *Journal of Business Venturing*, 10: 225–247; Teng, B.-S. 2007. Corporate entrepreneurship activities through strategic alliances: A resource-based approach toward competitive advantage. *Journal of Management Studies*, 44: 119–142.
9. Huston, L., & Sakkab, N. 2006. Connect and develop: Inside Procter and Gamble's new model for innovation. *Harvard Business Review*, 84: 58–63.
10. For discussions of this problem in general, as well as in the setting of entrepreneurship, see for instance, Hubbard, R. G. 1998. Capital-market imperfections and investment. *Journal of Economic Literature*, 36:193–225; Amit, R., Glosten, L., & Muller, E. 1990. Entrepreneurial ability, venture investments and risk sharing. *Management Science*, 36: 1232–1245; Casson, M. 1982. *The Entrepreneur*. Oxford, UK: Martin Robertson. Himmelberg, C. P., & Petersen, B. C. 1994. A panel study of small firms in high-tech industries. *Review of Economics and Statistics*, 76: 38–51.
11. Evans, D. S., & Jovanovic, B. 1989. An estimated model of entrepreneurial choice under liquidity constraints. The *Journal of Political Economy*, 97: 808–827.
12. Cooper, A., Dunkelberg, W., & Woo, C. 1988. Survival and failure: a longitudinal study. In B. Kirchhoff, W. Long, W. McMullan, K. Vesper., & W. Wetzel (Eds.), *Frontiers of Entrepreneurial Research*. Babson Park, MA: Babson College. Reynolds, P., & White, S. 1997. *The Entrepreneurial Process: Economic Growth, Men, Women and Minorities*. Westport, CT: Quorum Books; Gimeno, J., Folta, T., Cooper, A., & Woo, C. 1997. Survival of the fittest? Entrepreneurial human capital and the persistence of under-performing firms. *Administrative Science Quarterly*, 42: 750–783; Fagiolo, G., & Luzzi, A. 2006. Do liquidity constraints matter in explaining firm size and growth?

Some evidence from the Italian manufacturing industry. *Industrial and Corporate Change*, 15: 1–39.

13. Lerner, J., & Merges, R. P. 1998. The control of technology alliances: An empirical analysis of the biotechnology industry. *Journal of Industrial Economics*, 46: 125–156.

14. Hamm, S., & Ante, S. E. 2005. Beyond blue. *Businessweek*, (April 18): 68–76.

15. Bamford, J. D., Gomes-Casseres, B., & Robinson, M. S. 2003. *Mastering alliance strategy*. New York: John Wiley and Sons.

16. Johanson, J., & Vahlne, J.-E. 1977. The internationalization process of the firm: A model of knowledge development and increasing foreign market commitments. *Journal of International Business Studies*, 8: 25–34.

17. For a more detailed discussion of these questions and the examples noted in this section, see Oviatt, B. M., & McDougall, P. P. 1995. Global start-ups: Entrepreneurs on a worldwide stage. *Academy of Management Executive*, 9: 30–43.

18. These recommendations also come from Oviatt, B. M., & McDougall, P. P. 1995. Op. cit.

19. Penttila, C. 2005. Stop, thief! A joint venture with a big company sounds like a dream—until the company backs out, takes your idea with it and leaves you in the dust. *Entrepreneur.com*, June.

20. Axelrod, R., Mitchell, W., Thomas, R. E., Bennett, D. S., & Bruderer, E. 1995. Coalition formation in standard-setting alliances. *Management Science*, 41: 1493–1508.

21. Gomes-Casseres, B. 1996. *The alliance revolution*. Cambridge, MA: Harvard University Press.

22. Lovev, D., Lechner, C., & Singh, H. 2007. The performance implications of timing of entry and involvement in multipartner alliances. *Academy of Management Journal*, 50: 578–604.

23. See Contractor, F., & Lorange, P. 1988. *Cooperative strategies in international business*. New York: Lexington Books; Harrigan, K. R. 1986. *Managing for joint venture success*. New York: Lexington Books.

24. Zahra, S. A., Ireland, R. D., & Hitt, M. A. 2000. Op. cit.

25. Brau, J., & Fawcett, S. E. 2006. Initial public offerings: Theory and evidence. *Journal of Finance*, 61: 399–436.

26. http://www.blackstone.com/private_equity/investment.html.

27. Mayer Brown. 2007. China private equity: Blackstone's corporate partnership template helps Chinese firms "go global."

28. McGrath, R. G. 1997. A real options logic for initiating technology positioning investments. *Academy of Management Review*, 22: 974–996; McGrath, R. G. 1999. Falling forward: Real options reasoning and entrepreneurial failure. *Academy of Management Review*, 24: 13–30.

29. Kogut, B. 1991. Joint ventures and the option to expand and acquire. *Management Science*, 37: 19–33.

30. Reuer, J. J., & Leiblein, M. J. 2000. Downside risk implications of international joint ventures. *Academy of Management Journal*, 43: 203–214. Tong, T., Reuer, J. J., & Peng, M. 2008. International joint ventures and the value of growth options. *Academy of Management Journal*, 51: 1014–1029.

31. Dyer, J. H., Kale, P., & Singh, H. 2004. When to ally and when to acquire. *Harvard Business Review*, 82: 109–115.

32. Luehrman, T. 1998. Investment opportunities as real options: Getting started on the numbers. *Harvard Business Review*, 26: 51–67.

33. Kogut, B., & Singh, H. 1988. The effect of national culture on choice of entry mode. *Journal of International Business Studies*, 19: 41–432; Hennart, J.-F., & Reddy, S. 1997. The choice between mergers/acquisitions and joint ventures: The case of Japanese investors in the United States. *Strategic Management Journal*, 18: 1–12.
34. Balakrishnan, S., & Koza, M. 1993. Information asymmetry, adverse selection, and joint ventures. *Journal of Economic Behavior and Organization*, 20: 99–117.
35. Reuer, J. J., & Koza, M. 2000. Asymmetric information and joint venture performance: Theory and evidence for domestic and international joint ventures. *Strategic Management Journal*, 21: 81–88.

CHAPTER

ALLIANCE GOVERNANCE

INTRODUCTION

Calyx was an entrepreneurial firm that developed an innovative business model for flower retailing.[1] It departed from the standard channel in which growers sell to distributors in growing regions, who sell to wholesalers and ultimately to retail shops by using a combination of catalog sales, telemarketing, and ecommerce, along with overnight shipping by FedEx. This new business model enabled growers to ship flowers directly to consumers while the flowers were just blooming rather than ten or more days old, as was the case under the traditional business model. In setting up this new business model for selling flowers, Calyx therefore needed to orchestrate a network of relationships with thirty growers as well as an important relationship with FedEx to maintain control and flexibility.

Entrepreneurial firms face three important decisions related to alliance governance: (1) Is an alliance the best way to pursue a business opportunity, or is some alternative form of organization such as an acquisition preferable? (2) If an alliance is best, what type of alliance should be formed? (3) Finally, how should the various governance mechanisms be designed?

Alliance governance refers to the ways in which the exchange relationship will be monitored and coordinated, as well as to the safeguards and incentives that are in place that can promote relationship continuity and efficiency while protecting partnering firms' interests. Alliance governance is therefore one of the most important aspects of forming alliances and can have an important impact on the subsequent implementation of alliances as well as on whether alliances are effective in delivering upon parent firms' objectives for them. Chapter 2 considered the first question on whether an alliance or some other arrangement (e.g., mergers and acquisitions [M&A]) is optimal, and in this chapter we wish to cover the next two questions on different types of alliances and ways entrepreneurs can design governance mechanisms in detail.

CHOOSING AMONG DIFFERENT TYPES OF ALLIANCES

The entrepreneurial firm might employ an array of different forms of alliances, as introduced earlier, so a decision is needed as to which structure is most suitable. Alliances can take many forms, including R&D (research and development) contracts, supply agreements, copromotion arrangements, minority equity partnerships, joint ventures, and many other types of deals. As a result, an alliance type decision must be made to select among the various forms of alliances. In this chapter, we will discuss ways of categorizing alliances to help with this selection, and we will also cover some of the important criteria for choosing between one form of alliance over another.

DESIGNING ALLIANCE GOVERNANCE MECHANISMS

After the entrepreneur has concluded that an alliance is sensible and has decided upon the most appropriate form of collaboration, he or she then needs to actually structure the business relationship and craft the legal agreement in detail. Decisions need to be made, for instance, on the alliance's scope and division of labor, the specific provisions that should go into the contract, the interfaces between firms and, if the alliance will be a joint venture, how the joint venture's board should be structured. Each of these choices represents an alliance design decision that can have an important impact on the governance and subsequent management of the collaborative agreement. In addition to these formal governance mechanisms, informal governance mechanisms such as trust can facilitate interfirm cooperation. In this chapter, we devote particular attention to the alliance contract as a means of establishing the alliance's governance when forming collaborative agreements, and subsequent chapters will delve into trust and alliance process issues.

A DECISION-MAKING MODEL OF ALLIANCE GOVERNANCE

Figure 3.1 provides a general decision-making model of alliance governance that captures these classes of choices that entrepreneurial firms make when forming alliances. The figure depicts how alliance governance choices are made in sequence as well as become progressively more specific. As noted, firms first make broader decisions such as whether to collaborate versus use some other investment vehicle (i.e., the alliance investment decision; Chapter 2) and whether to use one form of alliance over another (i.e., the alliance type decision). Firms also need to make very specific decisions about particular clauses to put into the alliance contract, and we will later provide some specific examples of the number and complexity of these clauses.

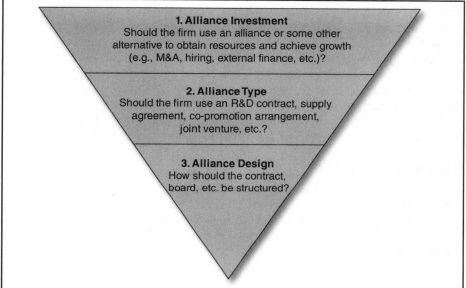

FIGURE 3.1   A Decision-Making Model of Alliance Governance

1. Alliance Investment
Should the firm use an alliance or some other alternative to obtain resources and achieve growth (e.g., M&A, hiring, external finance, etc.)?

2. Alliance Type
Should the firm use an R&D contract, supply agreement, co-promotion arrangement, joint venture, etc.?

3. Alliance Design
How should the contract, board, etc. be structured?

To begin these three decision-making steps concerning alliance governance, a number of basic preliminary matters will need to be clear at the outset, including:

1. What are the primary commercial objectives of the alliance?
2. What are the partners' anticipated resource contributions to the collaborative agreement?
3. What will be the alliance's product market scope and geographic scope?
4. What are the key hazards or risks that the parties face, and what are their interests in the collaboration?
5. What are the specific ways in which the parties will obtain financial or non-financial returns from the alliance?[2]

The partners will then make much more detailed choices on alliance contracts, boards, structures, and the like (i.e., alliance design decisions). This figure also summarizes the order of material presented in this chapter. We begin with alliance type decisions and then turn to alliance design decisions. The discussion of alliance design decisions highlights a few important legal issues with which entrepreneurs and general managers should be acquainted, though legal experts will be involved in the technical aspects of drafting particular provisions in alliance contracts.

DECISIONS ON ALLIANCE TYPE

One of the challenges that arises when considering the tradeoffs firms might take into account when selecting an alliance type is that there are so many different forms that alliances might assume, so it is simply not practical to attempt to compare them all at once. Despite the diversity of alliance types, however, fortunately they share some common underlying features that enable decision-makers to rule out certain alliances and flag others for additional evaluation. In broad terms, alliances can be aggregated into two distinct categories: nonequity alliances and equity alliances. Examples of each will be discussed in turn next, and criteria for selecting between nonequity and equity alliances will be developed.

NONEQUITY ALLIANCES

The distinguishing feature of nonequity alliances is that they are governed by a contractual agreement between the participating firms. This means that no independent business entity is created (e.g., as in an equity joint venture), and there are no cross-equity holdings between the partners. The following are several examples of nonequity alliances:

- Nuvelo, a small firm based in San Carlos, California, formed an alliance with Bayer Healthcare to develop and commercialize Alfimeprase, a drug for stroke and deep vein thrombosis. Nuvelo retained commercialization rights in the United States, while Bayer Healthcare was to distribute Alfimeprase outside the United States. Given the significant market potential of the drug and its late stage in development, Bayer agreed to make up to $385 million in payments as well as pay tiered royalties up to 37.5% to enter into this agreement with Nuvelo.
- Sipex and Eten Information Systems of Taiwan formed a strategic alliance to produce camera phones. The agreement not only covered manufacturing activities but also design activities as the firms collaborated to design a phone incorporating a high-powered LED flash using Sipex's integrated circuits to power the flash.

As these examples suggest, nonequity alliances can be used in all stages of the firm's value chain, ranging from R&D to production to marketing and distribution in order to tap into other organizations' capabilities and access new markets.

A natural question that arises is how such nonequity alliances differ from plain vanilla contracts or other transactions of a pure "market" variety. On some entrepreneurial firms' websites, for instance, one sometimes sees the phrase *our partners* to describe a new venture's business dealings with a range of vendors, value-added resellers, or customers. Are such relationships truly "alliances"? Returning to the definition set forth in Chapter 1, an alliance necessitates firms working together, or making some specific investments in the relationship, under an incomplete contract. So, vendors conferring special status or volume discounts are not necessarily alliance partners per se, nor are relationships in which a firm purchases technology or some other resource for cash in what might be termed an *arm's-length transaction* in which there is little or no ongoing interaction or coordination between the parties. In alliances, parties also customize contracts to a great extent, whereas in arm's-length transactions, or market-based contracts, the agreements will tend to be standardized. Given that the term *alliance* signifies a close working relationship and special status, however, it is natural for entrepreneurial firms to use this term rather broadly to garner endorsements from others or to obtain business in the future. It is even possible for firms to consider other organizations' partners even when no legal agreement governs their relationship with each other. The term *alliance* is therefore used in various ways in practice, and it can also be argued that the content, governance, and management of such relationships are more important than the precise terminology used to distinguish what is, or is not, an alliance.

EQUITY ALLIANCES

The second broad class of collaborative agreements is *equity alliances*. The feature that distinguishes this form of alliance is that shared ownership is added to a contractual agreement. Like nonequity alliances, equity agreements can come in several different forms, and some of the common types of equity alliances are summarized graphically in Figure 3.2 to distinguish different configurations of joint ownership. For instance, *minority equity partnerships* involve a parent firm (e.g., P_1) taking less than 50% ownership in some other firm (e.g., P_2) in its

FIGURE 3.2   Illustrative Equity Alliances

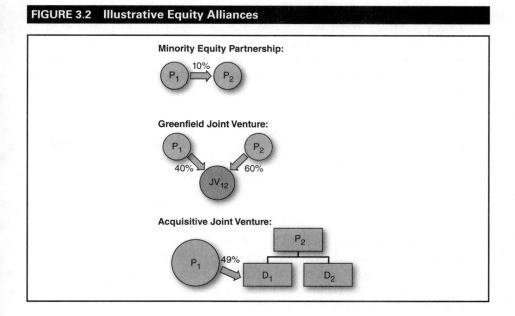

entirety. For example, P_1 might acquire a 10% ownership position in P_2. The following are some illustrations of minority equity partnerships:

- Healthcare organizations form minority equity partnerships by establishing limited liability corporations with a group of physicians and offering them capital and guidance to facilitate the venture's growth. For their part, the healthcare organization benefits from improved access to patients and managed care plans.[3]

- Realogy, a franchise system in real estate and relocation services, acquired a minority interest in Century 21 China Real Estate to capitalize on impressive growth opportunities in residential housing in China.

- Many entrepreneurial and high-tech firms have also been the object of minority equity investments. Cisco's minority equity stakes provide a case in point. For instance, along with Informix and Softbank Ventures, Cisco acquired a minority stake in VXtreme, a provider of high-quality streaming video for Internet and corporate networks, to ensure interoperability and to develop networking infrastructure.

It is also possible for firms to have equity cross-holdings, in which case P_1 owns an interest in P_2 and vice-versa. Often with such minority equity partnerships a firm can obtain some influence over the other firm because board representation accompanies the ownership position. Moreover, corporate venture capital can be seen as a type of alliance because these equity stakes are not just "market" transactions in which cash is invested in another company, but rather investing firms can shape the strategic direction and operational activities of portfolio companies, and substantial controls appear in such agreements (e.g., milestone agreements, liquidation preferences, etc.).

Equity joint ventures have the two firms, P_1 and P_2, jointly owning some distinct and separate business. For instance, one type of equity joint venture, the so-called greenfield joint venture, entails two partners setting up some new business, JV_{12}, and the two firms share in the joint venture's profit stream. For instance, P_1 might own 40% of the equity, and P_2 might own 60% of the new business. The following are several examples of greenfield joint ventures:

- At the end of 2005, Evergreen Solar and Q-Cell AG formed a 75.1–24.9% equity joint venture called EverQ to develop, manufacture, and distribute 30-megawatt solar wafers and solar cells in Germany. Within six months, the firms had taken on a third partner—Renewable Energy of Norway—to provide the joint venture with 190 metric tons of silicon annually. Renewable Energy acquired a 15% interest in the joint venture, Evergreen Solar's stake went to 64%, and Q-Cell's stake became 21%.

- Hewitt Associates and Human Link of Japan formed a small, 40–60% joint venture named Hewitt HLC to offer foreign companies in Japan human resource outsourcing services (e.g., pay and benefits, personnel administration, etc.). The joint venture was initially capitalized at only $90,000 and was expected to generate sales of $3.5 million within its first three years.

- Geron Corp. and Exeter Life Sciences entered into a 49.9–50.1% joint venture named Start Licensing to offer management and licensing services for a portfolio of intellectual property rights for animal reproductive technologies, including nuclear transfer cloning technology.

Another distinguishing feature of equity joint ventures is that a separate board is put in place to enhance joint control over the separate business. Representation by partners on the board of directors is generally consistent with their equity stakes, though this need not be the case. Firms have set up joint ventures with a 51–49% equity split or even a 50.1–49.9% division to have more control, but they have also been criticized for focusing on the division of ownership to the exclusion of other important aspects of joint venture governance and management. Indeed, ownership is not tantamount to control because firms can exert their control in many ways. For instance, a partner might have the ability to appoint the joint venture's general manager or fill other key posts despite not having dominant ownership.

There are also many other means of influencing the joint venture since specific control rights as well as ancillary agreements are also negotiable. As one illustration, in biotechnology–pharmaceutical alliances, twenty-five different control rights have been identified, falling into the following four broad categories: (1) key aspects of alliance management (e.g., rights to undertake process development, manufacture final products, market products, etc.), (2) determination of alliance scope (e.g., rights to terminate particular projects or the alliance without cause, expand or extend, sublicense, etc.), (3) control of intellectual property (e.g., rights to partial patent ownership, control of patent litigation, delay or suppress publications, etc.), and (4) governance (e.g., control of top project management body, board seats, participation in financings, ability to make public equity purchases, etc.).[4] Schering-Plough, for instance, uses an "alliance relationship launch" to examine challenges in working together with a partner, and during this process specifies in detail which decisions are likely to come up, which individuals on the alliance team will be making them, with whom they should consult, and which ones require the approval of senior executives.[5] Firms' control over their alliances is therefore determined by the total package of control rights they and their partners negotiate.

As in other forms of alliances, equity joint ventures might entail more than two firms being involved in the collaborative agreement, as the EverQ example illustrates.[6] The presence of multiple partners can enhance resource access, spread risks, or achieve other benefits. For example, in many high-tech alliances, constellations of established and entrepreneurial firms come together in short order in multiparty alliances to develop a technological standard, such as the operating software for workstations or the IEEE 802.11 dominant design in the wireless local area network (WLAN) industry.[7] However, increasing the number or diversity of partners in a given collaboration can also have adverse effects on performance for two reasons. First, it can be more difficult to draft a sufficiently complete contract because of divergent goals and the corresponding difficulties associated with specifying collaborators' rights and obligations. Second, as the number of partners increase, it can become more difficult for partners to achieve cooperation in joint ventures as partners can "free ride" off one another if monitoring mechanisms are difficult to design.[8]

Equity joint ventures can also be *acquisitive joint ventures*. For instance, if P_2 is a multidivisional firm and P_1 is a single business company, P_1 might want to acquire an equity position in an existing division of P_2 rather than form a brand new company with P_2 (i.e., greenfield joint venture) or purchase an ownership position in P_2 in its entirety (i.e., minority equity partnership). A famous example of this form of alliance is the joint venture between Philips and Whirlpool, in which the latter obtained an equity stake in Philips' domestic appliances business in particular, which it later acquired in full. Another form of joint venture, in which two firms acquire ownership in a preexisting organization, is the *platform joint venture*. For these types of deals, P_1 and P_2 jointly purchase some third firm, F_3, in whole or in part, such as when Cinergy and General Public Utilities jointly purchased Midlands Electricity. In this case, the joint venture represents a hybrid form of acquisition with more than one bidder taking over a third party.

A CONTINUUM OF TRANSACTION TYPES

That the equity/nonequity dichotomy is a useful means of categorizing alliances and deciding upon alliance governance can be seen by comparing both types of alliances with other ways of organizing transactions, including doing an activity yourself, or internal organization, on the one hand and market-based exchange on the other. Equity alliances are more similar to relationships that occur within organizations because equity alliances entail greater control due to the equity ownership and boards involved. Equity and nonequity alliances can therefore be placed on a continuum of transaction types in order to draw comparisons between these classes of alliances and begin to develop criteria for choosing between them (see Figure 3.3).

In order to understand when equity alliances should be used rather than nonequity alliances, it is necessary to understand what really changes if transactions are governed more to the left, or more to the right, along this continuum. We can

FIGURE 3.3　A Continuum of Transaction Types

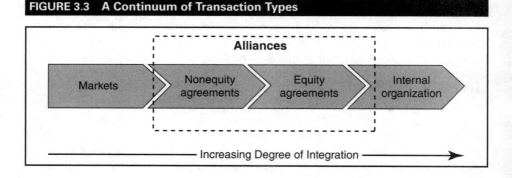

start with the two polar cases first. On the left-hand side, markets work well at handling certain types of transactions such as the purchase by the firm of standard components or commodity inputs like computer keyboards. For exchanges such as these, parties have similar information, price is a primary basis for making trades happen, and parties can switch at low cost if they are dissatisfied with each other for some reason. In situations such as these, the market functions quite efficiently.

However, for other types of transactions, using the market can become inefficient, providing a rationale for why exchanges happen within firms and for why firms exist in the first place rather than having all exchanges occurring over the market interface. For example, suppose a firm needs to make certain investments in plants, employee training, and so on, that are specific to a supplier or customer. If the relationship were to end, and if these investments could not be redeployed to another supplier or customer, switching becomes costly. When such problems exist, the firm is at risk of "holdup" by the supplier or customer, or having the supplier or customer seek to renegotiate terms of an agreement. As a second example, a firm might be at risk of others misappropriating its technology or not performing as agreed.

Under conditions such as these, exchanges happening within a firm can be more efficient than exchanges happening across firm boundaries in a market. This is because of the authority relationships existing in organizational hierarchies to facilitate exchanges and adjudicate disputes rather than relying on general competitive pressures or the court system, as is the case for market-mediated exchange, to make sure that parties do not act opportunistically. However, conducting exchanges within firms also gives rise to certain governance costs (e.g., levels of hierarchy, managerial overhead, etc.), which implies that comparatively simple transactions for which contracts can be drafted easily are better left to the market.

This logic reduces to an important rule of thumb for selecting transaction types along the continuum:

> The greater the threat of opportunistic behavior by another firm
> (e.g., renegotiating terms, cheating, misappropriating technology, etc.),
> the greater the need for integration, so transaction types to the right
> are to be preferred. The lower such threats, transaction types to the left
> are more efficient.

An example of this rule of thumb can be provided by the alternative ways that firms organize for innovation. Certain innovations require inputs that might be described as "autonomous," or ones for which improvements can be made in isolation without coordinating with other components of a product. These innovations can be outsourced, and often there are many qualified suppliers who are in competition to provide what a firm needs. A case in point is Motorola's external sourcing of nickel cadmium batteries for its wireless devices. By contrast, other innovations are "systemic," or ones that require substantial coordination with complementary technologies. Fuel cells or other advanced battery technologies would be examples of these innovations. Systemic innovations are better sourced in-house given the specific investments they require and their heavy coordination needs with other technologies managed by the firm. By sourcing such innovations in-house, Motorola is able to maintain control over the direction the technology takes, manage the timing of the innovation, and coordinate other related technologies.[9]

CHOOSING BETWEEN EQUITY AND NONEQUITY ALLIANCES

Because equity and nonequity alliances blend features of markets and internal organization yet are also ordered along the continuum in Figure 3.3, this rule of thumb for markets and internal organization can also be used for equity and nonequity alliances. Specifically, we can use it to derive conditions under which equity versus nonequity alliances should be selected based on their core underlying features. The differences in nonequity and equity alliances' governance properties can effectively be reduced to two fundamental distinctions. First, equity alliances afford greater *incentive alignment* between the parties compared to nonequity agreements since both firms have ownership in the collaboration. Take a two-party 50–50 joint venture as an example. Both firms are so-called residual claimants in the joint venture's operation, because they share the net profits from the collaboration. As a result, actions that harm the collaborative agreement have an adverse impact on both parties, so this encourages cooperation and reduces the incentives for parties to take actions to the detriment of the alliance. Second, equity alliances such as joint ventures afford greater *joint control* since a board of directors monitors behavior and performance in a separate business entity.

The choice between an equity alliance and a nonequity alliance is therefore a decision about whether incentive alignment and joint control are needed to mitigate opportunistic actions by another party (e.g., renegotiating terms, cheating, misappropriating technology, etc.), or whether firms are able to write a contract that is sufficient to govern the collaborative agreement without these additional protections and incurring greater governance costs.

These considerations lead to the following rule of thumb for the decision to enter into an equity versus nonequity alliance:

> If the threat of opportunistic behavior is high, the incentive alignment and joint control features of equity alliances will be attractive. If not, firms can use a purely contractual alliance (i.e., nonequity alliance) to govern their relationship efficiently.

DECISION-MAKING CRITERIA FOR EQUITY VERSUS NONEQUITY ALLIANCES

While there are many types of opportunistic behavior and factors influencing opportunism, the following are some specific questions entrepreneurial firms can ask to guide decisions about the use of equity versus nonequity alliances:

- Does the alliance involve significant *behavioral uncertainty*, or uncertainty about how each party will act once the collaborative agreement is executed?

When a partner's resources, expectations, incentives, or commitments in an agreement are not clear, behavioral uncertainty can be high. Under such conditions, the partner pays to use an equity alliance to help align incentives and enhance monitoring and control.

- How *complex* is the alliance? Complexity increases as the scope of an alliance (e.g., business, functional, or geographic) expands and if the alliance's division of labor is not sharp and the partners will need to coordinate their activities closely. Complexity also tends to increase as the number of partners in an alliance increases. If it is relatively easy to specify rights and obligations, activities, and contingencies affecting the collaboration, however, it is easier to write a contract and rely upon a nonequity alliance.

- Are significant *relationship-specific investments* needed in the alliance? Such investments might include outlays for equipment or plants that are tailored to the customers' needs. When such investments are made, holdup risk increases and necessitates the incentive alignment and control features of equity alliances.

- Do firms have *prior alliances* with one another? If so, they have probably developed routines for working together and might not need a separate organization to coordinate activities. The simple contractual interface provided by a nonequity alliance might be sufficient.

- Does the firm have *collaborative capabilities*? If not, it might be more exposed to the hazards presented by a nonequity alliance, compared to more experienced firms, and might need to use an equity alliance.

FURTHER BREAKDOWNS OF ALLIANCE TYPES

While the previous discussion aggregates together many forms of alliances into the broad categories of equity and nonequity governance structures, this is only a first step and clearly simplifies the selection of a particular type of alliance. In fact, the incentives, control rights, monitoring mechanisms, safeguards, and other aspects of alliance governance can vary a great deal within each of these two categories. For instance, within the nonequity category, contractual agreements that are unilateral in nature because one firm provides a technology or product and another party takes on a downstream function such as production or distribution (e.g., licensing agreements, supply contracts, etc.) might be distinguished from bilateral agreements (e.g., joint research, manufacturing, promotion, etc.). In the case of bilateral agreements, both partners tend to make specialized investments to the collaboration and such alliances tend to have improved incentive alignment compared to unilateral alliances.[10] While the alliance type decision we covered earlier helps to think about the features of broad classes of alliances, the drawbacks of aggregating diverse alliances into broader categories are also evident. Therefore a need exists to examine the details of alliance design in order to put in place the most appropriate governance mechanisms for a particular collaborative opportunity.

DECISIONS ON ALLIANCE DESIGN

Designing an alliance is considerably more complex than making decisions on alliance type because alliance design is multifaceted. Parties will need to agree on the alliance's scope, division of labor, interfaces between the organizations, control rights, contractual safeguards, and so on. In the remainder of this chapter, we will pay particular attention to the alliance contract. This is not only because other aspects of alliance design and governance (e.g., particular control rights) figure prominently in the collaborative agreement's contractual foundations but also because more knowledge exists on this aspect of alliance governance. It is also important to emphasize that we are presenting the decisions regarding alliance investment, types, and designs to reflect the increasing specificity of these choices, but the process by which decision-makers handle these choices need not be so linear.

INITIAL STEPS

When partners set out to design their collaborative agreement in detail, several initial steps are important to consider. The following eight questions can be used as an initial checklist before delving into more detailed commercial and legal issues that we will discuss:[11]

1. Is the feasibility study or business plan complete?
2. If confidential information will be disclosed, has a confidentiality or nondisclosure agreement been signed?
3. Is each party free to negotiate an alternative deal, or will "lockout" provisions preventing parallel negotiations be used?
4. Will a memorandum of understanding be used to outline the business principles of the alliance?
5. Do any of the parties have obligations for public announcements or shareholder approval?
6. What other authorizations, licenses, or other conditions must be met to begin the collaboration?
7. If the alliance is international, what effects will local laws have on the alliance (e.g., registration, taxes, profit repatriation restrictions, intellectual property rights, etc.)?
8. What governing laws should apply?

Confidentiality agreements can be used to safeguard sensitive information, particularly in the event that negotiations break down and the alliance is not formed. Such agreements can also be supplemented with additional protections such as restrictions on negotiating in parallel with other firms (e.g., "lockout" provisions) or limiting due diligence to a particular site or on a need-to-know basis.

Memoranda of understanding (MOU) need not be used to form an alliance, and one risk of such agreements is that firms enter into a legally binding agreement accidentally at an early stage, as in some legal regimes the MOU is already a binding agreement. Indeed, even simple oral discussions can become binding unless parties agree that they are "subject to contract." However, memoranda of understanding can be useful to help entrepreneurs or executives concentrate on the business fundamentals of an alliance before involving lawyers on the legal technicalities of a transaction. Memoranda of understanding can also be used for other purposes, including preparing public announcements and providing a platform for lawyers to work on the definitive contracts.[12] Table 3.1 provides an illustration of the contents that can be found in memoranda of understanding for alliances.

During these initial steps, the parties are laying the groundwork to structure the alliance legally. Even some matters that might seem self-evident or even trivial at first glance can be quite important to resolve at this stage. For instance, while the partners to the alliance might appear obvious, other parties might need to be part of the agreement for their obligations to be legally enforceable. These include a parent company of one of the parties, banks, or other associated companies that will have dealings with the alliance. It is also important in international collaborations to make decisions concerning what country's law will apply as partners can spend time dealing with this jurisdictional matter rather than on resolving substantive disputes that might arise after the alliance has been implemented.

TABLE 3.1 Contents of Memoranda of Understanding

1. Purpose of the agreement
   • Mission and value-added proposition
2. Spirit of the venture
   • Partners' commitment to the future
3. Key objectives and responsibilities
   • Targeted customers, products, etc.
4. Method of decision-making
   • Control rights
5. Resource commitments
   • Financial and "soft" resources
6. Financial philosophy
   • Pricing, costing, and transfer pricing
7. Assumption of risks
   • Expected rewards and profit division
8. Project specific issues
   • Intellectual property rights, handling of agents and distributors, etc.
9. Anticipated structure
   • Nonequity versus equity alliance
10. Transformation
   • Anticipated evolution or termination of the alliance

Source: Hewitt, I. 2005. *Joint ventures* (3rd Edition). London: Sweet and Maxwell.

CONTRACTUAL COMPLEXITY OF ALLIANCES

We will cover the various types of provisions that firms can negotiate into their alliance agreements, but it is important for partners to first consider in broad terms whether it is generally desirable or unattractive to seek to craft a complex legal agreement or a more open-ended agreement for the collaboration they have in mind.[13] On the one hand, alliance agreements will inevitability be incomplete, or will be unable to cover all potential contingencies that might arise and how firms will respond to them. It is also clear that designing a complex contract can consume significant resources since the services of lawyers, accountants, and consultants are costly. Perhaps even more importantly, protracted negotiations take executives away from other projects and activities that require their attention, and such protracted negotiations are also to be avoided when going to market quickly is one of the underlying rationales for the alliance. There is a myth of sorts of firms forming alliances in airport lounges on the basis of a handshake. However, it is also the case that firms enter into agreements under conditions of significant uncertainty, so partners place a premium on flexibility as well.

On the other hand, developing a more complex contract can serve several important purposes, even if it is not desirable or even possible to be exhaustive in specifying the contract. To begin with, it is valuable for partners to develop appropriate safeguards in alliance contracts to protect their technologies and other resources, customer base, and vital interests. Given the uncertain and ambiguous environments in which alliances are formed, it is also easy for partners to misunderstand each others' duties and interests. In the alliance contract, partners are able to ensure that certain rights are clear, and they commit to certain obligations by specifying the inputs to the collaboration, the ways in which firms will work together, and the outcomes they expect from the relationship. The process that underlies the development of the alliance contract also helps partners articulate, codify, and deepen the meeting of their minds for their collaboration. By forming a more complex contract, the partners can also place constraints and obligations on each other outside of the actual collaboration itself. Before the partners execute the agreement, they can limit information disclosures and, during the implementation of the alliance, the agreement can specify how the partners will interact with others, such as other associated companies, suppliers and customers, or the court system. Importantly, the contract can also govern how the alliance might be reconfigured or might come to an end.

These tradeoffs suggest that partners need to consider many different aspects of designing the alliance, both from a business and legal standpoint. Excessively complex agreements can limit flexibility under uncertainty and can also be costly. Overly simple agreements, by contrast, can expose the firm to various risks (e.g., appropriation of technology, liability, nonperformance, etc.) that can be mitigated through more deliberate contracting. The decision to bear the costs of negotiating a more complex or simple alliance contract is therefore similar to the decision to use an equity or nonequity agreement since the costs of contracting need to be

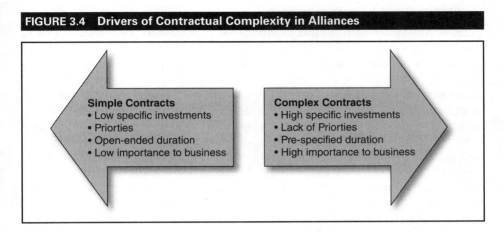

FIGURE 3.4 Drivers of Contractual Complexity in Alliances

Simple Contracts
- Low specific investments
- Priorties
- Open-ended duration
- Low importance to business

Complex Contracts
- High specific investments
- Lack of Priorties
- Pre-specified duration
- High importance to business

weighed against the risk of opportunistic behavior, which contractual safeguards can help curb.

Many factors influence the decision to use a more complex or simple contract, but we provide four illustrations here (see Figure 3.4).

Asset Specificity

Partners first need to assess the degree to which the alliance requires specific investments, or investments that are valuable for the implementation of the focal agreement but would have less value if used in some other relationship. At the extreme, sunk investments are those that would be effectively worthless if the alliance came to an end and, at intermediate levels, some investments might be redeployed but at significant cost if the alliance were to terminate (e.g., marketing, training, colocated facilities, etc.). As discussed earlier, when a firm makes a specific investment in an alliance, it exposes itself to the risk of "holdup" because the other firm can threaten to terminate the alliance, impose unfavorable conditions, or otherwise renegotiate its terms to extract some of this value. These potential risks make it advantageous to negotiate more complex contracts to safeguard the firms' commitments to the alliance. By contrast, when alliance termination would not impose a value loss on a company because its resource commitments are of a more general kind that can be easily redeployed to other relationships, such risks are low and fewer contractual safeguards need to be put in place.

Prior Ties

Partners might also consider whether or not they want to work with a familiar firm or a partner with whom they have not collaborated in the past, as well as how such prior ties could affect the negotiation and execution of the focal collaboration.[14] Successive collaborations between firms can reduce the need for complex contracts for two reasons. Prior ties can help cultivate trust as well as develop interorganizational routines that help make coordination more efficient. A Malaysian automotive components firm named Autobelt, owned in part by a Swedish firm, was introduced to Philippine Qualibrands by Embassy officials, and the firms had little or no common history together upon which to build a collaborative relationship.[15] Under circumstances such as these, executives not only might select an equity alliance over a nonequity structure to align incentives and exert more control, as discussed earlier, but also their contracts might be more complex to help coordinate activities. When partners have not worked together in the past, they are also likely to not understand each other's procedures, management systems, organizational cultures, and so forth, therefore it is particularly useful to articulate and codify how the alliance will be managed and governed. In successive collaborations, partners develop mutual understanding and reduce coordination, conflict resolution, or other problems and see less need to negotiate such provisions into alliance contracts. However, it is also the case that some conditions that were already discussed or agreed upon in the past can become "boilerplate" or common terms that are included in a new alliance contract at little or no additional contracting cost.[16]

Fixed Alliance Duration

Partners can also take into account the implications of alliances with a prespecified duration versus those that are open-ended in nature. Intuition suggests that alliances with a limited scope would have simpler contractual foundations. It is true that narrower alliances with very specific objectives present fewer obstacles for drafting more complete contracts, yet if we hold factors such as alliance purpose and scope constant, other considerations emerge. Specifically, whether or not alliances have a prespecified ending date or open-ended duration has an impact on partners' expectations for the alliance's future and can alter their incentives. For instance, in open-ended alliances that have the potential to last a long time, there is the prospect of future business that can make alliances "self-enforcing."[17] Given the opportunities for the parties to apply rewards and punishments to one another, the potential gains from future collaboration effectively safeguard the alliance from current opportunistic actions.[18] This so-called shadow of the future does not apply to short-term alliances with a prespecified duration, as partners' incentives are to look after their own short-term payoffs and extract as much value as possible before that ending date. It is also the case that the costs of contracting increase with the expected length of the collaborative agreement since it is difficult to foresee relevant contingencies and responses to them in the distant future,[19] whereas the set of relevant contingencies is easier to identify in short-lived agreements. Due to the positive incentives attached to open-ended agreements as well as the higher costs of negotiating contracts for such alliances, contractual safeguards for such collaborations tend to be less extensive than contracts for alliances with prespecified durations, holding everything else constant.[20]

Importance of the Collaborative Agreement

As a final illustration, partners need to assess the importance of the alliance to their entrepreneurial activities and overall business strategy. Several decades ago, most alliances were formed by large multinational companies and were often rather peripheral to their activities as they tended to operate in noncore businesses. However, for many entrepreneurial firms, alliances can be very important as a proportion of their overall business and therefore involve higher risks as a consequence. Alliances that are more important to the firm require more deliberation and clarity concerning the scope of the alliance, the division of labor amongst participants, rights and expectations, and the way the alliance will end, in order to avoid having valuable resources fall into the hands of a third party or inadvertently shoring up a competitor during the course of collaboration. As a consequence, these alliances demand greater safeguards and monitoring, and it pays to articulate and codify the mechanisms facilitating control of the alliance, the way disputes will be resolved, and the way termination will be handled. For alliances that are important to entrepreneurial initiatives or the firm's strategy, the entrepreneur has a greater incentive to bear the costs of negotiating more complex legal agreements in order to safeguard his or her interests in the collaboration.

CLASSES OF PROVISIONS IN ALLIANCE AGREEMENTS

The previous discussion has considered the tradeoffs between being exposed to the risks associated with opportunistic behavior and the costs of negotiating more complex alliance agreements in general. It is important to emphasize, however, that contractual provisions in alliance agreements come in many varieties and have very different purposes. It is therefore worthwhile to distinguish some of the most important classes of contractual provisions that appear in alliance agreements.

A search of the legal literature and interviews with senior executives have identified eight distinct classes of contractual provisions that firms put into their alliance agreements to deter opportunistic behavior.[21] These are listed in order of increased stringency, where Item 1 is the least stringent category of contractual provisions and Item 8 is the most stringent:

1. Periodic written reports of all relevant transactions
2. Prompt written notice of any departures from the agreement
3. Right to examine and audit all relevant records through a firm of certified public accountants (CPAs)
4. Designation of certain information as proprietary and subject to confidentiality provisions of the contract
5. Nonuse of proprietary information even after termination of the agreement
6. Termination of the agreement
7. Arbitration clauses
8. Lawsuit provisions

These provisions serve different purposes for the establishment and execution of the collaborative agreement. Items 4 through 8, for instance, can be seen as partner control provisions and govern firms' behaviors even outside of the alliance. Items 1 through 3, by contrast, are more informational in nature and deal with the operations of the alliance itself and the partners' need to coordinate. There are many other ways of categorizing the contents of alliance contracts that highlight the importance and functions of the alliance contract. For instance, all of the clauses within an alliance agreement can be viewed as having one of two important purposes: (1) mitigating opportunism by specifying terms and (2) accounting for contingencies and delineating guidelines for handling them.[22]

CONTENTS OF ALLIANCE AGREEMENTS

The contents of alliance agreements might also be distinguished based on the typical ordering of material appearing in actual contracts: After identifying the parties to the agreement, introductory paragraphs set forth the purpose of the contract and the role of the parties. The main body of the agreement follows, which discusses the terms of formation (e.g., goals, capitalization, etc.), operations and management (e.g., technology transfer, marketing, human resources, etc.), cooperation (e.g., duties, profit sharing, etc.), and termination (e.g., renewal, asset disposals, liquidation, etc.). Typically a number of "boiler plate" clauses appear that are standard clauses on items such as notifications, governing laws, dispute resolution procedures, and so forth. After the final signature and date clauses, often a number of schedules are included that provide more details on elements of the agreement.[23]

A more detailed classification of issues that must be considered when drafting an alliance agreement appears in Table 3.2. This table provides a useful checklist for joint venture contracts, prepared by the law firm Freshfields Bruckhaus Deringer. Each of these topics presents a number of sub-items that deserve consideration, and the law firm's complete checklist includes more than one hundred items, many of which apply to other forms of collaborative agreements.

Each of these categories of contractual provisions can involve a number of important considerations and specific clauses that parties might want to address in the alliance agreement. As one example, negotiating termination provisions can be one of the more contentious aspects of alliance contracting,[24] and parties will need to agree upon the triggers, procedures, and financial consequences of termination. Table 3.3 provides illustrations of contractual clauses that deal with the issue of alliance termination in outsourcing partnerships for logistics services.[25] Based on a sample of outsourcing agreements in Europe, the table also provides frequencies indicating how often certain clauses are used in such partnerships. The most common clauses are those relating to objective or performance triggers for termination (i.e., 71 and 77%, respectively), whereas termination without cause is less frequently negotiated into outsourcing partnership contracts (i.e., 28%). Automatic renewal clauses are commonly used in such

TABLE 3.2 Issues Covered in Joint Venture Agreements

1. Identity of parties
2. Conditions precedent (i.e., preconditions of completing the joint venture)
3. Business of the JV (e.g., scope)
4. Capital and funding
5. Constitution of the JV
6. Board of directors
7. Shareholder meetings
8. Matters requiring unanimity or special majority
9. Administrative or corporate matters
10. Profit distribution
11. Intellectual property
12. Restrictions on shareholders/parents
13. Change of control of shareholder
14. Transfer of shares
15. Ancillary contracts
16. Termination
17. Deadlock
18. Standard provisions

Source: Freshfields Bruckhaus Deringer. 2001. *Joint ventures and alliances: A guide to the legal issues*. London, UK.

agreements (i.e., 54%) and allow the contract to be extended unless a firm provides a partner with notification otherwise. Firms less frequently design a specific process for renegotiating contracts (i.e., 35%). It also appears that firms generally negotiate specific financial consequences of termination less often than the triggers of termination or the procedures for handling the termination of such outsourcing partnerships.

TABLE 3.3 Termination Provisions in Outsourcing Partnerships

1. Termination with cause (i.e., objective reasons) (71%)
2. Termination subject to performance reasons (77%)
3. Termination without cause (i.e., without objective reasons) (28%)
4. Contract renegotiation protocol (35%)
5. Automatic renewal clauses (54%)
6. Compensation and indemnities for assets (40%)
7. Compensation and indemnities for specific investments (36%)
8. Compensation and indemnities for people (25%)

Source: Arino, A., Reuer, J., Mayer, K., & Jane, J. 2008. Contracting costs in outsourcing partnerships: An investigation of termination provisions and prior ties. IESE Business School working paper.
Note: Frequencies of usage in logistics contracts appear in parentheses.

TABLE 3.4 Table of Contents of an Actual International Joint Venture Agreement	
1. Definitions and Interpretation	1
2. Completion	16
3. UK Business	18
4. Commencing Non-UK Business	18
5. Non-UK Sourcing of Product	23
6. Call Option/Establishment and Administration of Holding Companies	25
7. Put Option	29
8. Pre-emption Rights	35
9. Tag-Along/Drag Along	38
10. Transfer of Shares and Assignment	40
11. Company Business	42
12. Tax Matters	43
13. Confidentiality	43
14. References to the Independent Accountant	44
15. Costs	44
16. No Partnership or Agency	45
17. Entire Agreement	45
18. Further Assurance	45
19. Assignment	45
20. Goodwill and Competition	45
21. Invalidity	45
22. Release, Indulgence, etc	45
23. Remedies	46
24. Notices	46
25. Governing Law	47
26. Miscellaneous	47
27. Submission to Jurisdiction and Agents for Service of Process	48
28. Partner Guarantee, Indemnity and Warranty	49

Source: Campbell, E., & Reuer, J. 2001. International alliance negotiations: Legal issues for general managers. *Business Horizons,* 44: 19–26.

To illustrate the makeup of alliance contracts, Table 3.4 offers the table of contents of an actual international joint venture agreement. This table indicates the number as well as the potential complexity of the clauses appearing in alliance agreements. Some of the contractual provisions such as those involving shares (e.g., put option, preemption rights, transfers or shares, etc.) will not apply to alliances that are nonequity collaborations. In addition, while the technical and legal details of these different clauses will not be covered here, some brief mention of a few clauses is useful for illustrative purposes. As noted earlier, after identifying the parties and setting out the general purpose of the agreement, the main body of the agreement follows, which offers performance clauses that provide details on the firms' obligations and the restrictions they are placing on one another.

Examples of such clauses include warranties or minimum service levels for supplies a partner will be providing, which might also be covered in a separate contract. Restrictions cover limitations placed on competition between a parent firm and the alliance (noncompetition), on employing each other's staff (nonsolicitation), and on information or other assets (confidentiality). Partners must also decide on how to deal with liability, and it is possible that all liability be excluded, such that partners agree that they will not make claims against each other, or that partners hold each other liable to the full extent of the law or at some intermediate level. For instance, they might agree to monetary caps on liability.

All of these clauses concern the establishment of the alliance and partners' obligations and restrictions during the operation of the alliance, but many important agreements need to be made concerning particular postformation issues as well. Many alliances are renegotiated, involve disputes, and come to a planned or unexpected termination after several years, so a range of postformation changes to alliance agreements need to be contemplated. Partners should consider how they will make changes to the contract, and in a schedule they can agree upon what level of management must make changes to the agreement, a minimum number of meetings needed to review issues or concerns surrounding the alliance, a dispute resolution procedure, and whether the agreement can be assigned or transferred, for instance, in the event of corporate restructuring. Partners will also need to decide what deadlock means, whether external experts or internal panels are employed to resolve conflicts, and whether mediation or alternative dispute resolution procedures will be used. Regarding termination, partners will negotiate whether the alliance is meant to last a fixed or indefinite amount of time and, if the former, how long; circumstances that will automatically trigger termination of the agreement; rights of a party subject to breach of contract; notices required for termination; asset valuation methods and disposal procedures (e.g., auctions); and division of liabilities; among others.[26]

Conclusion

This chapter has presented a general decision-making model for alliance governance that illustrates how alliance governance decisions are sequenced and become progressively more specific and complex, and subsequent chapters of the book will devote more attention to the processes by which firms negotiate agreements as well as earlier and later processes. Firms first begin by addressing the fundamental alliance investment decision: Is an alliance an appropriate investment vehicle relative to other alternatives such as acquisition, internal development, and so forth?

If the answer to this question is yes, the next decision concerns what type of alliance is going to be most appropriate given the objectives the firm has for the collaborative agreement. We emphasized that alliances can be classified into two broad categories—equity and nonequity—and that the former offers greater incentive alignment and control than the latter, but involves greater governance costs as well. The question of whether an equity or nonequity alliance is most attractive therefore involves consideration of whether the incentive alignment and control features of equity alliances are needed, such as when the firm faces a serious risk of opportunistic action (e.g., holdup, misappropriation of key resources, etc.).

After this alliance type decision is made, the firm must decide on a number of important alliance design decisions, and in this chapter we have emphasized the contractual foundations of collaborative agreements deserving the attention of entrepreneurial firms, knowing that lawyers will be involved in the technical aspects of crafting alliance agreements. Entrepreneurial firms, for instance, can consider how complex or open-ended in general their collaborative agreements need to be, given the risks and costs they foresee for their alliance. They can also acquaint themselves with initial steps that should be addressed prior to contractual negotiations, the basic contents of memoranda of understanding, and the various classes of clauses that appear in alliance contracts. Given that very specific provisions concerning the transfer of shares and alliance termination affect the value they capture from alliance agreements and can also shape partners' incentives and behavior, it also pays for entrepreneurs and managers, rather than only lawyers, to have an understanding of alliance contracts.

It is also important to emphasize here that alliance governance not only involves *contracts* but also *contracting*. In other words, negotiating an alliance contract is not only about what terms appear, or do not appear, in alliance agreements, but about a process that involves multiple actors (e.g., commercial and legal representatives) that ultimately ends in the legal agreement being executed and the stage being set for the cooperative agreement. In this chapter, we have emphasized the formal aspects of alliance governance and the content of alliance contracts as a specific dimension of alliance governance. In subsequent chapters, we also consider alliance processes as well as discuss the informal, or relational, aspects of alliance governance that also have important implications for the management and outcomes of alliances.

Key Terms

- nonequity and equity alliances
- minority equity partnerships
- greenfield joint ventures
- control rights
- contractual safeguards

End of Chapter Questions

1. What is the purpose of alliance governance?
2. What challenges do entrepreneurial firms face in governing alliances?
3. What is the difference between a greenfield and acquisitive joint venture?
4. When should firms adopt equity alliances over nonequity alliances when forming collaborative agreements?

5. What are the tradeoffs presented by using more or less complex legal agreements to govern strategic alliances?
6. Under what conditions should firms use complex contractual devices such as Russian roulette clauses or call options to handle transfers of shares in equity alliances?

References

1. Calyx and Corolla, *Harvard Business School Case*, #592035.
2. Hewitt, I. 2005. *Joint ventures* (3rd Edition). London: Sweet and Maxwell.
3. Pavia, L. 1998. Achieving business growth through minority equity partnerships. *Healthcare Financial Management*, 52: 80–81.
4. Lerner, J., & Merges, R. P. 1998. The control of technology alliances: An empirical analysis of the biotechnology industry.*Journal of Industrial Economics*, 46: 125–156.
5. Hughes, J., & Weiss, J. 2007. Simple rules for making alliances work. *Harvard Business Review*, (November): 122–131.
6. Makino, S., & Beamish, P. 1998. Performance and survival of joint ventures with non-conventional ownership structures. *Journal of International Business Studies*, 29: 797–818.
7. Axelrod, R., Mitchell, W., Thomas, R. E., Bennett, D. S., & Bruderer, E. 1995. Coalition formation in standard-setting alliances. *Management Science*, 41: 1493–1508; Lavie, D., Lechner, C., & Singh, H. 2007. The performance implications of timing of entry and involvement in multi-party alliances. *Academy of Management Journal*, 50: 578–604.
8. Gong, Y., Shenkar, O., Luo, Y., & Nyaw, M.-K. 2007. Do multiple partners help or hinder international joint venture performance? The mediating roles of contract completeness and partner cooperation. *Strategic Management Journal*, 28: 1021–1034.
9. Chesbrough, H., & Teece, D. J. 1996. When is virtual virtuous? Organizing for innovation. *Harvard Business Review*, (January–February): 65–73.
10. Oxley, J. E. 1997. Appropriability hazards and governance in strategic alliances: A transaction cost approach. *Journal of Law, Economics, and Organization*, 13: 387–409.
11. Freshfields Bruckhaus Deringer. 2001. Joint ventures and alliances: A guide to the legal issues. London, UK.
12. Hewitt, I. 2005. Op. cit.
13. Ariño, A., & Reuer, J. 2004. Designing and renegotiating strategic alliance contracts. *Academy of Management Executive*, 18: 37–48.
14. Gulati, R. 1995. Does familiarity breed trust? The implications of repeated ties for contractual choice in alliances. *Academy of Management Journal*, 38: 85–112.
15. Lecraw, D. Autoliv QB: A proposed joint venture. Richard Ivey School of Business Case No. 9A97G00.
16. Ring, P. S. 2002. The role of contract in strategic alliances. In F. J. Contractor & P. Lorange (Eds.), *Cooperative strategic and strategic alliances*. London, UK: Elsevier Science.
17. Telser, L. G. 1980. A theory of self-enforcing agreements. *Journal of Business*, 53: 27–44.
18. Axelrod, R. 1984. *The evolution of cooperation*. New York: Basic Books.
19. Crocker, K. J., & Reynolds, K. 1993. The efficiency of incomplete contracts: An empirical analysis of Air Force engine procurement.*RAND Journal of Economics*, 24: 126–146.

20. Reuer, J., & Ariño, A. 2007. Strategic alliance contracts: Dimensions and determinants of contractual complexity. *Strategic Management Journal*, 28: 313–330.
21. Parkhe, A. 1993. Strategic alliance structuring: A game theoretic and transaction cost examination of interfirm cooperation. *Academy of Management Journal*, 36: 794–829.
22. Luo, Y. 2002. Contract, cooperation, and performance in international joint ventures. *Strategic Management Journal*, 23: 903–919.
23. Campbell, E., & Reuer, J. 2001. International alliance negotiations: Legal issues for general managers. *Business Horizons*, 44: 19–26.
24. Serapio, M. G., & Cascio, W. F. 1996. End-games in international alliances. *Academy of Management Executive*, 10: 62–73.
25. Ariño, A., Reuer, J., Mayer, K., & Jane, J. 2008. Contracting costs in outsourcing partnerships: An investigation of termination provisions and prior ties. IESE Business School working paper.
26. Freshfields Bruckhaus Deringer. 2001. Op. cit.

CHAPTER 4

FINDING THE RIGHT PARTNER

INTRODUCTION

In February 2007, Nano-Terra—a privately owned nano- and microtechonology R&D company founded in 2005—and Merck—the well-known global pharmaceutical and chemical company—announced a strategic alliance to develop innovative, nanotechnology-based solutions based on Merck's specialty chemical materials.[1] The purpose of this alliance was to create novel technologically sophisticated applications and products by changing the qualities of existing chemicals with the help of soft lithography—a set of techniques which is used for making microelectronic systems.[2] For instance, the new modified solutions would be used to create printable electronic components. Nano-Terra needed Merck's materials as well as the large company's experience in order to commercialize its unique soft lithography technology, while Merck benefitted by developing new properties for its materials, which made it possible to create new applications at lower investment levels. Why did Nano-Terra choose Merck as a partner? A number of reasons explain this decision: Merck is a world leader in the research-driven chemical industry, and has extensive experience commercializing new technology worldwide; innovation is at the core of Merck's corporate culture; Merck has a long history of successful partnerships with R&D companies worldwide; and Merck had long been interested in work done by Nano-Terra. Why did Merck decide to ally with Nano-Terra? Because no other company in the market could offer the solutions Nano-Terra possessed, and because Nano-Terra was backed up by Harvard University, which gave it initial credibility in the eyes of Merck management. The first products were launched in early 2008. Since both parties were satisfied with the alliance, they decided to extend the existing partnership till 2011.

Getting the right partner is of particular importance to alliance success.[3] In Chapter 1, we reported on a survey of CEOs by *Dataquest*: 75% of the participants deemed partner selection as a key success factor in managing alliances. Related, 49% thought lack of common benefits is a reason for alliance failure. Who the partner is shapes the combination of resources and skills that will be available to carry out the joint project. The combination of Nano-Terra's technology and Merck's materials along with its commercialization capabilities make the goal of their alliance feasible. Furthermore, who the partner is may reduce uncertainty in the alliance operation.[4] The fact that Nano-Terra is a start-up that enjoys the support of a leading university reduces the uncertainty Merck faces when entering this alliance. It becomes clear that getting the right partner has an important influence on the company's ability to achieve its strategic objectives.[5]

Getting the right partner involves three processes, as highlighted in Figure 4.1: searching for potential partners, selecting a preferred potential partner, and attracting the preferred partner. Although we present these processes in a rather linear manner, in practice they are not linear processes. Sometimes the discovery of entrepreneurial opportunities will trigger partner search and selection. On other occasions, having developed a good relationship with one partner will prompt both parties to search for opportunities to leverage the relationship, or even such opportunities will emerge naturally once the partners become familiar with each other. This is how the joint venture between a Russian start-up and a large Western European company started in the electric wire devices industry. The start-up had performed distribution functions for the large company. Its CEO reports: "From the very beginning we had very open relationships. So when [a few years later] I was offered to become a partner in a joint venture I thought it was a logical development of our previous relations."[6] Further, partner selection is not finalized with the initial selection of one particular company as preferred potential partner: This choice will be subject to confirmation throughout the negotiation process.[7] A richer knowledge of the preferred potential partner generated at this stage might indicate not to pursue the opportunity any further, which will prompt the selection of a new preferred partner or even the search for new potential ones. Similarly, failure to attract the preferred

FIGURE 4.1   Processes Involved in Getting the Right Partner

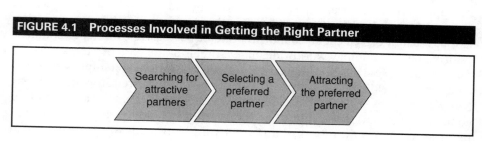

partner during negotiations will push the company back to initial stages to find a partner. Clearly, attracting the preferred partner is intertwined with alliance negotiation, and this will be dealt with in Chapter 5. Here, we focus on partner search and selection.

Partner search refers to acts involved in identifying potential partners.[8] Readily available information about potential partners is often insufficient.[9] Determining who may be a right partner takes much time and effort from senior management due to the lack of information.[10] Typically, searching for good partners is more costly to entrepreneurial companies than to established companies for several reasons. Entrepreneurial companies are less experienced at exploring partnership opportunities and are less likely to have set up partner search processes. Also, these companies lack the infrastructure and extensive contacts, making it extremely hard to find good partners.[11] Finally, they have fewer managers than established companies, thus partner search takes a higher proportion of precious management time and becomes relatively more costly to entrepreneurial companies.

Partner selection refers to acts involved in ascertaining the quality and intentions of potential partners.[12] It is necessary to make sure that the partner and the firm are compatible. Two main groups of selection criteria emerge in this respect: task- and cooperation-related.[13] Task-related selection criteria are associated with the strategic resources and skills that a firm requires for its competitive success, while cooperation-related criteria are associated with ascertaining how partnering firms can work together effectively.[14] Table 4.1 offers sample task- and cooperation-related criteria. Also, the Nano-Terra and Merck case helps illustrate the use of both types of criteria in their mutual selection. As indicated earlier, Nano-Terra chose Merck because of its leadership position and extensive commercialization experience (task-related criteria), and because of its innovation-centered culture and its history of successful R&D partnerships (cooperation-related criteria), while Merck chose Terra because it offered unique solutions (task-related criteria), and because of the credibility it offered (cooperation-related criteria). Usually, entrepreneurial companies are more dependent on getting a partner than established firms. In practice, this means they hurry more to get the deal, and at times they do so at the cost of paying insufficient attention to whether the identified partner should be selected or not.[15]

TABLE 4.1 Sample Task- and Cooperation-Related Partner Selection Criteria

Task-Related Criteria	*Cooperation-Related Criteria*
• Local market knowledge	• Extent of power delegation
• Technical know-how	• Decision-making speed
• Experienced personnel	• Management style
• Connections to government . . .	• Degree of flexibility . . .

In this chapter we will discuss the challenges entrepreneurial companies face in finding alliance partners, focusing on partner search and selection. We assume that the entrepreneurial company is the one taking the initiative to find a partner. At times, it may happen that an alliance project is presented to the entrepreneurial company by another initiating party. This will save partner search, but still managers in the entrepreneurial company will have to undergo a process of partner selection before committing to the new project.

CHALLENGES ASSOCIATED WITH FINDING ALLIANCE PARTNERS

A key element of the alliance implementation challenge discussed in Chapter 1 concerns finding alliance partners. This challenge stems from the fact that partners to an alliance remain independent organizations. To the extent that there is a good partner fit and they are compatible, the implementation challenge will be lessened. Search and selection processes are critical in assessing partner compatibility. Assessing fit is an ongoing process throughout partner search, partner selection, and negotiations, which entails exploration and discovery. The earlier (mis)fit is identified, the better for all companies and managers involved.

Fit may be assessed at various levels:[16]

- *Strategic fit:* the degree of compatibility between the goals each of the companies has for the alliance, and the extent to which the resulting combination of resources is appropriate to carry out the alliance project.

- *Organizational fit:* the extent to which the companies will be able to work well together.

- *Operational fit:* the extent to which it is in fact feasible that the resources each company contributes to the alliance be combined efficiently.

- *Human fit:* the extent to which the people involved in the alliance may feel comfortable collaborating.

Table 4.2 shows the different levels of partner fit and when they are evaluated in the absence of prior relationships with a potential partner. Typically,

TABLE 4.2	Assessment of Partner Fit in the Absence of Prior Relationships With a Potential Partner	
Levels of Fit	*Search and Selection Stages*	*Negotiation Stage*
Strategic fit	Initial assessment	Confirmation of assessment
Organizational fit:	Initial assessment	Confirmation of assessment
• External features	Assessment not feasible	Initial assessment
• Internal features		
Operational fit	Assessment not feasible	Initial assessment
Human fit	Assessment not feasible	Initial assessment

assessment of fit will start from visible partner traits, and as the search and selection—and negotiation—processes unfold, such assessments will move to features that are less observable to outsiders. If the company has a good knowledge of the potential partner from past relationships, the process is greatly simplified. This is why, in general, strategic and organizational fit are considered during partner search and selection, while most likely operational and human fit will be evaluated during negotiations as they are more difficult to assess from a distance.[17] And we say this is the general case because given the lack of resources most entrepreneurial firms have for searches, it is likely they often start with the human fit as proved in prior interactions. Also, some aspects of organizational fit will likely emerge during negotiations. Thus, the focus of this chapter will be on how to determine strategic and organizational fit.

Evaluation of strategic fit involves assessment of goals and resources. Organizational fit includes dimensions such as organizational structures, company size, national and corporate cultures, and so on. It is important to notice that fit does not imply that the two firms are identical on one or more dimensions. Rather, it is enough that partners be compatible. Differences in firms' resources and capabilities, which motivate the alliance in the first place, tend to be related to other differences in operation, structure, culture, and so forth. However, awareness of differences becomes crucial once the alliance is operational as such awareness helps to understand the origins of possible conflicts that may arise in the future, and to take the right corrective actions.

Later on, we will deal with the different levels of fit in more detail. However, we want to highlight here what's at the root of the alliance implementation challenge as related to partner search and selection. At a fundamental level, partners' goals should be compatible for the alliance to be executed appropriately and in this way meet the implementation challenge. The fact that partners remain independent organizations means that each one may have goals for the alliance which are not shared by the other partner. On the one hand, the partnering companies combine their resources to pursue certain common goals; on the other hand, since each partner is indeed a sovereign organization, they are sure to have their own agenda with different private goals for the alliance.[18] Due to the existence of these private goals, the behavior that serves one company's interests—the combination of its common and private goals—may not be the same as the behavior that helps meeting its partner's interests, which can make violation of the agreement an attractive alternative. Search and selection processes aim at ascertaining the extent to which a potential partner will help a company achieve its set of goals for the alliance, and this involves ensuring not only that the partner has the right resources but also that its goals are compatible with those of the entrepreneurial company. For instance, one small company in the automobile components industry had a joint R&D agreement with a larger company. As time went by, the small company observed that its counterpart was not bringing in the expected resources. They became suspicious and interpreted this as a signal that the partner might be letting them carry out the development work and would eventually try to appropriate the new product jointly developed. The

TABLE 4.3 Partner Search and Selection Tactics Under Different Scenarios

		Information Availability	
		Broad	*Limited*
Time Pressure	**High**	3. Development of efficient knowledge management tools	4. Strategic expediency
	Low	1. Rational decision-making	2. Development of effective search mechanisms

Source: Based on Bierly, P. E., & Gallagher, S. 2007. Op. cit.

small company's reaction was to withdraw resources. Eventually, the agreement was discontinued and neither company accomplished its goals for the alliance. This situation might have been avoided by a more careful assessment of the partner's interests at early stages. Admittedly, this is not always easy to do as at times interests may be subtle or even hidden deliberately.

Partner search and selection would be of no particular concern if managers had all of the relevant information or if they did not face time constraints. Of course, this is rarely the case. Usually, managers find themselves having to make decisions with incomplete information and under time pressure. Table 4.3 presents four scenarios depending on the availability of information regarding potential partners, and on the extent to which there is time pressure to form the alliance.[19] The more limited the available partner information, the higher the uncertainty about partner fit. The higher the time pressure faced, the more pressing the need to make the best out of whatever information is available. Based on these considerations, Table 4.3 suggests the tactics to use under each scenario:

- *Cell 1* in Table 4.3 represents the least frequent situation in which a company has broad information regarding potential partners and does not face particularly high time pressures to form an alliance. In this ideal situation, managers can take a rational, analytic decision-making approach where they systematically evaluate different alternatives and choose an optimal solution: they are able to analyze all available alternative partner companies along all levels and dimensions of fit. Based on this analysis, they will judge which partner is the most fitting for them.

- Companies falling in the scenario in *Cell 2* have limited information about potential partners. However, as they are not under a high time pressure they can take the time to develop effective information search techniques. Once the requisite information has been gathered they will find themselves in a Cell 1-type of situation.

- *Cell 3* presents the situation of companies with broad information about potential partners but in need to make quick decisions. So as to benefit from the available information, these companies need to find ways to manage their knowledge effectively.

- Finally, companies in *Cell 4* are the most pressed ones as the information available to them is limited and they do not have the time to acquire more. In this scenario, strategic expediency—the capability to make rapid, high-quality decisions within a simplified framework—becomes most useful to identify potential partners and select a preferred one.[20] Managers of these companies have to make important trade-offs in balancing the need for information to back their selection of a preferred partner and the need to make quick decisions which limits how much information they can gain prior to deciding who that preferred partner might be. Interestingly, most entrepreneurs will likely find themselves in Cell 4 as discussed next.

While there are reasons why entrepreneurial companies might fall into any of the cells in Table 4.3, most would appear to be in Cell 4 as information availability and time pressure depend on who the company under consideration is and not only on environmental conditions. Admittedly, circumstances external to the company play a role here. For instance, in some sectors industry associations play a more active role than in others, making it easier to identify potential partners, have a good sense of how valuable their resources may be, and so on. Also, different industries pose different levels of time pressure on companies. Fast-moving industries like biotech or networking technology require faster decision-making than more stable ones. The fact that the two dimensions we are considering—information availability and time pressure—are partly driven by environmental factors, independent of the company means that entrepreneurial companies may find themselves in any of the cells in Table 4.3. However, company-level factors also influence information availability and time pressure levels. Entrepreneurial companies lack contacts as well as the infrastructure and resources to engage in substantial research, making it hard to find partners.[21] Thus, entrepreneurial companies may have less information on available partners than established firms. Also, their resource bases are often limited and they face more financial constraints than large firms, thus time pressure for finding partners that give them access to the requisite resources may be higher than for established firms.

It becomes clear that managers at entrepreneurial companies confront a difficult trade-off. On the one hand, the benefits of reducing uncertainty indicates a need to gain partner information both at the search and selection stages, but this takes time. On the other hand, time pressures make it requisite not to delay decision-making, but the danger here is falling into rash behavior[22] as well as into the trap to limit the search for alternative solutions to ready-made ones (what is known as the "limited search trap"), and in this way unduly restricting beforehand the range of companies to examine as potential partners.[23] Thus, managers at entrepreneurial companies should think about the following questions:

- How to gather and use information on potential partners?
- How broad a partner search should be?

- When and why are certain partners more attractive than others?
- Which partner selection criteria should be considered and how to weigh them?
- How to balance expediency against falling into the limited-search trap?

SEARCHING FOR PARTNERS

Partner search refers to acts involved in identifying potential partners.[24] The expected outcome from the search process is a short list of attractive potential partners from which the preferred potential partner will be drawn. An attractive partner is one that the initiating firm considers as desirable, favorable, appealing, and valuable.[25] These considerations are driven by initial assessments of strategic and organizational fit we referred to earlier.

One first question related to partner search is how to gather and use information on potential partners? Partner search involves collecting and evaluating information about companies that might fit with the initiating firm. This process may be more, or less, formalized depending on the company being examined.[26] At one extreme, partner search is a highly formalized process based on formal routines and procedures for information search. Companies with a formal alliance function are illustrative. Large companies heavily involved in alliances leverage their experience by creating an alliance office that allows transfer of collaborative know-how across their various alliances (we will touch upon the creation of an alliance office in Chapter 8). Eli Lilly in pharmaceuticals and Philips in electronics are examples of companies with such an organizational unit.[27] An alliance office may help in partner search by designing partner screening forms and activity domain maps that help managers in identifying potential allies. At the other extreme, partner search is based on simple decision-making rules and even on gut feeling regarding, for instance, which information sources or which partner selection criteria to use. Most entrepreneurial companies fall closer to this end of the partner search continuum, which is depicted in Figure 4.2.

FIGURE 4.2 Partner Search Continuum

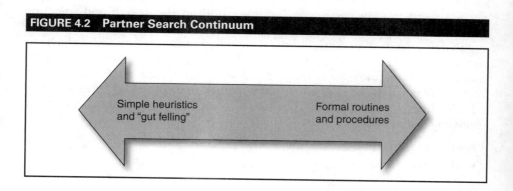

Simple heuristics and "gut felling"

Formal routines and procedures

Despite the benefits of using formal procedures for partner search, few companies use them. One study on search and selection practices of international trading partners by small Dutch firms shows that few companies have formal procedures to find trading partners.[28] Although international trade partners are not necessarily strategic partners, insights from this report are illuminating for entrepreneurial companies in search of strategic alliance partners. In this study, close to half of all companies had no formal procedures or a clear road map guiding the search process, and 22% had few or very informal procedures. Only 10% had well-developed procedures. Thus, most small companies in this study fall close to the "simple heuristics and 'gut feeling' " extreme in the continuum presented in Figure 4.2, while very few lie at the other extreme, namely "formal routines and procedures." To the extent that companies look for partners only infrequently, managers may think that developing formalized search procedures may not be worthy. However, the same study found that the degree of formalization in search procedures makes a significant difference in finding an appropriate partner. This is not to say that formal procedures are a substitute for managers' experience regarding information sources and how to assess different alternatives. In fact, this study found that experience exerts an even stronger influence than formalized procedures in finding an appropriate partner, so both appear important.

Entrepreneurial companies are therefore advised to establish procedures to search for potential alliance partners. For instance, the open innovation trend referred to in Chapter 2 offers an ocean of opportunities for technological start-ups.[29] Large companies are adopting business models that embrace open innovation as a way to counteract two pressures: the rise in R&D costs and the decrease in revenues that stems from shorter product life cycles. Open innovation helps companies counteract these pressures as it involves a greater use of external technology which brings about savings in both time and money. Companies with open innovation programs are eager to find partners with innovation capabilities. For instance, with its "Connect + Develop" program, P&G (Procter & Gamble) seeks innovation partnerships and this is made widely public at its web page.[30] They publicize their innovation needs and request partnership proposals to help them meet these needs. The list of needs is constantly updated. In turn, P&G allows external partners to use their internally developed assets and know-how. They also make information about these assets public. Entrepreneurial companies with established procedures to search for alliance partners are more likely than other companies to become aware of opportunities like those offered by P&G and in this way identify attractive potential partners. Computers, search engines, and pattern matching may be used for partner selection.[31] Of course, this is but one example and there are sources of information about potential partners other than the Web.

Broadly speaking, search mechanisms fall into one of two categories: institutionalized mechanisms and social mechanisms.[32] Table 4.4 compares both types of mechanisms. In some instances, institutions such as organized markets, chambers of commerce, or the Internet exist that offer information about potential

TABLE 4.4 Characteristics of Partner Search Mechanisms	
Institutionalized Mechanisms	*Social Mechanisms*
• Costly	• Cheap
• Lengthy	• Fast
• Broad	• Narrow

partners. Searching through these institutionalized mechanisms entails costs: from those of compiling contact information to the time invested in looking for information about relevant partner characteristics. Partner search through institutionalized mechanisms is not always cost effective. At times, information may be too scattered as it happens when potential partners are geographically dispersed. At other times, information may be too sparse and inaccurate as is the case in some emerging markets where in the extreme these mechanisms might not even exist.

When partner search through institutionalized mechanisms becomes problematic, turning to social search mechanisms may be more efficient.[33] The managers' network may be an effective, cheap, and fast source of information about potential partners. To a large extent, this depends on the network composition—the number of contacts, their diversity, and their domains of competence in terms of function, industry, or geography. Broad networks help make partner search effective in that they provide a wide range of information sources. They also make searching cheap and fast as on the one hand managers already have an idea about whom to contact, and on the other hand the person being contacted is requested to provide information he or she already has or which he or she might come across in the normal course of events. In fact, research shows that entrepreneurial firms form more alliances when their top management teams are large, experienced, and well connected,[34] as such teams enjoy broad networks. This role is played as well by some of the investors in entrepreneurial firms, such as venture capitalists and business angels. Part of what they are asked to contribute to a small firm is their connections for resources, including alliance partners. This was the original strategy used by Critical Mention, a privately held New York company that pioneered the field of Web-based television search and monitoring services.[35] From the very beginning, CEO Sean Morgan attracted a diverse group of investors with strong contacts and invited experienced individuals on the board of directors and advisory board. The networking approach became the key mechanism to searching for potential partners. As a result, during its first year of operations Critical Mention managed to have more than sixty corporate and governmental companies—including some Fortune 500 corporations—sign up for its services. Strategic alliances with well-established giants such as CNBC, BBC, and the Associated Press allowed Critical Mention to offer top quality content and, consequently, to attract new customers.

Entrepreneurial companies face a number of challenges in using search mechanisms. On the one hand, these companies have scarce resources and might not be willing to engage in a costly search using institutionalized mechanisms. On the other hand, their networks may not be as extensive as to make searching through social mechanisms effective. Thus, the next question managers from entrepreneurial companies should address is how broad a partner search should be?

Given the challenges we described, the temptation might be to not engage in partner search and move directly into selecting partners among the pool of current or previous ones.[36] By doing so, entrepreneurial companies might fall into the limited-search trap we discussed earlier and which easily results in failed decisions.[37] Research on decision-making shows that in four out of five decisions only one idea is given serious thought.[38] Forming a new alliance with an already proven partner is an easy way out for managers. However, this should not be the only option considered. Before making this decision other alternatives should be contemplated, or entrepreneurial companies might be driven by inertia, whereby past solutions to old problems become the starting point for new searches.[39] Prior ties may act as blinders and an unconscious excuse to avoid analysis, for instance. Driven by a desire to act swiftly, managers may rush to judgement.[40] A European company that was trying to enter the market for medical equipment in Latin America faced an experience similar to the one just described. An alliance with a local company enjoying good distribution access was a mindful option to this end. Advised by an independent director, the European company's managers initiated formal conversations with an Argentine company whose owners were acquaintances of the director of the European company but they did so without searching for alternative potential partners. During negotiations that lasted about eight months they realized there was not enough partner fit to justify forming the alliance. Had they done a thorough analysis prior to engaging in formal negotiations, they would have saved a precious time—which they could have invested in carrying out a broader partner search. By contrast, engaging in partner search beyond the immediate pool increases the likelihood that the chosen partner is an appropriate one for the task at hand, even if the end result might still be to form an alliance with a previous partner.

Let us keep in mind that the purpose of partner search is to identify a list of potential attractive partners. To do so, managers have to be clear about what makes an attractive partner, and which type of information they need to make this type of assessment. Thus, in order to answer the question whether to engage in a broad search for potential partners, managers should consider the related question: When and why are certain partners more attractive than others? Given the costs of search and the scarce resources of entrepreneurial companies, managers of such companies should focus their efforts. In addition, partner search is more successful when a clear objective has been set.[41] At the same time, while having a clear picture of attractive partner traits would be ideal, this is not always possible. When facing great time pressures—as is the case in emerging markets such as those being created due to new technological possibilities—it may be difficult to determine exactly what a satisfactory partnership might look like. In these situations, it is enough to have a general guide on what is desirable rather than a detailed map. But still, we need some picture of expected results even if it is just a general guide. Without clarity, the different people involved in partner search will form different impressions about what is wanted[42] and the search will not be effective.

At a general level, this picture of what managers expect as a result from search efforts should provide some basic indication of the type of features that are most critical for the alliance success. We indicated earlier that task- and cooperation-related criteria are two main groups of criteria to ensure partner compatibility.[43] Depending on the nature of the project at hand, one or another group may become more important. The implementation process may be more difficult to manage in certain types of alliances than in others.[44] If the process is relatively easy to manage, task-related criteria and complementarity of skills and resources somewhat ensure that the outcomes will be beneficial to all involved parties. On the contrary, if the process is relatively difficult to manage, cooperation-related criteria and trustworthiness are important features of an attractive partner. For instance, horizontal alliances in which firms pool together activities at the same stage of the value chain are generally easier to manage than vertical alliances in which firms combine activities at different stages of the value chain. Take the case of a horizontal alliance in the early 2000s between a dot-com company and the online arm of a traditional bricks-and-mortar firm to combine their Internet operations. The former might contribute e-commerce capabilities and the latter its volume with the associated purchase economies with the common end of leveraging their strengths to create a more powerful competitor than either of them would have been on their own. Now think of a vertical alliance between a small innovative firm and a large firm holding the assets required to take that innovation to the market. It is easier for the large firm to absorb the innovation and realize its market potential than for the small firm to develop the necessary organizational capability to grow by itself. This situation is a difficult one to manage for the small firm, as it may create a relationship of dependency by the small firm on the large firm, which in time may come to impose unreasonable demands. Likely, this vertical alliance will be rockier than the horizontal one. Alliances with a narrow scope are also easier to manage than those whose scope is broad.

But isn't trustworthiness always a desirable feature that makes a partner attractive, even if the alliance process were an easy one to manage? Definitely, yes: Trustworthiness is always a plus. Searching among friends is easy and not so costly. However, it's a matter of relative terms and the different partner features have to be weighed. For instance, new partners might bring novel capabilities or access to new markets compared to prior partners and may be preferred when such benefits are sought.[45] The crucial point is to make sure that trust is used as a response to uncertainty, not as an excuse to avoid or delay analysis.[46]

This gives a hint as to how broad or narrow partner search should be. Potential partners might be thought of as friends, acquaintances, or strangers.[47] Friends are potential alliance partners with whom the initiating firm has had multiple positive previous interactions, acquaintances are those that the firm knows through a few previous interactions, and strangers are potential partners who are unknown to the firm. The firm does not trust each type of potential partner to the same extent. If task-related criteria are more important than cooperation-related criteria and trust, then a broad search of strangers via institutionalized mechanisms may be conducted, as may an extensive search of acquaintances through the company's network. On the contrary, if cooperation-related criteria and trustworthiness are more important features of an attractive partner, then firms are better advised to use their networks of friends in searching for potential partners.

In sum, when deciding the type of partner search to initiate, entrepreneurial companies are better off thinking ahead and reasoning backwards. Figure 4.3

FIGURE 4.3 Steps to be taken in Finding the Right Partner

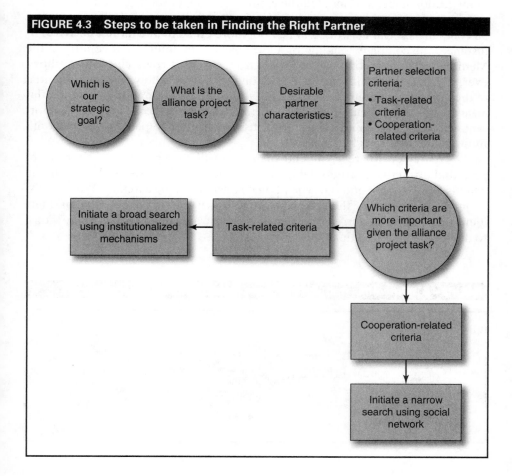

summarizes the steps entailed in finding the right partner. The first step is to consider the requisite characteristics sought in a partner given the alliance project task, which in turn depends on the company's strategic goal. Having established these, even if at a rather general level, will shed light on the relative importance of task-related and cooperation-related partner selection criteria. While the former allows us to identify the strategic similarities and differences between the partners and detect potential conflicts deriving from the differences, the latter helps determine the degree of organizational fit between the two companies. It is vital to find out whether the organizations are similar in structure and size, and whether the cultures are compatible. While organizational identity is not the aim, awareness of organizational differences and flexibility to adapt to them make the difference. Having a clear idea of the relative weights of task-related versus cooperation-related criteria sheds light onto the type of search process to engage in. If task-related criteria are relatively more important, an entrepreneurial company may be better off by engaging in a broad search by means of institutional mechanisms. On the contrary, if cooperation-related criteria are relatively more important, a more focused search by means of the entrepreneurial company's social network will be both more efficient and more effective. For instance, one company looking for a local partner to enter a new country in the Mediterranean basin first tried the help from a market research company; however, what yielded fruit was the mediation of a person who was very influential in the area. In that country, personal relations are valued and they would influence the alliance execution. Thus, cooperation-related criteria were very important, and having been introduced by a trusted person helped ensure a smooth future relationship for both sides.

As search efforts reach an end, managers will have produced a short list of potential attractive partners, which may in fact be not so short, depending on what is being sought and the type of mechanism used in searching. With the list at hand, managers face the task of selecting which among the potential partners identified is their preferred one. Figure 4.4 illustrates this process. We now turn to discuss partner selection.

FIGURE 4.4   Outcomes from Partner Search and Selection Processes

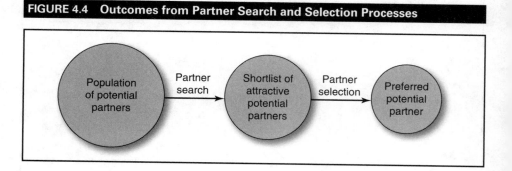

SELECTING PARTNERS

In the introduction to this chapter, we presented the notion that *partner selection* refers to acts involved in ascertaining the quality and intentions of potential partners.[48] The expected outcome from the selection process is the identification of a preferred potential partner (see Figure 4.4)—or maybe a rank list of a few candidates—for the managers of entrepreneurial companies to approach with a proposal to form an alliance. Prior to making a choice, the criteria to guide it must be identified and weighed. However, important as this is, it is not enough. Managers should assess not only how potential partners meet their company's needs, but also how their company meets those of the partner. Assessment of fit should be two-sided.[49]

In identifying which is the preferred potential partner, a critical question managers face is which partner selection criteria should be considered and how to weigh them? We have already advanced the two broad categories of criteria that form the basis of partner selection and the more intensive processes that support this decision: task-related criteria and cooperation-related criteria. Task-related criteria aim at evaluating strategic fit. As shown in Table 4.5, there are two primary dimensions of strategic fit: the partner's goals and its set of resources and skills. With regard to strategic goals, we have already discussed that these should be compatible with those of the entrepreneurial company. In the absence of better information or resources to make such assessments, a prospective partner's mission statement may be a good initial source of information about its goals. Something to keep in mind is that strategic goals tend to change over time. If this is considered when choosing a partner, different future scenarios may be envisaged. In this way, managers may anticipate possible changes in the potential partner's goals and analyze how they might affect the alliance and their own company.

With regard to the set of resources and skills, assessment of fit will be in close connection to the company's strategic goals and its own set of resources, as this is what determines the company's needs. For instance, one study in the semiconductor industry found that large firms with leading technologies are valued as

TABLE 4.5 Types of Partner Selection Criteria and Levels of Fit

Types of Partner Selection Criteria	*Level of Fit Assessed*	*Dimensions of Fit Levels*
Task-related criteria	Strategic fit	Strategic goals • Resources and skills
Cooperation-related criteria	Organizational fit	Organizational structures • Company size • Corporate culture • National culture

partners by entrepreneurial companies because young and small firms often lack the resources to access such technology.[50]

Despite the variety in task-related criteria, we first want to draw attention to one type of resource commonly sought by entrepreneurial companies: legitimacy.[51] Gaining legitimacy in this way helps entrepreneurial companies overcome their inherent liability of newness, as discussed in Chapter 2. At times, even if the alliance goals end up not being met, a heightened reputation from having survived the due diligence of a prominent partner may be an important benefit in and of itself. Gaining a well-reputed alliance partner signals the quality of an entrepreneurial company. It creates a public conviction that its products are valuable, and in this way it helps the company in its efforts to gain customers. This is the case, for instance, of Internet-based start-ups whose success depends largely on how broad their network of consumers is, which in turn hinges upon the breadth of the product–supplier network. The presence of strong partners legitimizes the start-up company and enhances the development of its consumer and supplier networks.[52] Think of Brightcove, a start-up in the young and rapidly evolving Internet TV industry.[53] Brightcove chose to build a network business that involved various types of participants, including producers of Internet TV content, companies that want to advertise their products through Internet TV, and end users who want to view online video content. Content producers will join the network only if it links them to paying advertisers; advertisers will join only if the network can deliver consumers; consumers will join only if they find a desirable content offer. As a newly created company, it is very hard for Brightcove to enjoy the legitimacy to attract content producers, advertisers, and consumers. Gaining a prominent partner heightens the requisite legitimacy to attract others to the network.

Also of importance to entrepreneurial companies is making sure the potential partner has enough financial strength, especially so if it is another entrepreneurial company. Its credit record may serve as an indicator.[54] Also, valuable information may be obtained from common suppliers. If the company enjoys a good relationship with them, they might be willing to share information such as if they are paid on time by the potential partner, and so on.

The implicit idea already advanced is that assessment of strategic fit has to be two-sided. The entrepreneurial company has to evaluate not only how a potential preferred partner fits its needs but also how it fits those of the preferred partner. Careless attention to this will result in wasting both money and time. In addition to the direct costs associated with spending time in hopeless negotiations, there are opportunity costs related to other activities or projects to which managers could devote attention during that time. Even worse, in some cases wasting time in undue negotiations may lead to forgone alliance opportunities, or eventually worsen the company's competitive position. On the contrary, having considered fit from a two-sided perspective paves the way to valuable opportunities in an efficient and timely manner. This is the approach taken by Seattle's RadioFrame Networks.[55] When looking for a partner, RadioFrame's CEO paid special attention to what his company could offer to a big player. Two American entrepreneurs created RadioFrame with the idea of installing radio transmitters inside buildings to allow for a clearer phone signal. Therefore, in their partner search they focused on companies that had low network capacity and thus were likely to value their offer. The strategy worked well. In 2001, Nextel, one of the major U.S. wireless carriers, was lagging behind its competitors in terms of the coverage it offered and when RadioFrame approached them with its offer, Nextel happily jumped on board. The cooperation resulted in a productive alliance which significantly enhanced Nextel's wireless coverage and allowed RadioFrame to secure cash, infrastructure resources, and guaranteed sales.

Furthermore, dynamic considerations are important when assessing mutual fit. Each company's contribution must be valuable to the other and sustainable over time. For instance, a large, established firm may be moderately dependent on the resources provided by an entrepreneurial company to the extent that the future of the large firm depends on factors other than the resources contributed by the entrepreneurial company. Yet the latter may be heavily dependent on the large firm's resources. This will lead to an imbalance of power and mutual need within the alliance which may encourage the large company to end the alliance as circumstances change. In that sense, the more complementary the partners are (with respect to know-how, markets, resources, etc.), the greater the chance that the alliance will survive in the long term, as the partners will be more dependent on one another.

Cooperation-related criteria are intended to determine organizational fit. Assessing organizational fit is easier to do when the potential partner under scrutiny is known to the entrepreneurial company because of previous relationships than when it is an unfamiliar party, especially so for the less visible partner traits that are less known to an external examiner. As suggested in Table 4.5, the following are the main dimensions of organizational fit that managers have to examine: organizational structures, company size, and corporate and national cultures.[56] If the partners have very different organizational structures, the relationship is likely to be more difficult. If one partner has, for instance, a decentralized structure while the other is highly centralized, decision-making is bound to be very different. To a certain extent, organizational structure is related to company size. If the potential partner's size is similar to that of the entrepreneurial company, it will be easier for them to establish a good working relationship. If the two companies are very different in size, the entrepreneurial company may be suspicious that the larger one might plan to take it over sooner or later and trust will be harder to build.

Both corporate and national cultures have to be analyzed carefully. A good way to do so is to draw up a profile of each company's culture. This will make it easier to detect areas where cultural conflict is most likely to arise. An illustration of how to draw such profiles is offered in Figure 4.5. Conflict may be due to differences of attitude with respect to issues such as the willingness to make short- or long-term decisions, the preference for risk-taking or for caution, incentives offered to employees, styles of communication, etc. If the

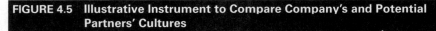

FIGURE 4.5 Illustrative Instrument to Compare Company's and Potential Partners' Cultures

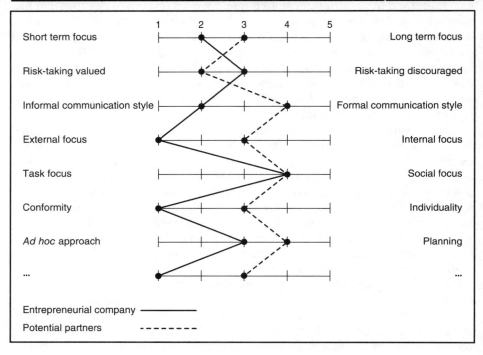

company is not aware of these differences, it is likely to misinterpret the partner's actions. For example, making quick decisions may be a sign of efficiency for one partner, while the other may consider it a sign of rushed behavior. Cultural incompatibility is not easy to overcome, especially if the partners are not aware of the differences. There may be a very close strategic fit between the partners and yet, if the company perceives its partner as having a too different management style then that partner may not be a very good choice. Conversely, if there is cultural compatibility, the relationship may prove very rewarding.

Cultural compatibility is even more difficult to achieve when the companies are from different countries. Added to the likely differences in corporate culture, there will be differences between the two national cultures. This may mean that the two companies have very different decision-making processes, meeting cultures, etc. Unless both companies are aware of these differences, it will be very difficult to establish a good working relationship.

However, for an alliance to be effective, the two cultures do not necessarily have to be very similar; what is needed is an attitude of openness and understanding toward differences, and a willingness to talk things over when those differences lead to problems. It is very unusual to find two companies with similar cultures, particularly when they are from different countries. Also, the fact that two companies have different cultures may enrich the relationship, as they will have the opportunity to learn from one another.[57] Furthermore, in some cases such differences are unavoidable. For instance, if a high-tech start-up seeks an alliance with an established and less innovative firm, there are obviously going to be cultural differences. Therefore, what the entrepreneurial company should look for in a partner is the flexibility to understand and adapt to cultural differences so as to be able to work together. In turn, managers in the entrepreneurial company, too, must try to develop the same flexibility.

Usually, it is not possible to find a partner that meets all of the selection criteria, and managers will have to weigh these criteria. The relative weights assigned to each one vary across situations. For instance, as discussed earlier, the level of difficulty in managing the alliance implementation process should be considered in placing the weight on task- versus cooperation-related criteria. The more difficult this process is anticipated to be, the more important cooperation-related criteria turn out to be. Prioritization of criteria becomes more important if fewer potential partners are available. In this case, it is more difficult to find an exact-fitting match, and partners have to be chosen based on meeting fewer specific constraints.[58] Thus, under these conditions managers should be very clear on what are "musts" and what are "wishes."

The next question managers from entrepreneurial companies confront is how to balance expediency against falling into the limited-search trap? Any manager involved in partner selection should have a mind-set that values the potential contributions of each partner.[59] Thus, it is also important to have an open discussion from which internal consensus emerges about what is crucial in a potential partner. The higher the time pressure, the more important it becomes to have a simplified framework to help managers make rapid but high-quality partner selection decisions.[60] And it is not rare for alliances to be formed under time pressure: "it is not a coincidence that the rapidly changing, high-technology industries, such as biotechnology, semiconductors and software, that value time as a strategic resource, are also the industries where alliances occur most frequently (as) alliances are very effective in . . . helping firms respond quickly to external opportunities and threats."[61]

Entrepreneurial companies may benefit from developing such a simplified framework early on, as in this way decision-making becomes less dependent on the entrepreneur, who otherwise ends up turning into a bottleneck that slows down growth. It is helpful to develop a template that embodies a broad range of variables to help managers make sense of potential partners. Individual managers can use the template as a guide to frame and establish boundaries for their partner selection decisions, and still rely heavily on their intuition in choosing a specific partner. Early development of such a template is helpful as it can

FIGURE 4.6   Illustrative Template to Guide Partner Selection

Alliance project:		
Potential partner: Company A		
Characteristics sought	**Minimum level required**	**Level displayed by A**
A. Product market overlap (1=very low to 5=very high)	2	3
B. Geographic market overlap (1=very low to 5=very high)	1	5
C. Access to distribution (1=very low to 5=very high)	5	2
D. Decision-making speed (1=very slow to 5=very fast)	4	2
E. Flexibility (1=very low to 5=very high)	1	4
F. ...	...	...

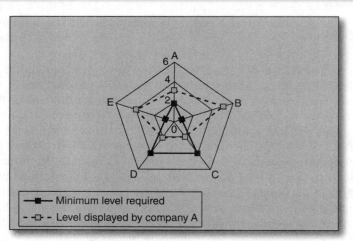

- ■ — Minimum level required
- - -□ - - Level displayed by company A

Note: If any of the characteristics falls below the minimum level required, the company should be dismissed as an attractive potential partner.

be done in a methodical way and without the pressure faced when selecting a partner. Also, this gives time for debate and disagreement that otherwise might not happen. The template should be revised periodically so as to incorporate the experience managers gain with practice. Figure 4.6 offers an illustrative template to guide partner selection.

Conclusion

This chapter has presented the processes entrepreneurial companies have to undergo so as to find the right partner. These processes include partner search and selection. Still, the task is left to attract their preferred potential partner at the negotiation stage. Also during this stage, the choice of a preferred partner will be subject to further exploration and confirmation, especially so for the least visible traits.

Partner search and selection are not always as rational as depicted in Figure 4.3. The level of information availability and the time pressure experienced by the entrepreneurial company will indicate particular partner search and selection tactics to use under different scenarios, as suggested in Table 4.3. Managers "need to become more comfortable with ambiguity and be willing to make speedy decisions in the absence of complete, unequivocal data or support."[62] Figure 4.3 provides guidance for decision-making as related to partner search and selection.

The homework has to be done before approaching a preferred potential partner with a proposal to ally. However, managers charged with this task should be aware that the initial analysis is subject to confirmation and update throughout the negotiation stage, as valuable information will be revealed at this time that may support or invalidate the homework done. We turn to discuss the alliance negotiation process in Chapter 5.

Key Terms

- partner search
- partner selection
- selection criteria
- partner fit

End of Chapter Questions

1. What are the main challenges entrepreneurial companies face in searching for and selecting an alliance preferred partner?
2. Why is it advisable for entrepreneurial companies to establish partner search procedures?
3. Which mechanisms can entrepreneurial companies use to identify attractive potential partners? When does it pay to use one or another type of mechanism?
4. How can entrepreneurial companies establish the criteria to use in selecting a preferred potential partner? Under what conditions are task-related criteria more or less important than cooperation-related criteria?
5. How can entrepreneurial companies ensure that participants in partner search and selection share a common understanding to guide their efforts?

References

1. http://www.nanoterra.com/press_release_2_20_07.asp
2. http://www.nanoterra.com/soft_lithography.asp

3. See for example, Park, S. H., & Ungson, G. R. 1997. The effect of national culture, organizational complementarity, and economic motivation on joint venture dissolution. *Academy of Management Journal*, 40: 279–307.

4. Nielsen, B. B. 2003. An empirical investigation of the drivers of international strategic alliance formation. *European Management Journal*, 21: 301–322.

5. Geringer, J. M. 1991. Strategic determinants of partner selection criteria in international joint ventures. *Journal of International Business Studies*, 22: 41–62.

6. Personal communication.

7. The idea that partner search and negotiations overlap to a certain extent is highlighted as well by Ring, P. S. 2000. The three T's of alliance creation: Task, team and time. *European Management Journal*, 18: 152–163.

8. Rangan, S. 2000. The problem of search and deliberation in economic action: When social networks really matter. *Academy of Management Review*, 25: 813–828.

9. Rangan, S. 2000. Op. cit.

10. De Mattos, C., Sanderson, S., & Ghauri, P. 2002. Negotiating alliances in emerging markets—Do partners' contributions matter? *Thunderbird International Business Review*, 44: 701–728.

11. Nijssen, E. J., Douglas, S. P., & Calis, G. 1999. Gathering and using information for the selection of trading partners. *European Journal of Marketing*, 33: 143–162.

12. Rangan, S. 2000. Op. cit.

13. Michael Geringer was the first one to categorize partner-selection criteria in his article published in 1991 (op. cit.). He identified two categories which he labeled *task-related* and *partner-related criteria*. Here we depart from his nomenclature and talk about task-related and cooperation-related criteria under the understanding that *task-related criteria* also refer to the partners.

14. Geringer, M. 1991. Op. cit.

15. See for example, Alvarez, S. A., & Barney, J. B. 2001. How entrepreneurial firms can benefit from alliances with large partners. *Academy of Management Executive*, 15: 139–148.

16. Douma, M. U., Bilderbeek, J., Idenburg, P. J., & Looise, J. K. 2000. Strategic alliances. Managing the dynamics of fit. *Long Range Planning*, 33: 579–598. These authors also consider cultural fit as one of the fit levels. However, we consider it as embedded in organizational fit.

17. As suggested, operational and human fit may already be evaluated during partner search and selection if managers in the entrepreneurial company have had some type of previous interaction with the potential partner and/or its managers.

18. Ariño, A. 1995. Inter-firm collaborative ventures: Performance and cooperative behavior. Unpublished doctoral dissertation. The Anderson School, University of California, Los Angeles.

19. We draw here from useful considerations offered by Bierly, P. E., & Gallagher, S. 2007. Explaining alliance partner selection: Fit, trust and strategic expediency. *Long Range Planning*, 40: 134–153.

20. Bierly, P. E., & Gallagher, S. 2007. Op. cit.

21. Nijssen, E. J., Douglas, S. P., & Calis, G. 1999. Op. cit.

22. Bierly, P. E., & Gallagher, S. 2007. Op. cit.

23. Nutt, P. C. 2004. Expanding the search for alternatives during strategic decision-making. *Academy of Management Executive*, 18: 13–28.

24. Rangan, S. 2000. Op. cit.

25. Shah, R. H., & Swaminathan, V. 2008. Factors influencing partner selection in strategic alliances: The moderating role of alliance context. *Strategic Management Journal*, 29: 471–494.

26. Nijssen, E. J., Douglas, S. P., & Calis, G. 1999. Op. cit.

27. For an insightful discussion of how to organize a dedicated alliance function see Dyer, J. H., Kale, P., & Singh, H. 2001. How to make strategic alliances work. *MIT Sloan Management Review*, 42: 37–43.

28. Nijssen, E. J., Douglas, S. P., & Calis, G. 1999. Op. cit.

29. Chesbrough, H. 2007. Why companies should have opens business models. *MIT Sloan Management Review*, 48: 21–28.

30. http://pg.t2h.yet2.com/t2h/page/homepage

31. Pidduck, A. B. 2006. Issues in supplier partner selection. *Journal of Enterprise Information Management*, 19: 262–276.

32. Rangan, S. 2000. Op. cit.

33. Rangan, S. 2000. Op. cit.

34. Eisenhardt, K. M., & Schoonhoven, C. B. 1996. Resource-based view of strategic alliance formation: strategic and social effects in entrepreneurial firms. *Organization Science*, 7: 136–150.

35. http://www.forbes.com/columnists/2005/12/07/startup-strategicalliance-entrepreneur-cx_tt_1207straightup.html

36. Ellis, P. 2000. Social ties and foreign market entry. *Journal of international Business Studies*, 31: 443–469.

37. Nutt, P. C. 2004. Op. cit.

38. Nutt, P. C. 2004. Op. cit.

39. Li, S. X., & Rowley, T. J. 2002. Inertia and evaluation mechanisms in interorganizational partner selection: syndicate formation among U.S. investment banks. *Academy of Management Journal*, 45: 1104–1119.

40. Nutt, P. C. 2004. Op. cit.

41. Nutt, P. C. 2004. Op. cit.

42. Nutt, P. C. 2004. Op. cit.

43. Geringer, M. 1991. Op. cit.

44. Shah, R. H., & Swaminathan, V. 2008. Op. cit.

45. Li, D., Eden, L., Hitt, M. A., & Ireland, R. D. 2008. Friends, acquaintances, or stranger? Partner selection in R&D alliances. *Academy of Management Journal*, 51: 315–334.

46. Bierly, P. E., & Gallagher, S. 2007. Op. cit.

47. Li, D., Eden, L., Hitt, M. A, & Ireland, R. D. 2008. Op. cit.

48. Rangan, S. 2000. Op. cit.

49. Douma, M. U., Bilderbeek, J., Idenburg, P. J., & Looise, J. K. 2000. Op. cit.

50. Stuart, T. E. 2000. Interorganizational alliances and the performance of firms: A study of growth and innovation. *Strategic Management Journal*, 21: 791–811.

51. Stuart, T. E. 2000. Op. cit.

52. Manral, L., & Harrigan, K. R. 2006. Alliances in the new economy. In O. Shenkar & J. J. Reuer (Eds.), *Handbook of Strategic Alliances*. Thousand Oaks, CA: Sage.

53. Hagiu, A., Yoffie, D. B., & Slind, M. 2007. Brightcove and the future of Internet television. HBS case 9-707-457.

54. Wallace, R. L. 2004. Strategic partnerships: An entrepreneur's guide to joint ventures and alliances. Dearborn Trade Publishing.

55. Bick, J. 2003. Gold bond: Expanding with a business alliance. *Entrepreneur Magazine,* 31(3): 54.
56. Ariño, A., & Concha, A. 2001. Partner selection in strategic alliances. IESE Business School document DGN-612-E.
57. Child, J., & Faulkner, D. 1998. Strategies of cooperation: Managing alliances, networks, and joint ventures. Oxford, UK: Oxford University Press.
58. Pidduck, A. B. 2006. Op. cit.
59. De Mattos, C., Sanderson, S., & Ghauri, P. 2002. Op. cit.
60. Bierly, P. E., & Gallagher, S. 2007. Op. cit.
61. Bierly, P. E., & S. Gallagher. 2007. Op. cit., 145.
62. Garvin, D. A., & Roberto, M. 2001. What you don't know about making decisions. *Harvard Business Review*, 79(8): 108–116. Quote from p. 116.

CHAPTER 5

NEGOTIATING ENTREPRENEURIAL ALLIANCES

INTRODUCTION

Filled Bagel Industries LLC is a family-run bakery whose product line is recognized for its New York-style bagels filled with fresh cream cheese produced using family secret recipes.[1] Its owner Gary Schwartzberg had been trying to sell his product to supermarkets on his own; however, after an unsuccessful attempt he realized he needed a well-established brand to achieve wide distribution. Kraft Foods, Inc.—the global food and beverage company—might be the right partner for him. However, how could a small company such as his gain the attention of such a large company involved in hundreds of projects? He found a creative way and mailed Kraft a box of cream-cheese-filled bagels along with a business proposal. And he got their attention! Kraft had been working on a similar project looking for new opportunities to market its cream cheese in the portable-breakfast category. What they lacked, however, was bagel-making expertise. Kraft executives got interested in Mr. Schwartzberg's proposal and created an internal team to evaluate the possibility of manufacturing a new product on a national scale. Finally a strategic alliance was established, a result of which was products known as Bagel-Fuls, which were to be based on Filled Bagel Industries' recipes and expertise but filled with Philadelphia Cream Cheese and branded as a Kraft product. The first Bagel-Fuls went to U.S. stores in April, 2008.

Prior to sending the box of bagels to Kraft, Mr. Schwartzberg and his team one way or another underwent the type of search and selection processes discussed in Chapter 4. As a result, Kraft was selected as their preferred partner.

In this chapter we discuss the processes that take place in between partner selection and alliance formation—the type of processes that the management team at Filled Bagel Industries had to undertake to attract Kraft to a partnership and which finally led to the creation of their alliance with Kraft.

Negotiating an entrepreneurial alliance entails two key processes: the intrafirm preparation to negotiate, and the actual interfirm negotiation. In preparing to negotiate, managers from the initiating company have to consider how to attract and maintain their preferred partner's attention, and how to ensure that the preferred partner will choose their company as well. This takes persuading the partner-to-be that their company can help them satisfy the partner-to-be's strategic needs. This can be more challenging for entrepreneurial companies than for established ones. Oftentimes, entrepreneurial companies lack legitimacy in the marketplace, and it is expensive for them to overcome this drawback so that their preferred partners decide to ally with them.

Negotiating the alliance is an interactive process between the initiating company and their preferred partner, and it provides an opportunity to confirm the company's initial assessments of partner fit. As discussed in Chapter 4, the earlier a (mis)fit is identified the better for all companies and managers involved. This means that one possible outcome of the alliance negotiation is the discovery that, contrary to initial expectations, the chosen partner presents a misfit, and the two companies will be better off not continuing the relationship any further. The time pressures experienced by entrepreneurial companies may push them to expedite the process. However, in doing so, they may forget that assessment of partner fit was not finalised when making their preferred partner choice. As a matter of fact, a survey carried out among owners or general managers of small and medium-sized companies revealed that more than 70% of the respondents perceived partner agreement on clear and realistic objectives to be very important for alliance success.[2] This supports the idea that unless the partners-to-be are well suited to each other and able to reach agreement on goals at the negotiation stage, they are better off not entering the alliance.

If the companies decide to go ahead and create the alliance, the resulting outcome is not only a set of formal contracts (in the case of a joint venture), but a new legal entity, which make up the alliance structure. As a result of the ongoing interactions during negotiations among managers from both companies, a psychological contract also emerges. And there is a relational outcome as well: As a consequence of those interactions, the involved managers develop a certain level of relational quality—which should be positive or at least not negative for the alliance to be formed—that will have an influence on subsequent alliance execution. We will elaborate on the negotiation outcomes later on.

In this chapter we will consider the challenges entrepreneurial companies face in creating an alliance with their preferred partners, and we will discuss how to prepare to negotiate as well as issues to keep in mind when negotiating alliances. Our purpose here is not to provide a detailed guide to negotiations and the tactics involved—for that we refer the reader to the well-established literature on negotiations[3]—but to uncover issues peculiar to negotiating entrepreneurial alliances. Consistent with our approach in Chapter 4, we assume that the entrepreneurial company is the one taking the initiative to form the alliance. If this were not the case, the reader may easily adjust the ideas we present here.

CHALLENGES ASSOCIATED TO NEGOTIATING AN ENTREPRENEURIAL ALLIANCE

Part of the alliance implementation challenge is how to negotiate the alliance with the preferred partner identified at the partner search and selection stages. The first challenge associated with alliance negotiations stems from the need to attract the preferred partner's attention. Given how time-constrained busy executives are, they have to focus their attention screening out some information and narrowing what is left[4]. But getting an executive's attention is not only a matter of surpassing an initial screen as Mr. Schwartzberg managed to do by sending the box of cream-cheese-filled bagels along with a business proposal. He and his team also faced the challenge to maintain Kraft's attention throughout the negotiation process. And it is easy to imagine how many projects compete for the attention of executives in a $37 billion sales company like Kraft Foods. For instance, Novo Nordisk reports having received 236 proposals for new alliance opportunities in 2008, out of which 146 were further evaluated, and only 3 deals were made.[5] If the preferred partner is another entrepreneurial company, attracting and maintaining its managers' attention is equally challenging as the managers are likely to have a preconceived business plan for their new undertaking and might see the proposal to form an alliance as deviating their attention from that plan.

Gaining and maintaining this attention is especially difficult for small, entrepreneurial companies as they are not well known in the market place, and executives in their preferred partner company will not have an initial inclination to pay attention to a proposal coming from an unknown firm. It falls on the entrepreneurial company to make a good case for how their proposal to ally will benefit their potential partner. But in doing so, managers from the entrepreneurial company confront the danger of disclosing too much information. In some cases, once the potential partner has that information, it might go ahead with the business opportunity, leaving the entrepreneurial company aside. Knowledge-based businesses—such as science- or information technology-based businesses—are more prone to this conundrum than others as they are subject to the so-called information paradox:[6] You can't value information until you know what it is; but once you know it, why would you pay for it?

Other challenges associated with alliance negotiations stem from the time pressures entrepreneurial companies face typically, as we discussed in Chapter 4. Eager to get the deal done, managers at entrepreneurial companies may rush into negotiations, which can bring about a number of undesired consequences. One such a consequence is that they may yield power to the other company, and this is more the case if the counterpart is a large corporation. There is some evidence that the smaller firm is often asked to take on the higher level of risk.[7] The stakes in the alliance may not be as critical for a large partner as for an entrepreneurial company. Executives in a large corporation may assign a lower priority to getting it done than their entrepreneurial counterparts, especially so when the former are not the initiating party. In an attempt to keep the deal moving ahead, entrepreneurial managers may fall into making concessions too quickly to the demands of the large company. Also, research shows that the larger the difference between the company's size and that of the potential partner, the shorter the time it takes to negotiate a partnership, an indicator that small companies may yield to the requests of their large counterparts more easily than when negotiating with companies of a similar size.[8] Quite the contrary, entrepreneurs should remember the homework they did when selecting their preferred partner: If they evaluated partner fit as suggested in Chapter 4, then they chose that one company because the alliance they propose is as good a fit for the potential partner as it is for their own company. Thus, the entrepreneur's job is to show their preferred partner what's in the alliance for them. Once the preferred partner becomes interested, the entrepreneur will not feel as pressured to yield to all of their requests.

Another undesired consequence of rushing through negotiations is that the insufficient levels of mutual knowledge and understanding achieved make final fit assessments difficult. Accelerating negotiations may result in establishing an alliance in which partner fit is insufficient or in which partners are not mutually aware of their differences and, when conflict emerges later on, this unawareness will make it harder for them to figure out how to solve that conflict. This was the case in the alliance between Toysmart—an Internet retailer of educational toys—and Disney.[9] Initially, Toysmart's CEO David Lord considered a strategic alliance with Disney to develop a virtual store specializing in selling nonviolent toys to be a perfect match. After the partner search, he determined there was a strong strategic fit. Disney had a major resource that Toysmart was dying to have, namely a brand that would translate into visibility and growth for Toysmart. At the same time, Toysmart could offer its dot-com experience that would allow Disney to reach to more customers. Moreover, the two companies seemed to share the same vision: Disney was viewed as a family-oriented company and Toysmart focused exclusively on selling nonviolent toys. Assuming the fit was there, David Lord signed a strategic alliance with Disney. A year later Toysmart ceased all its operations and went out of business.

When analyzing his company's failure, David Lord mentioned that he should have chosen his partner more wisely. If he had paid more attention to gaining a better understanding of Disney during the negotiation stage, he might have avoided a fatal mistake: He would have understood that while the fit was there, it was insufficient and that the companies differed too much to come to common grounds. First of all, the companies had somewhat conflicting goals: Toysmart focused too much on establishing its brand while Disney was solely concerned with making a profit. This initial incongruity in goals became conspicuous during the advertising campaign and eventually led to discord: Disney felt Toysmart's advertising was aimed at establishing the company's brand rather than at attracting more customers to its website, the address of which disappeared too quickly from the screen. Moreover, a few months after having signed the alliance agreement, Disney decided to switch its goals and focus on books and entertainment rather than on toys. Yet another problem in the relationship stemmed from organizational misfit; there was a clear cultural clash that impeded the work of the alliance. Being a big corporation, Disney operated on a much more bureaucratic level, which meant decisions took a long time. By contrast, Toysmart wanted to make decisions "right now" and was reluctant to wait. Many important deals were approved by Disney long after the end of the important Christmas shopping period. As a result, Toysmart was short of cash. If both companies' executives had given more weight to these issues during the negotiations period, they might have avoided the pitfalls or may have chosen to seek other partners.

As a result of these challenges, managers at entrepreneurial companies face several important trade-offs: First, getting the partner's attention requires information disclosure, but if they disclose too much information they risk loss of critical intellectual property; second, they need to move the process ahead given the time pressures suffered, but in doing so they may lose power to their partner, and they may end up entering an alliance for which partner fit is inadequate. Clearly, how they solve these trade-offs has an important impact on the value the alliance will create eventually, and on how this value will be distributed between the entrepreneurial company and its partner. A good negotiation preparation that leads to a thoughtful negotiation helps in solving these trade-offs, and we turn now to discussing how to prepare for negotiations.

PREPARING TO NEGOTIATE

In preparing to negotiate with a preferred potential partner, managers of entrepreneurial companies should keep in mind three considerations of a general nature (summarized in Table 5.1) before getting down to the details of the negotiation. The first general consideration is to keep in mind that the purpose is to use the alliance to cocreate value along with the partner. This sets the context for the negotiation, and it should influence the style—competitive or cooperative—to be adopted. In most cases, potential alliance partners do not have the exact

---

TABLE 5.1   General Considerations to Prepare for Alliance Negotiation

- Keep in mind that the alliance is meant to cocreate value along with your preferred potential partner: Take a cooperative approach to negotiation.
- Analyze both your needs and those of your preferred potential partner: Carry out a two-sided analysis.
- Remember you still have to confirm the fit with your preferred potential partner: Design the negotiation process in a way that allows you to make the necessary assessments.

same strategic objectives. As a result, their views of value creation will likely be different. Nevertheless, how an entrepreneurial company will benefit from the alliance depends on the extent to which value is actually cocreated. Unless value is in fact created, the eventual partners may have nothing to share. Thus, alliance negotiation is not only a process of value exchange but one of value creation.[10]

A value creation focus calls for a cooperative approach to negotiation, whereas a focus on value distribution is more attuned with a competitive style. While in cooperative negotiations the aim is to create a bigger pie, this does not necessarily mean that all parties win to an equal extent: It is enough if one gains without the other one losing as a result. When a negotiation is strictly competitive—a zero-sum game as it is often called—anything one side wins the other side will lose.[11] Interestingly, most people are inclined to view negotiations as a competition between parties quarrelling over the biggest piece of a fixed pie. Even when both parties prefer the same outcome, the tendency is to believe that the other's interests are conflicting with one's own.[12] The fact that the partners' goals are not identical need not be a significant issue as long as the goals are compatible and each party understands the potential partner's objectives.[13] Entrepreneurial managers preparing to negotiate will be better off focusing efforts at understanding which are the interests of both their own company and their preferred potential partner.

In practice, most entrepreneurial alliance negotiations are neither purely cooperative nor purely competitive, but a mix of the two. Therefore, it is vital to know when to cooperate and when to compete, when to focus on value creation and when on value capture. This means that alliance negotiators must "walk a fine line between strong negotiating tactics and the realization that the party across the table will become a partner, possibly for many years if the negotiation is successful."[14] In this game creativity is of the essence and the best support for creativity is sound analysis.[15]

This brings us to the second general consideration, that the analysis to prepare an alliance negotiation should be based on a good understanding not only of the entrepreneurial company's needs but also of those of the preferred partner.[16] Managers tend to be better equipped to deal with the first part of the analysis than with the latter. Putting oneself into the other's shoes not only means acknowledging the mutual interdependence that will be created once the alliance is formed. It also means acknowledging the fact that while managers from the initiating company may have a very clear idea of what they want for themselves, the other party may enter the negotiations without such a clear idea. Thus, entrepreneurs should be open to helping their preferred potential partner understand what's in the alliance for them[17] by identifying why the potential partner should be interested in the alliance, explaining how the new resource combination is a winning proposition, and generating alternatives that are attractive to potential partners.

The previous discussion implies that entrepreneurs have to be ready to share information during negotiations in a way that makes it easier for the potential partner to make their business case and analyze what they can gain from the alliance. Driven by a desire to increase the probability that the alliance will be formed in order to put their company on the path to having its goals met, entrepreneurs have strong incentives to communicate as much information as they can to the potential partner,[18] and at times this may be too much. Thus, they have to find a balance between providing enough information to make the alliance attractive to the counterpart, and giving away too much information inadvertently. This balance may partly come from the pace at which information is shared. If information is revealed in an incremental fashion, this gives the partner a chance to reciprocate to this openness, and in this way entrepreneurial managers are in a better position to estimate how the partner might behave in the future.[19]

The third general consideration in preparing to negotiate an alliance is to keep in mind that throughout the negotiations the assessment of the suitability of the counterpart as the preferred partner is still to be confirmed. Going back to Table 4.2 in Chapter 4 will remind us that initial assessments of strategic and organizational fit are to be confirmed during negotiations. Also, this is the time to make initial assessments of organizational fit with regard to internal features, as well as of operational and human fit. This has implications for designing the negotiation process. For instance, the need to assess human fit should be considered when deciding who will participate in the negotiations.

Once these general considerations have been thought through, managers of entrepreneurial alliances will be in good shape to start detailing their negotiation plan.[20] Points to bear in mind include who will be on the negotiation team, and how to make a sound two-sided analysis of each party's interests. First, it is worth pausing to consider who should take part in the negotiation team. The default composition tends to be the entrepreneur and possibly some other executives in the top management team. Of course, their participation is necessary. However, entrepreneurs should bear in mind that the alliance negotiation may fulfil other purposes in addition to getting the deal signed. As discussed earlier, it is during negotiations that the level of partner fit is finally evaluated and confirmed. This requires an active approach at seeking mutual knowledge and understanding of the parties. The people who will actually manage and keep the alliance working are in the best position to ask tough questions early in the process, and they will want answers to key operational questions.[21] Thus, their inclusion in the negotiation team is crucial to make a sound assessment of operational fit. Also, they will have to manage the relationship with the partner. As a consequence, assessment of human fit will be possible only if the working managers are involved in the process. Finally, an open team makes the internal sale of the alliance easier, something critical in ensuring support throughout the lifetime of the alliance.

Second, and obvious as it may sound, managers have to make a thorough two-sided analysis of each party's interests. Of course, this will be different in every single case, and what we offer here are the critical cornerstones that should be considered. Table 5.2 offers guidelines for such an analysis. Managers need to understand the real interests at stake in the negotiation, and not just those stated explicitly. A good preparation will help reveal common and complementary

TABLE 5.2 Guidelines for a Two-Sided Analysis of Negotiation Positions		
Dimensions for the Analysis	*Entrepreneurial Company*	*Preferred Partner*
What do we/they want? (needs, interests, . . .)		
What if we don't reach an agreement? (best alternative to a negotiated agreement, or BATNA)		
What is it that we have to negotiate?		
• Resource contributions		
• Other conditions (illustrative):		
• Location		
• Calendar		
• Management positions		
• Patents and intellectual property rights		
Which contextual conditions will influence the negotiation outcome?		
• Time		
• Information		
• Negotiation power		
• Approach to negotiation		

Source: Based on Ariño, A. & Montes, J. S. 2001. Op. cit.

objectives rather than emphasizing conflicting ones[22]—even if these should be acknowledged and discussed as well. Before negotiations begin, managers should have a clear idea of negotiable and nonnegotiable issues. Over time, alliance-experienced firms may learn what works and what doesn't work for their organizations. Entrepreneurial companies with limited alliance experience can therefore have a more difficult time determining what details are essential.[23]

Also, entrepreneurial managers must be aware of the alternatives and outcomes if the alliance is not successfully negotiated. They have to establish the best alternative to a negotiated agreement (BATNA) for each party as this provides a comparison level that serves as a baseline of the negotiation: Trespassing that limit would mean that no agreement would be possible. Thinking through the first two rows of Table 5.2 should help managers have a good understanding of what is at stake and what the boundaries of a potential agreement are.

But this is not enough to make a sound two-sided analysis. Entrepreneurial managers also need to consider the dynamics that may drive the negotiation in one direction or another within the boundaries just defined. Thinking about the parameters of the negotiation—what has to be negotiated—will help in this regard (see the third row in Table 5.2). These may include issues such as: Where will the business be located? What is the timeline to set up the business? How will the different management positions be shared? And, most importantly, the resources each party has to contribute. A list of potential contributions may help negotiations move as well as establish a path for discussion to understand each other's views.[24] Clearly, the entrepreneurial managers' assessment of their company's contribution is likely to differ from that of the potential partner, and vice versa. These differences must be taken into account so as not to misjudge the partners' respective contributions. Also, not all points under negotiation are equally important, and applying weights to them may help establish their relative significance.

The challenge here is for entrepreneurial companies to counterbalance the potential partner's power. When partners-to-be are of a similar size, chances are that they perceive themselves as equals in power. However, when there are important size differences it may easily happen that both see the entrepreneurial company as more dependent on the large one than vice versa. And in fact, this may be the case so far as entrepreneurial companies tend to be focused on a single business and their survival is contingent on how well they do in it. To the extent that the alliance is central to their business, they may need the large corporation more than the large corporation needs them. When size difference is combined with the time pressures described in Chapter 4, managers in entrepreneurial companies run the risk of forgetting that they have valuable contributions they can offer to their counterpart. Entrepreneurs should recognize that their companies have specialist knowledge that gives them critical expertise.[25]

Oftentimes, entrepreneurs at technological start-ups think of their companies as contributing only a particular technology to the alliance. Even if this technology is cutting-edge, a savvy-enough partner may absorb it with relative ease. And once this happens, the partner will not need the entrepreneurial company any longer. However, an entrepreneurial firm may contribute other resources to the alliance as well. Most importantly, they may contribute their inventive capability, provided they can show they have such a capability.[26] If the entrepreneurial firm can promise to bring in new technologies in the future, then the partner will have a strong incentive to continue investing in the relationship, which will continue as long as they still have valuable things to learn. This approach is well illustrated in the following comment by an alliance executive from an entrepreneurial drug delivery company:[27] "It's not an alliance, it's a series of alliances. It's a series of technologies that put proteins into a sustained-release format. That can be done with many proteins. We have two publicly announced agreements. One was with a large firm for human-growth hormone. And we have a number of others that we're working on; they just haven't been disclosed yet. And there's a subsidiary technology as well that we've just taken over that expands that capability into small molecules, and we just announced two days ago an agreement with a large firm for an unnamed compound."

Entrepreneurs shouldn't forget the homework they did when selecting their preferred partner: They chose that one company because the alliance they propose is as good a fit for the partner-to-be as it is for their company. At the same time, entrepreneurs have to be careful not to overpromise on what they can contribute to the alliance.[28] Their optimistic nature may betray them. And, this reinforces the need for a good two-sided analysis when preparing for the negotiation.

In addition, some contextual conditions may influence the result of the negotiation, as outlined in the last row of Table 5.2:

- *Time:* Usually, the time available for the negotiation is not the same for all parties. Most likely, the entrepreneurial company will have a tighter deadline than the preferred partner—and especially so when initiating the alliance, as we assume to be the case. The time pressure may affect the initial exploratory talks and the options that are generated, limiting dialogue in the hurry to get a deal signed. Awareness of this situation will help managers of entrepreneurial companies keep calm and not to yield to the counterpart's requests unnecessarily.

- *Information:* Given the uncertainty surrounding an alliance negotiation, managing the information one has and investigating the information provided by the other party are important tasks for the negotiation team. Negotiation boundaries—what's on the table and what's not—should be made clear. Also, entrepreneurial managers should keep in mind that unmentioned details are what get the partners into serious conflict later on. While ignoring certain issues may hasten an agreement, it will also make the alliance unstable in the future. There is a vast volume of negotiation items in most alliances, which makes the partners unwilling to open up that box at all. However, these issues, if pushed to the background during negotiations, may create lack of trust as partners may interpret ambiguous issues differently.

- *Power:* Managers have to think about the sources of both their company's and the preferred partner's power. Also, they should consider which external changes might happen that would increase or decrease that power. Usually, when power is balanced, a cooperative approach to negotiation becomes more natural. On the contrary, when there are important imbalances, there is less incentive to cooperate. Of course, having power does not mean it should be put into use: It is enough for the preferred partner to be aware of the entrepreneurial company's power for it to have its effect. And explaining it during both the early exploratory talks and the actual negotiations is a delicate and crucial part of effective negotiation.

- *Type of relationship:* When negotiating an alliance, the envisioned relationship is based on shared expectations of long-term, ongoing exchange, and the negotiation involves multiple dimensions. Under these conditions, the approach to negotiation should be more cooperative. The parties should realize that it is in their interest to foster cooperation, because without it, the value of their respective contributions will be greatly diminished and the expected return will decrease. Nonetheless, it is worthwhile for managers of entrepreneurial companies to pause and reflect whether this is the case, and how they expect the preferred partner's approach to be—cooperative or competitive. Let's not forget the earlier remark that most people are inclined to view negotiations as a competition.[29] Identifying the partners' most likely motives with the help of the guidelines in Table 5.2 (first row) may generate a better understanding of the likely approach to be taken.[30]

By following our guidance in preparing for negotiations, entrepreneurial managers should be prepared and able to avoid starting an alliance on blind faith,[31] based on certain expectations about the counterpart that run the risk of being unrealistic and, as a result, likely unattainable. However, even if the preparation has been thorough, entrepreneurial managers should be aware that often it is not until they actually start negotiating that the partners are able to pin down exactly what each one is looking for. In a way, negotiation is a learning process about mutual interests and goals. The better prepared the process, the more fruitful it will be. We turn now to discuss how to approach the negotiation itself.

CARRYING OUT NEGOTIATIONS

Entrepreneurial managers will start negotiations with certain expectations about their preferred partner.[32] These expectations have been formed throughout the previous partner search and selection processes and while preparing to negotiate. Also, the experiences—if any—that both parties have had with each other or other firms on previous occasions shape those expectations. The negotiation over the alliance will confirm or rectify these expectations. Thus, the negotiation can be characterized by the breadth and intensity of the mutual understanding process, which we may call the negotiation's "bandwidth." The negotiation can be a "broadband" process in which the value of the proposed alliance is explored and it is sought to confirm one's expectations about the partner. Alternatively, it can be a "narrowband" process, focused mostly on the particulars of who will carry out which tasks and who will contribute which resources but without actively seeking any broader mutual understanding (see Figure 5.1).

When engaging in a broad bandwidth negotiation, managers go beyond the immediate aspects of the alliance deal. This gives entrepreneurial managers an opportunity to observe the business judgment, reliability, and functional competence of the preferred partner. In other words, it provides entrepreneurial managers with a basis to finalize their assessment about partner fit. Also, a broadband approach allows entrepreneurial managers to signal their commitment to the relationship. They can take actions—like incurring certain negotiation costs—that show their willingness to make short-term sacrifices to realize longer-term benefits,[33] as both companies need to rest assured that the other has similar incentives to move the work forward.[34]

Entrepreneurial managers may use negotiations to showcase their entrepreneurial skills.[35] Often, large partners look for entrepreneurial skills that can break moulds, and entrepreneurial talent that can help solve their problems. The negotiation period provides entrepreneurs an opportunity to showcase the skills they have to create new solutions.

Negotiations also provide an excellent opportunity for the entrepreneurial company to demonstrate its reliability so that it becomes a preferred partner as well. Frequently, large corporations fear that a small company might not be

FIGURE 5.1 Negotiations Bandwidth

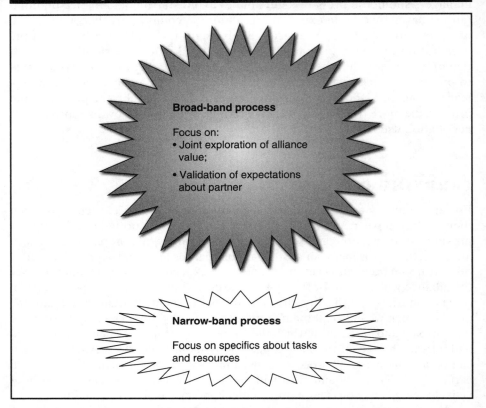

Source: Based on Ariño, A., de la Torre, J. & Ring, P. S. 2001. Relational quality: Managing trust in corporate alliances. California Management Review, 44: 109–131.

reliable in delivering upon its operational commitments. One manager from a large telecom company reported his concerns with small partner companies:[36] "the penalties that I have to pay for delaying a $2M shipment are massive compared to what they have to pay us for delaying a $20K shipment. The latter, however, is a prerequisite for the former." Overcoming this type of prejudice may be necessary to the creation of the alliance. For instance, Canadian wireless Internet provider Spotnik approached Telus—the second largest telecommunication company in the country—with the proposal to form an alliance to build a public wireless Internet network in hotspots across Canada.[37] Telus was convinced to partner with this small, unknown company because of the elaborate business plan Spotnik presented. Thanks to this alliance, in a few years Spotnik had turned into Canada's leading wireless Internet service provider.

Broadband negotiations also help to build trust. Entrepreneurial managers should be aware of the initial level of trust.[38] As Inkpen and Li put it:[39] "When

TABLE 5.3 A Guide to Evaluate the Alliance Project

- Are both companies committed to the alliance project?
- Does the project create value for the customers?
- Do both companies agree on resource contributions and the timeframe for this?
- Is there a clear project timeline?
- Does a detailed plan accompany the project?
- Has project success been defined?
- Have both companies agreed to a kick-off date?

Source: Based on Wallace, R. L. 2004. Op. cit.

partners have not collaborated in the past, the possibility of untrustworthiness is heightened because relations are in a developing stage and managers are uncertain about the skills, knowledge, and objectives of their counterparts. Without strong relationships between individuals at this stage, trust will not develop. In a worst-case scenario, if enemies are created in the negotiation process, it is unlikely any cooperative agreement that emerges will be successful." Nonetheless, beware that while low levels of initial trust are difficult to overcome, too high levels may give the parties a false sense of security and cause them to overlook potential conflicts of interest.

In sum, when the partners view the negotiation as a "broadband" process, it is more likely to end in an agreement which will serve as a foundation for the alliance design than if the negotiation is a "narrowband" process. Table 5.3 offers guidance to evaluate the soundness of a potential alliance. Affirmative answers to the questions in Table 5.3 are a sign that the partners have reached a mutually agreeable deal, and they are ready now to undertake the alliance.[40] Alternatively, they may decide it is better not to form the prospective alliance, a desirable outcome if partner fit was poor.

As negotiations progress, partners will become involved in more formal dealings so as to reach agreement on what the specific terms and conditions will be.[41] Once managers have a clear idea of the nature of the business deal, the time may have come to involve a lawyer to draft a contract that makes it happen. In Chapter 3 we already offered some considerations regarding when it is desirable or not to craft a complex contract or to leave it more open-ended. Also, we covered various types of provisions that firms can negotiate. Here, we just want to add some thoughts regarding how the contracting period itself may be used to enhance the inter-partner relationship.

There is a fine line in between bringing lawyers and other professionals on stage too early or too late. Bringing them in too early may prevent business negotiators from gaining a rich-enough mutual understanding. Bringing them too late entails a risk of making commitments while being unaware of their unintended legal implications. Deciding the right timing for introducing lawyers to negotiations is a fine art for which there are no ready-made recipes. A general rule to help make the decision is: Bring them in early enough that they may gain a good understanding of both companies' interests, but late enough that they do not interfere in the companies' efforts at making sense of the business deal.

If brought in at the appropriate time, lawyers may facilitate a good discussion that helps partners articulate, codify, and deepen the meeting of their minds, as we advanced in Chapter 3. Good professionals will ask the right questions, and will not fall into the extreme reported by a lawyer representing a small company:[42] "This law firm [the one representing their counterpart] has poisoned the negotiations by creating a set of 'what if' clauses, totally out of scope. The Memorandum of Understanding is 35 pages long. It should be no longer than 3."[43]

Generally, large companies take a more formal approach to contracting than entrepreneurial firms do. This provides the latter with an invaluable opportunity to learn from the former. For instance, the two types of companies approach due diligence differently.[44] Large companies often have long due-diligence checklists that help them evaluate a potential partner. However, a number of reasons prevent entrepreneurs from taking this crucial step to making a sound judgement of their preferred partner:[45] it is time-consuming, and it risks offending the other party. But perhaps the more important reason is that entrepreneurs are optimistic in nature and tend to assume they can make any business opportunity work out that appears to be sound. They prefer to get the deal than to take the time to make sure that the first impression is correct. Yet, as already discussed, taking this time pays off sooner or later, and entrepreneurial companies may benefit from investing in their own due-diligence checklists.

Also, large companies may have a well-structured approach to handling the transacting phase of the negotiation process from which entrepreneurial companies may learn. Finmeccanica—Italy's premier aerospace, defense, and security company—may be taken as an example of this.[46] During negotiations with Alcatel to create the Space Alliance, the Finmeccanica team maintained a list of unresolved issues detailing Finmeccanica's position, Alcatel's position, and the main reasons behind each other's argument. Also, the team had a timetable of activities, which outlined target dates for each specific issue. Throughout the negotiations, the list of unresolved issues constantly changed. Given the large amount of items to get through, the list helped the negotiation team to manage their time. Also, it made it easier to give periodic updates to their top management as the negotiators could explain all of the issues and the approach they were going to follow. Table 5.4 illustrates one way to keep track of unresolved issues.

The outcome from alliance negotiations goes beyond the alliance structure that is implemented.[47] By the end of negotiations, the managers involved will have generated a psychological contract,[48] possibly without even knowing it.[49] The mind frame and openness with which management carry out the negotiations set the stage for how they will interact once the alliance becomes operational. Arguably, both a sound legal contract and a psychological contract are necessary for an alliance to develop favorably.[50] On the one hand, an excessive focus on legal issues may lead to distrust among parties. On the other hand, the absence of formal legal structures paves the way to an abuse of trust. Thus, a

TABLE 5.4 Illustrative Instrument to Keep Track of Unresolved Issues				
Unresolved Issues	*Entrepreneurial Company's Interests and Position*	*Preferred Partner's Interests and Position*	*Actions to Help Solve the Issues*	*Target Deadline for Action*

balance between formal and informal aspects of contracting is desirable. A certain level of relational quality is also built as a consequence of the interactions during negotiations. Figure 5.2 shows the outcomes from the negotiations and their influence at the alliance execution stage.

A well-managed contracting period centered in gaining mutual knowledge and understanding can produce both a tight legal contract that sets specific terms and plans ways to adapt to a number of contingencies, as well as a psychological contract that allows the parties to reach mutually satisfactory agreements when facing unforeseen circumstances. One small German company in the tool industry decided to focus on some special markets.[51] So as to have the appropriate products for these markets, they negotiated contractual alliances with two key, noncompeting suppliers—small companies as well. Negotiations with one of them were very hard: "It seemed to me that they did not trust us at all. The contract was fixed after two years of discussions (adding another year before to interest them in the idea). Since the time we closed the contract we have never

FIGURE 5.2 Outcomes from Alliance Negotiations

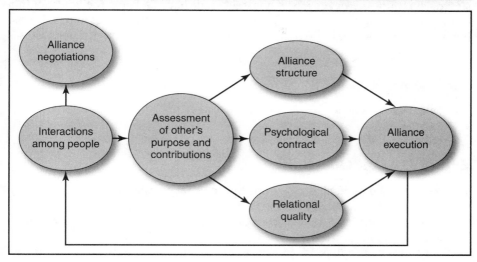

talked about it anymore. It just works very well. When they receive an inquiry they immediately transfer it to us and our conversations can be very open as no one has to hide any information. The success is excellent." In contrast, negotiations with the second supplier appeared very easy: "I told them about the idea to work together in those markets, they came to our company and after a discussion of two hours we signed the contracts. I was very surprised after my experiences with the previous one. The problems began later: the supplier cannot deliver all special products for the market, and we are suffering very long delivery times and losing reputation with big customers." This should not be read as if the longer the negotiation, the better. Rather, the message is that a contract should not be signed until the partners have reached a mutually acceptable agreement, and to reach this within reasonable time limits entrepreneurs should prepare well.

To the extent that prospective partners take a mutual value creation, perspective characteristic of a broadband approach, openness, and trust are more likely to develop throughout the negotiation process. The relational quality generated in this way will be an important input to how the alliance will be executed once it becomes operational.

Conclusion

This chapter has discussed the two key processes that the negotiations of an entrepreneurial alliance entails. These include the intrafirm process of preparing to negotiate, and the actual process of interfirm negotiation. As a result of negotiations, the partners-to-be will have a clear idea of the alliance project.

The next step is to go ahead and sign the deal. Still, entrepreneurs should ask themselves the killer question: "When the time arrives for my company to exit this alliance, will the company be stronger and more powerful than when we entered in?"[52] If the answer is yes, then the time has arrived to take the pen and sign each one of the pages in the contract, and then . . . leave the contract in a drawer as the company enters the alliance. A new set of challenges appear on the horizon to make it work.[53] We turn our attention to alliance execution processes in Chapter 6.

Key Terms

- negotiation preparation
- negotiation process
- negotiation outcomes

End of Chapter Questions

1. What are the main challenges entrepreneurial companies face in preparing to negotiate an alliance? And in carrying out the negotiations?
2. Why is it better to take a cooperative than a competitive approach to alliance negotiation?
3. Why does a broadband approach to negotiation work better than a narrowband approach?

4. What are the main outcomes from the negotiation process? What is the importance of each one?
5. How can lawyers help in the negotiation process?

References

1. "Running the show: My brain, your brawn: Big companies are on the prowl for small businesses that will hand over their best ideas in exchange for the piece of the action." *The Wall Street Journal*, (October 13, 2008); "Kraft's bagel idea spreads cheese line." *Chicago Tribune* (October 03, 2008).
2. Hoffman. W. H., & Schlosser, R. 2001. Success factors of strategic alliances in small and medium-sized enterprises—An empirical survey. *Long Range Planning*, 34: 357–381.
3. Fisher, R., & Ury, W. 1981. *Getting to yes: Negotiating an agreement without giving in*. Boston, MA: Houghton Mifflin.
4. Davenport, T. H., & Beck, J. C. 2001. *The attention economy: Understanding the new currency of business*. Boston, MA: Harvard Business School Press.
5. Grøndal, C. Development of a corporate alliance management function. Presentation at the 2nd Annual Copenhagen Conference on Partnerships: Creating innovative solutions through collaboration. November 17–18, 2008, Copenhagen, Denmark.
6. Arrow, K. J. 1973. *Information and economic behavior*. Stockholm: Federation of Swedish Industries.
7. Sulej, J. C., Stewart, V., & Keogh, W. 2001. Taking risk in joint ventures: Whose throw of the dice? *Strategic Change*, 10: 285–295.
8. Ariño, A., Reuer, J. J., Mayer, K. J., & Jané, J. Negotiating outsourcing partnerships: An investigation of termination provisions and prior ties. Work in progress.
9. Information on the Toysmart-Disney alliance may be found at McGarvey, R. 2000. Find your partner. *Entrepreneur Magazine*, 28(2): 72; King, J. 2000. CEO: Partnership hurt toysmart. *Computerworld*, 34(26): 1; Das, T. K. 2006. Strategic alliance temporalities and partner opportunism. *British Journal of Management*, 17: 1–21 Germain, D. Disney grabs online toy business, The Associated Press (August 08, 1999).
10. Inkpen, A., & Li, K.-Q. 1999. Joint venture formation: Planning and knowledge-gathering for success. *Organizational Dynamics*, (Spring): 33–47.
11. Ariño, A., & Montes, J. S. 2001. Negotiating strategic alliances. IESE Business School document DGN-558-E.
12. "Are you *really ready to negotiate?*" 2007. Editorial note in *Negotiation. Helping you build successful agreements and partnerships*, 10(9): 1–3.
13. Inkpen, A., & Li, K.-Q. 1999. Op. cit.
14. Inkpen, A., & Li, K.-Q. 1999. Op. cit.
15. Ariño, A., & Montes, J. S. 2001. Op. cit.
16. Ariño, A., & Montes, J. S. 2001. Op. cit.
17. De Mattos, C., Sanderson, S., & Ghauri, P. 2002. Negotiating alliances in emerging markets—Do partners' contributions matter? *Thunderbird International Business Review*, 44: 701–728.
18. Alvarez, S. A., & Barney, J. B. 2001. How entrepreneurial firms can benefit from alliances with large partners. *Academy of Management Executive*, 15: 139–148.
19. Wallace, R. L. 2004. *Strategic partnerships. An entrepreneur's guide to joint ventures and alliances*. Chicago, IL: Dearborn Trade Publishing.
20. This discussion draws heavily from Ariño, A., & Montes, J. S. 2001. Op. cit.
21. Inkpen, A., & Li, K.-Q. 1999. Op. cit.

22. De Mattos, C., Sanderson, S., & Ghauri, P. 2002. Op. cit.
23. Inkpen, A., & Li, K.-Q. 1999. Op. cit.: 39.
24. De Mattos, C., Sanderson, S. & Ghauri, P. 2002. Op. cit.
25. Sulej, J. C., Stewart, V., & Keogh, W. 2001. Op. cit.
26. These ideas were first introduced by Alvarez, S. A., & Barney, J. B. 2001. Op. cit.
27. Alvarez, S. A., & Barney, J. B. 2001. Op. cit.: 145.
28. Wallace, R. L. 2004. Op. cit.
29. "Are you *really ready to negotiate?"* 2007. Op. cit.
30. De Mattos, C., Sanderson, S., & Ghauri, P. 2002. Op. cit.
31. Inkpen, A., & Li, K.-Q. 1999. Op. cit.
32. These insights are based on work by Ariño, A., de la Torre, J., & Ring, P. S. 2001. Relational quality: Managing trust in corporate alliances. *California Management Review*, 44: 109–131.
33. Shah, R. H., & Swaminathan, V. 2008. Factors influencing partner selection in strategic alliances: The moderating role of alliance context. *Strategic Management Journal*, 29: 471–494.
34. Wallace, R. L. 2004. Op. cit.
35. Mockler, R. J., & Gartenfeld, M. E. 2001. *Strategic Change*, 10: 215–221.
36. Personal communication.
37. Nicholls-Nixon, C., & Litman, O. 2003. Spotnik Communications—Partnership in action (B) and (C). Richard Ivey School of Business cases 9B03M030 and 9B04M037.
38. Ariño, A., de la Torre, J., & Ring, P. S. 2001. Op. cit.
39. Inkpen, A., & Li, K.-Q. 1999. Op. cit.
40. Ariño, A., & Reuer, J. J.. 2004. Op. cit.
41. Ring, P. S. 2000. Op. cit.
42. Personal communication.
43. Personal communication from one of the involved lawyers.
44. Alvarez, S. A., & Barney, J. B. 2001. Op. cit.
45. These explanations are offered by Wallace, R. L. 2004. Op. cit.: 120–121.
46. Ariño, A., Ozcan, P., & Mitchell, J. IESE Business School case. Finmeccanica: The Space Alliance with Alcatel (B). Work in progress.
47. Ariño, A., de la Torre, J., & Ring, P. S. 2001. Op. cit.
48. Ring, P. S., & Van de Ven, A. H. 1994. Op. cit.: 100 characterize psychological contracts as consisting of "unwritten and largely nonverbalized sets of congruent expectations and assumptions held by transacting parties about each other's prerogatives and obligations." In other words, "expectations of what each party will give to, and receive from, the relationship."
49. Ring, P. S. 2000. Op. cit.
50. Ariño, A. & Reuer, J. J. 2006. Alliance contractual design. In O. Shenkar & J. J. Reuer (Eds.), *Handbook of Strategic Alliances*: 149–167. Thousand Oaks, CA: Sage.
51. Personal communication from one of the involved managers.
52. Wallace, R. L. 2004. Op. cit.

CHAPTER 6

EXECUTING ENTREPRENEURIAL ALLIANCES

INTRODUCTION

In 2001, start-up SCo was approached by LCo with the proposal to create a joint venture.[1] SCo was an entrepreneurial manufacturer of industrial components in an emergent country, and LCo was a large Western European multinational in the same industry. The two companies had worked together for a few years, with SCo already having acted as LCo's distributor in the emergent market. The new joint venture—which would perform both manufacturing and distribution functions— saw the light in 2002. From the very beginning, the partners faced a number of important difficulties.

The first difficulty was finding the right leader. Due to each partner's internal policies, they decided that the CEO should be an external person. The first CEO was found by the entrepreneurial company SCo. She managed the joint venture's start-up phase, but failed in the second stage when sales had to be built. LCo's reps decided to find a more experienced person and hired a fifty-year-old CEO. SCo was against him because, even at first sight, he seemed too slow for the young company. But SCo respected LCo's choice and finally accepted its proposal. For a year sales were stable at an extremely low level. Eventually, the partners decided that the CEO had to be replaced. This time, LCo trusted SCo to offer a candidate. The new CEO built a strong team and doubled sales in one year, exceeding the forecast. The entrepreneur's conclusion was "even in difficulties and when you make evident mistakes, in an alliance you have to be able to understand and to forgive your partner, to take responsibility for your own mistakes and go further. If parties are looking at the future and trust each other, they will overcome past mistakes."

A second difficulty was the decision to dilute SCo's share. The joint venture's results were not that good in the first year, and LCo had to extend more and more trade credits to the joint company. While LCo was ready to give a loan, increasing equity by the same amount as the dollar value of the loan was an attractive alternative from a tax perspective. Clearly, SCo's share in the joint venture would be diluted significantly. SCo could insist on keeping the loan but, taking into account LCo's interests and benefits and looking forward to the joint venture's future, SCo accepted the proposal. In exchange, LCo promised that SCo would recover its share of equity in the future, at least partially. Two years later, LCo fulfilled its promise and offered to transfer SCo for free an important part of the joint venture's shares whose worth had increased significantly. The entrepreneur's learning was that "even an unclear and, at first sight, potentially conflictive situation can be turned developmental and beneficial for the joint venture and for partners' relationships."

A third important difficulty arose when, according to the business plan, the joint venture had to acquire a plot of land in order to build a plant. After months of searching, SCo's entrepreneur found a perfect site with buildings owned by a large, local company. It had all of the desired features, but also one problem: The local company was selling a package of two companies—one owned the real estate, and the other operated in these facilities and employed people. LCo didn't want to buy a company with many problematic workers. Fearing that the opportunity might be lost, SCo offered to invest its own money and buy the two companies, solve the issues with workers, and sell only the real estate company to the joint venture without taking any fees for this operation. Naturally, LCo accepted, and the operation was completed in a record time of five months. "Sometimes, partners have to be very flexible and creative in order to push the joint venture development and not to lose time. It is impossible to reflect all of these issues in any contract, and only real interest to the mutual project's survival is the clue," concluded the entrepreneur.

Despite these hurdles, the alliance was a great success, and by 2007 sales were growing at a yearly rate of 60%. The two companies had been able to overcome difficulties thanks to, in the words of SCo's founder, "reliable and open relationships between partners, sharing of strategic goals, and flexibility and trust when problems and changes appeared, in addition to the right selection of key personnel."

As this story illustrates, executing an alliance is no easy task. Managing within such a nonhierarchical setting is not an easy endeavor, and it requires a combination of skills—large doses of entrepreneurship, corporate experience, and cross-cultural diplomacy—that are rarely found to coexist in any organization, including entrepreneurial companies.[2] *Alliance execution* refers to the activities involved in operating the alliance, adjusting it to changing circumstances, and terminating it eventually. Inappropriate execution of the alliance results in failure to meet the "alliance implementation challenge." As we discussed in

Chapter 1, the lack of trust, poor communication, cultural differences, lack of adaptation, and inadequate coordination or conflict resolution procedures are all examples of problems that can occur during the execution of alliances.

The fact that alliance partners remain independent organizations means that each one may have its own private goals for the alliance which are not shared by the other partner. It also means that each company brings in its own organizational characteristics—organizational structure, company size, as well as corporate and national culture—that have to coexist with those of the partner company. If managers of entrepreneurial companies have done a good job at the partner search and selection, and at the negotiation stages, they will have a good sense that the two companies present reasonable degrees of fit at the different levels (we refer the reader back to Table 4.1) or else they would be better off not initiating the alliance. But still, because the partners remain independent, there will always be some uncertainty as to what one party is counting on the other to do.[3] Despite the fact that SCo and LCo had worked together before creating their joint venture, the way they handled emerging difficulties could not be predicted beforehand.

Both the entrepreneurial company and its partner will have to cooperate if the alliance is to deliver the envisioned results. As they work together, partners' expectations will be confirmed or disconfirmed, which generates an internal dynamic that may foster cooperation or, conversely, undermine the relationship and possibly even lead to dissolving the alliance. The way SCo and LCo reacted to the difficulty in finding the right leader for the joint venture showed their mutual commitment and willingness to make things happen, in turn paving the way to a positive resolution of the next difficulties.

In this chapter we discuss the challenges entrepreneurial companies face in executing their alliances. We pay attention to ways of managing conflict so that it becomes healthy for the relationship; in particular, we portray formal mechanisms that rule decision-making, and elaborate on how to nurture relational quality. Then we turn to addressing the need to restructure an alliance that emerges at times, and the decision of when to terminate a restructured alliance.

CHALLENGES ASSOCIATED WITH EXECUTING ENTREPRENEURIAL ALLIANCES

Alliance execution is an important element of the alliance implementation challenge. Of course, the better the job that entrepreneurial managers have done at selecting their partner and negotiating and designing the alliance, the better position they'll be in to address this challenge. Certainly, the outcomes from negotiation—the alliance structure, a psychological contract, and a certain level of relational quality, as pictured in Figure 5.2—exert a significant influence on how managers from the partner companies behave once they are in the alliance. For instance, the way the alliance is structured has important consequences on how decisions will be made. The psychological contract sets the agreement boundaries which are delimited by the understanding each company has about its own, and the partner's expected contributions and the tasks each one should carry out drive their behavior as well as their perceptions of the partner's behavior. And the level of relational quality will influence how tolerant they are to deviations from their agreements and how they will react to the other stepping out of the anticipated boundaries.

Even if all of these initial conditions were positive and pointing in the right direction, entrepreneurial managers have to bear in mind a number of issues that add complexity to executing an alliance. First, the partner companies remain independent organizations with their own goals, identities, and cultures, and at times the consequences of these healthy differences may result in a clash. Second, and although not a prevalent reality, the partner company may hold a hidden agenda that has gone undetected in earlier stages and which may damage the entrepreneurial company's interests. Third, alliances are dynamic, as are the partner companies and the environment in which they operate. Thus, the interests that both entrepreneurial companies and their partners have in the alliance may vary and eventually turn into a conflict of interest. Finally, as the alliance develops, managers involved in it will update their psychological contract and relational quality, and may face the need to formally revise the alliance structure or even terminate the alliance in due course.

In practical terms, what this means is that entrepreneurial managers have to be ready to face conflict when executing their alliances. The main areas of conflict correspond to the levels of partner fit outlined in Table 4.2. Even if, by the end of negotiations, entrepreneurial managers have assessed that the partners-to-be fit reasonably well such that it makes sense to carry out the alliance, this fit will never be perfect, and, furthermore, mistakes may have been made along the way. To add complexity, the dynamic nature of alliances, partner companies, and the environment may result in situations of unanticipated conflict. Thus, the main challenges in alliance execution relate to overcoming the different conflicts that will emerge—strategic, organizational, operational, and human conflicts—and to adapting the alliance to changing conditions (see Figure 6.1).

Strategic conflicts may appear that relate to the goals each partner pursues for the alliance. When the alliance starts, the partners have agreed upon an agenda of common goals. However, conflict comes into play because the benefits each company expects to gain may not be the same. Apart from the common goals that both partners share, each firm may have its own private goals with respect to the strategic alliance that are not shared by the other partner. The level of conflict depends on the combination of private and common goals; that is, the level of match between the various goals and the importance given by each participant to each group of goals. A strategic alliance in which compatible common and private goals prevail will operate more smoothly than one in which incompatible private goals are stronger for one or both partners. In the worst scenario, the alliance may contribute to creating a competitor. This may be the case more frequently in vertical than in horizontal alliances.[4] In vertical alliances, each partner contributes different resources and capacities to the strategic alliance. This

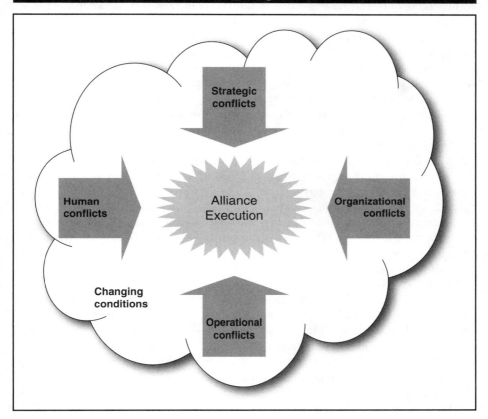

FIGURE 6.1 The Alliance Execution Challenge

situation enables firms to learn from the partner and internalize its contributions. Thus, they can embark upon the so-called learning race, where whoever wins will no longer need its partner.[5]

This may easily happen in a strategic alliance between a small innovative firm and a large firm holding the assets required to take that innovation to the market—such as manufacturing, marketing, sales, distribution, financial, or managerial resources. The entrepreneurial firm runs the risk of losing the learning race, as it is easier for the large firm to absorb the innovation and realize its market potential than for the small firm to develop the necessary organizational capabilities to grow by itself. This situation leads to a relationship of dependency by the small firm on the large firm, which in time may come to impose unreasonable demands.[6] This was the case for an entrepreneurial company that entered into an alliance with a large firm in order to commercialize an important new technology they had developed for the biotechnology industry.[7] In a few years, the large firm had gained access to the new technology and had successfully commercialized it, while the entrepreneurial company was bankrupt. A senior manager from the entrepreneurial company described the situation: "it was very much a David and Goliath story. There was nothing that we could do to stop them. It was cold and calculated on their part. And the real losers are strewn about the roadway here—our employees, the 160 people who lost their jobs between June and September last year." Entrepreneurial managers may avoid become trapped in this situation by positioning their company not just as contributing one innovation but as bringing in their innovation capability. For a large company, it is much harder to appropriate or develop such a capability than a single innovation.

Strategic conflict may result as well from differences in the psychological contract regarding resources and contributions. As referred to in Chapter 5, the expectations of what each partner will give to, and receive from, the relationship that the psychological contract entails may allow the parties to reach mutually satisfactory agreements when facing unforeseen circumstances. But this will be so to the extent that partners' expectations are congruent, which is not always the case—especially so if, during negotiations, insufficient attention was paid to achieving mutual knowledge and understanding. Trolltech, an open-source software start-up based in Norway, experienced the negative consequences of incongruent expectations.[8] Trolltech established a contractual alliance with a Japanese manufacturer with a Linux-based software platform for personal digital assistants. The alliance turned into a nightmare for Trolltech as differences surfaced between what the Japanese company thought it would get and what the start-up felt it should provide. If this happens, entrepreneurial managers are well advised to engage in discussions with their partner so as to clarify the situation. Possibly, these discussions will bring up the need to adjust the alliance terms, something we'll discuss more in depth later in this chapter.

Organizational conflicts often arise which relate to differences in partners' organizational structure, size, and corporate and national cultures. At the end of the day, these differences come down to different managerial practices. Unless taken into account, such differences may bring all kinds of misunderstandings that prevent managers from a prompt execution of the alliance.

There are no two identical companies. Thus, entrepreneurial managers will face organizational conflicts in any alliance they undertake, be it with another entrepreneurial company or with an established one, with a domestic firm or with a foreign company. Still, the more prominent the differences, the greater the potential for conflict is. For instance, the innovative culture of a start-up easily clashes with the bureaucratic style of a large company. This happened in the alliance between entrepreneurial Alza and large Ciba-Geigy that was mentioned in Chapter 2.[9] Alza discovered the bureaucratic and hierarchical nature of Ciba-Geigy, whose personnel was in turn shocked by Alza's behavioral style. Their interactions were more painful and progress was slower than expected.

Other notorious cultural differences are those faced by born-global companies. These start-ups take an accelerated path to internationalization, as from the very beginning they seek to build their competitive advantage from operating in multiple countries.[10] Achieving a global reach requires that they build alliances with companies based in other countries, and they have to cope with all types of differences in national cultures. Going back to the alliance between Norwegian Trolltech and its Japanese partner, when the latter suspected that Trolltech wouldn't deliver the software on time, it offered to send over a team of software engineers through the Christmas break so as to meet a deadline. While this would have been acceptable in Japan, Trolltech refused, alluding to the importance of the Christmas vacation in Norway. The relationship was at the edge of collapse. This illustrates the complexity of dealing with cross-border cultural differences, and suggests the elevated level of difficulties that may arise when the number of partners' countries is large, as with born-global start-ups.

Dealing with organizational conflicts requires a certain level of cultural intelligence:[11] understanding why people from the partner company act as they do will help entrepreneurial managers improve how they relate to their counterparts. Cultural intelligence can be developed: First, entrepreneurial managers should try to understand the motives and thoughts underlying their counterparts' actions and intents; second, apparent misunderstandings should not restrain entrepreneurial managers from engaging in new interactions with their counterparts; finally, they should show appreciation for the other's practices.

Operational conflicts may develop as partners realize that the efficient combination of their resources is not as easy as it might have appeared at the outset. These conflicts relate to the compatibility of the committed resources, be these information technology systems, manufacturing facilities, distribution systems, or any other type of resource committed to the alliance.[12]

Entrepreneurial companies may face operational conflicts in alliances created both with other entrepreneurial companies and with already established ones. For instance, a group of small companies may decide to set up an alliance to make joint purchases. By pooling together they may achieve efficiencies through scale which otherwise they would not be able to reach. However, they may run into trouble if the technical requirements of their products are not compatible, making it unfeasible to source components jointly. In the case of alliances with an established company, operational conflict may result from the entrepreneurial company's difficulties in delivering on schedule or in growing at the pace the large company would need it to. A manager from a large automobile manufacturer reported: "we haven't had a good experience with small partners. In fact, they can't invest. We've been in situations in which we had no car delivery, no spare parts."[13] Something similar happened in the alliance between Microsoft and Sendo, a start-up UK wireless phone manufacturer.[14] The alliance was set up with the goal of creating a new generation mobile phone based on Microsoft's Smartphone cell phone operating system. The alliance started showing the first failing signs soon after clinching the deal. Sendo claimed it could not proceed with its work because Microsoft was delivering a defective operating system while Microsoft was accusing Sendo of not meeting the deadlines. These crisscross accusations resulted in the final split of the alliance.

Smoothing operational conflicts does not mean turning the entrepreneurial company—or the partner company—upside-down. Rather, managers from both partner companies should agree to the minimum requirements for working together, and decide which of their procedures need to be adjusted and to what extent. For instance, some reporting practices may need to be modified, but this does not imply that the whole accounting system has to be redesigned.

Human conflicts may appear when the people involved in the alliance feel uncomfortable working together. Oftentimes, alliances require exchange of confidential information, and unless everybody is comfortable with one another the needed exchange is unlikely to take place. While these types of conflicts are latent in any alliance, when they involve entrepreneurial companies an added element comes into play: The egos of the entrepreneurs tend to clash.[15] Doubtless, entrepreneurs' egos are a must to bringing their venture to fruition, but at times egos may get entrepreneurs into trouble. Related, entrepreneurs are used to being the ones running the show, and at times it's hard for them to share decision-making power. That was the case of an entrepreneur in biotech.[16] A pharmaceutical company acquired a 20% stake in the start-up. The entrepreneur had been used to flying solo, so he was uncomfortable with the financial and operating restrictions imposed by the pharma company and specified in the shareholders' agreement. But—as reported by one participant in the deal—"one thing is to be uncomfortable with new ways of doing things, and another to approve the annual accounts without the joint venture's general shareholders meeting taking place!" Personal conflict may be even more pronounced if two entrepreneurs get together in one alliance.

Entrepreneurial managers may avoid being driven out by human conflicts in their dealings with the counterpart by fostering humble attitudes.[17] They should be open to new ways of doing things, eager to learn from their partner, acknowledge their own limitations and mistakes, and accept that failure presents a learning opportunity.

Sooner or later, entrepreneurial managers will face one or another type of conflict. While a certain level of conflict may be healthy, it may become harmful if not properly managed. Two main avenues open here. The first relates to setting up formal mechanisms that establish the rules of the game for decision-making. The second avenue involves nurturing the right relational quality between the partners. We discuss these next.

DECISION-MAKING RULES

The extent to which an entrepreneurial alliance will in fact create value to be shared by the partners depends on decisions that are made as the alliance becomes operational. Some of these decisions are related to governing or overseeing the alliance, and some to managing it on a daily basis. There is a range of mechanisms to make these decisions, depending on the alliance structure type. In Chapter 3 we introduced two distinct structural categories: nonequity alliances and equity alliances. In the case of nonequity alliances, governance decisions are made by a committee that represents each of the partner companies at a high level, and this committee might be as simple as two entrepreneurs talking on the phone. Management decisions are made by those in charge of the alliance's daily activities, who might be the entrepreneur or some key executive. In the case of equity alliances, governance decisions are made by the board of directors that represents the partner companies, and day-to-day decisions are made by the alliance executive committee.

In establishing decision-making rules,[18] entrepreneurial managers should keep in mind that job titles may mean different things in different contexts, and this is especially the case in an international environment. Unawareness of this may result in situations that complicate alliance execution. This was the case of an equity joint venture between a French (50.01% equity) and a Swedish (49.99% equity) partner.[19] It had been agreed that the joint venture chairman would come from the French firm and the CEO from the Swedish company. The Swedish firm thought that the chairman would simply look after board meetings, and the CEO would take care of the day-to-day business. To their surprise, in France, the chairman, or président directeur général (PDG), usually acted as both the chairman and CEO. It turned out that the PDG was a very authoritarian manager who intended to manage the joint venture his way. The Swedish CEO appointee was relegated to a non-CEO role leading to an intense conflict between the parent firms.

The lesson is that decision-making rules must be clearly defined, even in fairly simple alliances, and they must answer the following questions: Which are governance decisions? Which are management decisions? Which decisions must be referred up to the partner firms? What are the reporting lines? What information must be provided and when? What budgets and business plans must be approved? And so forth. Even if people making both governance and management decisions were the same, it should be clear to everybody which hat they are wearing each time: that of overseeing the alliance or that of managing its daily operations.

GOVERNANCE DECISIONS

When defining rules for governance decisions,[20] entrepreneurial managers should strive for one basic principle to be applied, and this is that the people brought by both partners must have the same level of discretion to commit their company to the alliance. Otherwise, they will not have the same decision-making capacity, which is a source of conflict. Very often, entrepreneurs are the ones representing their own companies along with a few key managers. If the counterpart is another entrepreneurial company, chances are that the directors will be of the same stature. However, if the counterpart is a large company, their natural choice might be someone at a relatively lower rank. Entrepreneurs should insist on having discussions with people who have enough decision-making power or else this may be a source of frustration to them. Also, it is very important to determine

TABLE 6.1 Available Mechanisms for Breaking Deadlocks in Entrepreneurial Alliance Governance Decisions
Casting vote of the Chairperson.
This mechanism is not very popular as it means tipping the balance of control toward one of the parties. However, it can be mitigated by rotating the chairmanship between the partners.
Casting vote of an independent director.
The difficulty lies in finding a person with the right experience who is acceptable to both parties.
Refer the matter to a third party, who could be an expert in the subject in question or an arbitrator.
This mechanism is not appropriate when the differences between the partners are due to their different approaches to the business.
Refer the matter to the partners' top managers, if they are not directly involved.
Sometimes, this can be the most practical solution, as the desire to prevent the matter from escalating upward can induce the directors to reach an agreement.

the confidentiality of information. If information is to be shared freely with other people in the firm, this must be clearly acknowledged in writing—even in the legal documents, if these exist, imposing confidentiality at partner-firm level.

Two difficult situations may arise, depending on the type of decision-making rules at work. First, if decisions are made by consensus, this can give rise to deadlocks. The challenge is to prevent this from happening. Table 6.1 offers some of the mechanisms for breaking deadlocks. Second, if one of the parties has a controlling vote, usually this partner wants to have the last word and control decision-making. One way to protect the minority partner is to provide it with a veto power in particularly important issues. Exercising the veto right may lead to a deadlock in a decision, but this can be avoided by implementing the mechanisms mentioned in the case of consensus-based decision-making.[21]

MANAGEMENT DECISIONS

The distribution of management responsibilities does not necessarily have to be equalitarian; one of the parties can even take on full responsibility for day-to-day business through a management contract with the alliance. The guiding principle should be to assign responsibilities according to excellence levels in the different areas.

Managers assigned to the alliance should think of their responsibilities broadly. To the extent they do so, these managers may play an active role in preventing conflict from arising. That's what a newly hired executive achieved in a joint venture between a Southern European entrepreneur and a Northern European company.[22] The joint venture had been plagued by conflict deriving from cultural, operational, and organizational conflicts. The Southern shareholder was also the CEO of the joint venture and information didn't flow in a very transparent way to the partner, under the prejudice that they couldn't understand the Southern way of doing business. A new executive was hired in the middle of this war and, to the surprise of the CEO, she was not on his side nor the Northern company's. Her transparency and honesty was a surprise for the partners, who started to trust her. She always claimed to work for the joint venture company and would try to do the best for it and not for one or other shareholder. This position cost her much disappointment from the CEO but in the end the CEO admitted that her position helped both parties become closer to each other. Once differences were admitted, they began working together to make the maximum profit of this alliance.

To this point, a number of areas worth alliance managers' attention include: making sure the alliance business objectives meet all partners' needs and expectations; evaluating whether the alliance's importance to each partner is of a similar degree; evaluating the similarities and differences in the partners' organizational structures; and specifying how alliance conflicts regarding strategic issues are to be handled.[23] To the extent the alliance managers pay attention to these issues they may spot areas of potential conflict which, if managed properly, might strengthen the alliance and improve partners' relational quality, but otherwise will prove unhealthy.

NURTURING RELATIONAL QUALITY

In Chapter 5 we identified relational quality[24] as one of the outcomes from alliance negotiations. The level of relational quality is a consequence of the partners' contacts during the negotiation phase—and also of previous relationships they may have had. When managers initiate the alliance execution, relational quality is like a blank page with not too much—either positive or negative—history written on it. At the end of the day, partners have agreed on the goals and laid down the initial rules of the game—but they haven't played the game yet!

Research has shown that most alliances are dissolved in their first two years of operation, although those that last beyond this threshold have a much better chance of survival.[25] This suggests that, in most cases, dissolution happens prematurely, before any of the partners have achieved their goals for the alliance. A premature alliance termination would hurt entrepreneurial companies especially hard because of two reasons.[26] First, the resources an entrepreneurial company invests in an alliance are a large proportion of its overall resources, including management time. Second, an alliance may have an important influence in the strategic direction of an entrepreneurial company. Entrepreneurs need to have realistic time horizons in mind when forming and attempting to manage an alliance.

Clearly, the threshold will not be exactly two years in every case, but the idea is valid of an alliance start-up period, which is critical for relational quality to strengthen. It is during this period that precedents are set which will largely determine the extent to which the relationship will be cooperative or not. For instance, in the aforementioned alliance between Microsoft and Sendo, when Sendo sent its first complaints Microsoft did not prove cooperative.[27] Microsoft's initial noncooperation generated unwillingness to cooperate on the part of Sendo as well.

Although cooperativeness is necessary for the successful development of an alliance, it does not happen automatically. Entrepreneurial managers and their counterparts will face numerous decisions of the "should I cooperate or shouldn't I?" type, as the story of the joint venture between SCo and LCo that opened this chapter illustrates well. What the managers end up doing affects their mutual perceptions, and rules of reciprocity—that is, rules of how to respond to the other's actions—emerge that will improve or deteriorate their relational quality and their willingness to trust each other in their relationship. As relational quality improves, the partners become more tolerant of minor deviations from what was planned. On the contrary, if the relational quality deteriorates, each one may decide to act only in accordance with its own interests, and the relationship gradually worsens. In this case, as the alliance develops, the relational quality will evolve in a positive or negative direction, as Figure 6.2 illustrates.[28]

Entrepreneurial managers should be aware of their capacity to shape relational quality: So long as they cooperate, their counterparts are more likely to reciprocate and behave similarly. This is how the entrepreneur at SCo managed to create an atmosphere of cooperation that endured the relationship. SCo submitted to hiring a CEO suggested by LCo even if they didn't like him fully. Aware that their first choice had worked well only at the beginning, they did not want to overimpose their opinion and went with LCo's proposal. In turn, when the mistake was evident to LCo they didn't hesitate in trusting SCo to offer a new candidate. This positive opening began shaping rules of reciprocity that would drive future behaviors.

FIGURE 6.2   Relational Quality Dynamics

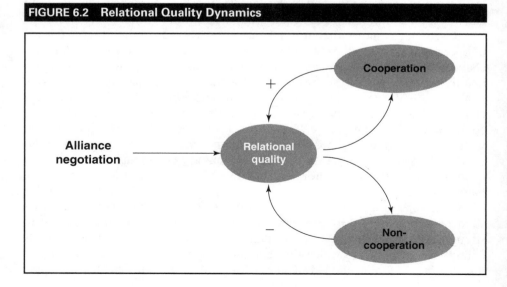

The point to drive home is that entrepreneurial managers should take an active attitude to build relational quality and not leave it to their partner only or rely on wishful thinking that things will work out with the partner. However, entrepreneurs have to be watchful and mind their partner's behavior as everyone should be cooperative for the alliance to succeed. If the partner turns out not to reciprocate the entrepreneur's efforts at promoting cooperation, the entrepreneur is better advised to open a discussion with the partner to try and redirect the situation. But if the partner persists to the point that the entrepreneur's interests are seriously jeopardized or simply go unserved, the time may have arrived to bring the alliance to an end—something we will discuss at the end of the chapter.

Satisfactory conflict resolution is an excellent means of building trust and adjusting expectations. Hence, it is important for entrepreneurial managers to seek consensus and take the partner's interests into account. Conflict resolution has a cumulative effect that may change the dynamics of the relationship. The way conflicts are dealt with sets precedents and will either strengthen or weaken the relationship. Thus, when a conflict arises within the alliance, entrepreneurial managers should ask themselves not only how to resolve it efficiently, but also how the chosen solution will affect the future relationship with the partner. Again, how SCo handled the decision to dilute its share and how they solved the problems faced in acquiring the needed land illustrate this point well. For instance, taking differences into account does not mean they should be eliminated—rather, partners may leverage them to create value.[29] Entrepreneurial managers should remember that they sought an alliance with their partner precisely because their differences offer the potential to create value. However, when these differences show up, entrepreneurial managers and their counterparts are often uncomfortable with them and with the conflict they bring. An attempt at leveling those differences sends the message that the differences are bad and hides conflict without resolving it. On the contrary, an open discussion about how those differences are perceived and whether they might benefit the alliance if they are not ignored or suppressed helps use those differences to create value.

If wisely used, the formal conflict resolution procedures in Table 6.1 will contribute to generating a positive dynamic among the partners. This will help prevent unnecessary friction and will facilitate effective joint problem-solving. And entrepreneurial managers should remember that it is always better to persuade one's partner to go in a particular direction than create the impression that they are trying to impose their will on their counterpart. This was the experience of a manager from a family-owned company involved in a 50/50 joint venture:

> . . . the most important thing you can do is trying to avoid deadlocks by investing a lot of time in the relationship, talking a lot with your partner, understanding their worries and feelings, and not rushing into a decision unless you are sure that your partner feels 100% comfortable with it. This sounds nice but it is extremely tiring sometimes . . . Sometimes you

see very clearly that a decision needs to be taken very soon and because your partner is not so sure you cannot take it and you have to wait until the consequences are bigger and your partner understands it.[30]

In this way, trust or mistrust builds. Trust is much more fragile during the start-up phase than once the relationship has matured. Mutual understanding among the partners smoothes the relationship. This characterized the successful alliance between Uniformity, a Los Angeles-based start-up manufacturer of fashionable school uniforms, and Macy's West, a subsidiary of Macy's chain of retail department stores which offers apparel, furniture, and household goods.[31] Both parties worked out a clear managerial scheme of the alliance operation which put regular communication flow at the heart of their business. For instance, Uniformity received weekly sales reports from Macy's West. The companies had regular monthly meetings at the executive level, and both parties evaluated each other's progress regularly and offered their recommendations. After successfully cooperating for more than a year, the companies decided to extend their partnership with more Uniformity boutiques opening in Macy's stores over the following two years.

The following recommendations may help to make cooperation happen, especially during the start-up stage of alliance execution:

- devote time to informal discussions with managers from the partner company;
- organize meetings between employees from both companies at all levels, and not just at the top management level;
- visit the partner's facilities, and invite the partner to visit yours;
- devote time and energy to conveying the alliance purpose to the rest of your organization; and
- establish permanent channels of communication with your partners.

This was the route traveled by managers from a particular family-owned business. One of them shared their positive experience with us:

We usually go to the country where the joint venture operates for a week with [the managers from the partner company] and we travel in the same plane, we stay in the same hotel, we have lunch and dinner together, so there is time to build a relationship and share our experiences in all areas of our business. We have discussed technical issues, organizational issues, the role of the owners in the company and our experiences in other countries. You also learn a lot by observing how they address the issues that we discuss about the joint venture, to which things they pay more attention to, what is their point of view, how they analyze, etc.[32]

However, entrepreneurial managers should be warned not to take a naïve attitude. In particular, they should be aware of the possibility mentioned earlier in this chapter that the alliance becomes a learning race. The dilemma faced here is that, on the one hand, partners need to share information to carry out their joint activities, while, on the other hand, information disclosure may contribute to creating a competitor in the market place. This happened to an entrepreneurial logistics operator that created an alliance with a more established one from another country.[33]The entrepreneurial operator contributed its market knowledge and the established one its operations know-how. Within a year, the entrepreneurial company had lost its market to the partner. Entrepreneurial managers should understand the extent to which the partner's goal is to learn from their company. The challenge is to share the relevant information necessary to support the alliance while simultaneously protecting proprietary knowledge.[34] Important decisions in this respect include how the partner's information requests are to be channeled and who will control those information flows. Needless to say, relational quality becomes increasingly negative in learning-race situations.

At the same time, entrepreneurial managers should not forget that some alliances are temporary arrangements. As circumstances change, the alliance may require some adjustments or even termination. We turn to this in the next two sections of this chapter.

RESTRUCTURING ALLIANCES

Entrepreneurial alliances are dynamic:[35] With time, managers may find the alliance was not structured properly, partner companies may experience strategic or organizational alterations, or the environment in which the alliance operates may change. Under these circumstances, entrepreneurial managers should think about the need to adjust their alliances. However, restructuring and renegotiating an alliance may be fairly expensive—even if it were only in terms of the entrepreneur's time and energies, thus entrepreneurial managers should carefully consider the need to do so.

Like anyone else, entrepreneurial managers are subject to mistakes when choosing how to structure the alliance. One mistake they may make is to overstructure the deal by establishing a complex structure for a simple relationship. In 2000, entrepreneurial Amazon.com and Toys "R" Us launched a cobranded website to sell toys online. Amazon operated the site, and handled distribution and customer service, while Toys "R" Us was responsible for merchandising. The relationship was governed by a contractual agreement by which Toys "R" Us financed the inventory of toys in Amazon warehouses and recorded the sales as its own. In return, it paid Amazon.com a percentage fee to cover the costs of order handling, and an annual fee.[36] For a well-specified relationship involving a single activity with modest coordination needs, such as the relationship between Amazon.com and Toys "R" Us, the creation of a separate business entity with shared equity and the institution of a board to oversee the collaboration is not required. Indeed, such an overstructure might bring about slow decision-making and high organizational costs. Entrepreneurial managers may also make the opposite mistake: understructuring the agreement by using a simple arrangement when an equity alliance would be required. For a complex relationship with a broad scope and high coordination needs, and in which partners' rights and obligations are difficult to specify before entering the alliance, an informal agreement may not facilitate coordination. Also, it may not provide sufficient incentives to avoid opportunistic behaviors from either party.[37]

If entrepreneurial managers and their counterparts made a mistake in deciding the appropriate alliance structure, they may find the benefits from restructuring the alliance outweigh the costs of doing so. There is evidence that renegotiation is more frequent in overstructured than in understructured alliances.[38] This may indicate that the costs of overstructure are greater than those of understructure, as the former are actual—slow decision-making, organizational costs—while the latter are potential—possible opportunistic behavior. Research also suggests that small firms make fewer contractual adjustments in the face of structure misfit than large firms do, probably because the latter are more powerful and, consequently, are in a better position to adapt their relationships over time.[39]

Naturally, the conditions dictating the structure of the alliance will also change over time, and such changes may prompt adaptations in the alliance's structure. In particular, entrepreneurial managers should consider whether restructuring is necessary when there have been changes in any of the partners' strategy or organizational structure, or in the environment in which the alliance operates—of course, provided those changes affect the alliance in an important manner. Strategic alliances become intertwined with the partners' strategies and evolve with them, so that when the partners' strategies change, the structure of the strategic alliances may need to be changed.[40] An entrepreneurial company in the flexible packaging industry entered an alliance with a label manufacturer to capture multinational clients.[41] At the very beginning both companies seemed to have the same interests, and worked well together since they had many similarities in terms of organization, operation, culture, and goals. But as time passed the partner's behavior signaled a lack of commitment and low interest in new projects. Their strategy had changed to keep only high-margin clients, and they did not see the new projects as long-term opportunities.

Relatedly, profound organizational changes may bring about new strategic priorities that make it necessary to revisit an alliance structure. A small, innovative, niche player in the electronic hardware market entered a strategic alliance with a larger competitor to commercialize a new product that the former had developed. The strategic alliance was working relatively well. However, when the large firm's main competitor purchased the entrepreneurial company it all went horribly wrong. Management tension and conflict lead to price wars and legal battles.

Whatever its root might be, the development by one firm of a new strategy may imply that the resources contributed by the partners are not as valuable as they were when the alliance was created. The opposite may happen as well: An alliance may become more valuable for its partners. Similarly, environmental changes may lead to changes in entrepreneurial managers' assessment of an alliance. When changes in the environment affect a strategic alliance, managers change their opinion about its value.[42] In such circumstances, they are more

---

FIGURE 6.3   A Guideline to Assess the Need for Alliance Renegotiation

Do you have an equity alliance for a relatively simple transaction?

Yes ☐   No ☐

Is your alliance contract fairly simple?

Yes ☐   No ☐

Did your strategy or that of your partner change in a way that affected the alliance significantly?

Yes ☐   No ☐

Did your organization or that of your partner change in a way that affected the alliance significantly?

Yes ☐   No ☐

Did the environment change in a way that affected the alliance significantly?

Yes ☐   No ☐

The more positive answers, the more convenient alliance renegotiation will be.

Source: Based on Ariño, A. & J. J. Reuer. 2004. op. cit.

likely to renegotiate the terms of the contract so that they match the new conditions more closely.

A guideline to consider the desirability of restructuring an entrepreneurial alliance may be found in Figure 6.3. At times, changes are important enough that pose a question mark on the need for the alliance. Entrepreneurial managers should consider whether the time has arrived to put an end to it: a question to which we turn next.

TERMINATING ENTREPRENEURIAL ALLIANCES

In the previous section we noted that new circumstances may advise alliance restructuring. It is wise to periodically reassess the desirability of keeping the alliance alive or terminating it. In this way, entrepreneurial managers will avoid the error of maintaining the alliance just out of inertia.[43] They should keep in mind that terminating an alliance does not mean it has failed. Alliance termination may have been planned from the beginning. Also, entrepreneurial managers may decide to terminate an alliance once the goals for which it was created have been achieved. In such cases, putting an end to the alliance is a sign of success.

Two situations may call for terminating an alliance: First, if the alliance no longer helps meet the goals for which it was created; and second, if the costs it entails surpass the benefits it yields. The first situation may arise for reasons both internal and external to the alliance. The internal reasons include the learning races we mentioned earlier in this chapter. Once the firm is capable of carrying out the alliance activity on its own, it may be better off putting an end to the strategic alliance. The external reasons include changes in one of the partners' strategy or organization and in the environment, which we addressed in the previous section. Environmental changes may be either specific to the industry (strong consolidation, growth slowdown, etc.) or more general (technological, political or economic changes, etc.).

The following example illustrates this situation well. In the "dot-com" era, Petco—a leading brick-and-mortar retailer of premium pet food and supplies—decided to extend its capabilities and started looking for a partnership with an online pet store.[44] The chosen partner was Petopia.com—a private San Francisco-based start-up which was founded as an online pet supply retailer offering a variety of pet-related items ranging from pet food to healthcare products and expert advice. The goal of the alliance was to unite Petopia's expertise in online retail with Petco's top-quality products and wide distribution network in order to create a top-notch online supply service for pet lovers. The partnership turned out to be extremely successful and in a few months Nielsen NetRatings placed Petopia.com as the number one pet products e-commerce website in terms of the number of buyers and "stickiness" of the website. Petopia was enjoying the highest gross margins in its industry. The alliance had been operating for a year when the pet supplies market became saturated to the degree where there was too much competition and too little room for all the companies operating in the sector. One by one, all Petopia's competitors were leaving the stage. One year after having been acquired, Petopia suffered the first downturn. The company had to lay off about 60% of its employees and postponed the IPO (initial public offering) that it had filed six months earlier. Heavily in debt, Petopia.com was gobbled by its partner eighteen months after the alliance's launch. This example illustrates how environmental changes can influence the progress of the alliance. When the dot-com market emerged, the investors were excited, seeing in it the alternative to the traditional retail model. However, over time it became obvious that Web-based retail was only an integral part of multichannel shopping that was developing within traditional brick-and-mortar establishments. In addition, the need for the alliance had waned over time as Petco developed the system to operate its own e-commerce channel.

The second situation that may advise terminating an alliance—that the alliance's costs surpass its benefits—may occur as the alliance's coordination and management costs increase. This may happen when differences between the partners emerge as the relationship develops: incompatible goals, different philosophies in decision-making, design of noncooperative compensation systems, asymmetry in the power held by each partner in the strategic alliance, and so on. A manager from a large chemical company that had an alliance with a small firm illustrated how they discovered alliance costs were surpassing the benefits it brought:

> One of our Licensed Industrial Applicators patented an application for the paper industry using our product. The partner was a small company in Finland which did not have the resources to sell outside their country.

Consequently, we signed a contract with them for the rights to sell their application worldwide and paid a royalty as compensation for the use of the patent. Once we started to introduce the patented technology worldwide, we realized that the costs of applying the product (one technical person had to travel to the paper mill for each application) reduced our margins significantly. Hence, we tried to renegotiate the contract in two ways: First, we wanted to just ship the product directly to the paper mill and train the customer to apply it (in order to eliminate travelling costs for our technician). Secondly, we tried to reduce the royalty as the size of revenues brought by our Finnish partner were very small compared to the amount of sales that we were bringing in. At the end, our partner did not want to give the technology to the paper mills, even though it was patented. Furthermore, they objected to reduce the royalty, which triggered us to break the contract and drop any activity in this market.[45]

Sometimes it is not easy for the partners to agree about when and how to end the strategic alliance, particularly if the termination is due to an impasse between the partners. This is why it is highly advisable to specify the circumstances in which the strategic alliance will be ended. Eventually, all partnerships come to an end, whether planned or not, but having planned that end may avoid later problems at the final stage of collaboration and reduce the costs of termination.[46] Termination provisions vary in terms of how easy (fast and inexpensive) or hard (lengthy and expensive) exiting an alliance will be.[47] While easy exit offers flexibility, hard exit promotes dedication to the alliance even in rough times. The more an entrepreneurial company depends on the alliance, the harder it should try to make it for the partner to leave.

Conclusion

This chapter has presented the challenges entrepreneurial companies face in executing their alliances. These challenges relate to the conflicts—strategic, organizational, operational, and human—that will likely emerge as the alliance unfolds. Both formal mechanisms and a good relational quality may help in managing these conflicts and preventing them from becoming unhealthy for the alliance. Still, entrepreneurial managers should keep in mind the temporary nature of strategic alliances, which might better be renegotiated or even terminated if circumstances dictate.

The focus on this chapter and Chapters 4 and 5 has been on dealing with the alliance implementation challenge. They have concentrated mostly on alliances between two companies, at least one of which is entrepreneurial in nature. The complexities of meeting alliance challenges grow with the number of companies involved in an alliance, as well as with the number of alliances one company participates in. Chapter 7 discusses so-called multiparty alliances and alliance portfolios.

Key Terms

- decision-making rules
- relational quality
- alliance renegotiation
- alliance termination

End of Chapter Questions

1. What are the main challenges entrepreneurial companies face in executing an alliance?
2. Which problems may arise from consensus-based decision-making rules? And from rules based on having a dominant partner? How can these problems be solved?
3. How can entrepreneurial managers foster cooperativeness in the alliance?
4. Under what conditions are the costs of renegotiating an entrepreneurial alliance worth incurring?
5. When should entrepreneurial managers consider terminating an alliance?

References

1. This account is based on personal communications from SCo's entrepreneur.
2. Ariño, A., de la Torre, J., & Ring, P. S. 2001. Relational quality: Managing trust in corporate alliances. *California Management Review*, 44: 109–131.
3. Inkpen, A. C., & Li, K.-Q. 1999. Joint venture formation: Planning and knowledge-gathering for success. *Organizational Dynamics*, 27: 33–47.
4. The reader may review the concepts of vertical and horizontal alliances in Chapter 1.
5. Hamel, G. 1991. Competition for competence and interpartner learning within international strategic alliances. *Strategic Management Journal*, 12: 83–103.
6. However, it should be remembered that it is up to the partners to choose the type of SA to build (see García-Canal, E., & Valdés-Llaneza, A. 2006. Direct competition, number of partners and the longevity of stakes in joint ventures. *Management International* Review, 46: 307–326). A strategic alliance does not automatically become a "learning race" but rather this occurs as a consequence of the partners' intention and behavior. If the partners conceive the alliance as a long-term relationship and avoid opportunistic conducts, the alliance may become a "learning cycle" in which the increased mutual knowledge enables the partners to identify new business opportunities which they can embark upon together.
7. Alvarez, S. A., & Barney, J. B. 2001. How entrepreneurial firms can benefit from alliances with large partners. *Academy of Management Executive*, 15: 139–148.
8. Daniel, J. Isenberg. 2008. The global entrepreneur. *Harvard Business Review*, 86(12): 107–111.
9. Doz, Y. L. 1996. The evolution of cooperation in strategic alliances: Initial conditions or learning processes? *Strategic Management Journal*, 17 (Summer Special Issue): 55–84.
10. For further insights on born global companies, refer to Shrader, R. C., Oviatt, B. M., & McDougall, P. P. 2000. How new ventures exploit trade-offs among international risk factors: Lessons for the accelerated internationalization of the 21st Century. *Academy of Management Journal* 43: 1227–1247; and to Oviatt, B. M., & McDougall, P. P. 1994. Towards a theory of international new ventures. *Journal of International Business Studies*, 25: 45–64.

11. Earley, P. C., & Mosakowski, E. 2004. Cultural intelligence. *Harvard Business Review*, October: 139–146 offers interesting insights on navigating through foreign cultures.
12. Das, T. K., & Teng, B.-S. 2002. The dynamics of Alliance conditions in the alliance development process. *Journal of Management Studies*, 39: 725–746.
13. Personal communication.
14. Nimtschek, J., Hulsen, R., Wong, S., & Pestana, F. 2003. The Sendo–Microsoft Alliance. IESE Business School, unpublished report.
15. Wallace, R. L. 2004. *Strategic partnerships. An entrepreneur's guide to joint ventures and alliances.* Chicago, IL: Dearborn Trade Publishing.
16. Personal communication from one of the lawyers involved in the deal.
17. Dusya, V., & Rodriguez-Lopez, A. 2004. Strategic virtues: Humility as a source of competitive advantage. *Organizational Dynamics*, 33: 393–408.
18. This section is based on Freshfields Bruckhaus Deringer. 2005. Joint ventures and alliances. An introductory guide; available at http://www.freshfields.com/publications/pdfs/practices/12561.pdf. We draw as well from Ariño, A. 2005. Strategic alliances: An option to enable corporate growth. IESE Business School document DGN-648-E.
19. This example appears in Inkpen, A. C., & Li, K.-Q. 1999. Op. cit.
20. For an account of the challenges faced by joint venture Boards beyond those faced by the Boards of a typical company, see Bamford, J., & Ernst, D. 2005. Op. cit.
21. Killing, P. 1982. How to make a global joint venture work. *Harvard Business* Review, May/June: 120–127 offers useful insights about the pros and cons of dominant versus shared governance of a joint venture.
22. Personal communication.
23. These useful suggestions are offered by Ireland, R. D., Hitt, M. A., & Vaidyanath, D. 2002. Op. cit.
24. This section draws from Ariño, A., & Montes, J. S. Strategic alliances: Managing the relationship with the partner. 1999. IESE Business School document DGN-562-E; and from Ariño. A. 2005. Op. cit.
25. Bleeke, J. & Ernst, D.. 1992. *Collaborating to compete*. New York: Wiley & Sons.
26. Kelly, M. J., Schan, J.-L., & Joncas, H. 2000. Collaboration between technology entrepreneurs and large corporations: Key design and management issues. *Journal of Small Business Strategy*, 11: 60–76.
27. Nimtschek, J., Hulsen, R., Wong, S., & Pestana, F. 2003. Op. cit.
28. Ariño, A., & de la Torre, J. 1998. Learning from failure: Towards an evolutionary model of collaborative ventures. *Organization Science*, 9: 306–325.
29. Hughes, J., & Weiss, J. 2007. Simple rules for making alliances work. *Harvard Business Review*, November: 122–131. These authors suggest the idea that differences may be leveraged to create value, and we draw from them here.
30. Personal communication.
31. Brown, C. M., & McGee, S. A. 1998. Individuality without compromise, *Black Enterprise* 28(12): 30; Page, H. 1998. United we stand, *Entrepreneur Magazine*. www.entrepreneur.com/magazine
32. Personal communication.
33. Personal communication from one of the managers involved.
34. Ireland, R. D., Hitt, M. A., & D. Vaidyanath. 2002. Op. cit.
35. We draw here from Ariño, A., & Reuer, J. J. 2004. Designing and renegotiating strategic alliance contracts. *Academy of Management Executive*, 18: 37–48.
36. Waters, R. 2000. Amazon, Toys R Us in web link. *Financial Times*, August 11: 15.

37. See Oxley, J. E. 1997. Appropriability hazards and governance in strategic alliances: A transaction cost approach. *Journal of Law, Economics, and Organization*, 13: 387–409.

38. Reuer, J. J., & Ariño, A. 2002. Contractual renegotiations in strategic alliances. *Journal of Management*, 28: 47–68.

39. Ariño, A., R. Ragozzino, & J. J. Reuer. 2008. Op. cit.

40. See Koza, M. P., & Lewin, A. Y. 1998. The co-evolution of strategic alliances. *Organization Science*, 93: 255–264.

41. Personal communication from one of the managers involved.

42. See Doz, Y. L. 1996. Op. cit.; and Ariño, A., & de la Torre, J. 1998. Op. cit.

43. Inkpen, A. C., & Ross, J. 2001. Why do some strategic alliances persist beyond their useful life? *California Management Review*, 44: 132–148

44. McGarvey, R. 2000. Find your partner. *Entrepreneur Magazine,* www.entrepreneur. com/magazine; Enos, L. Petco Gobbles up Petopia's assets, *E-Commerce Times,* http://www.ecommercetimes.com/story/5880.html; Portsmouth, I. Postcards from the future, *Profit,* 19(7); and PETCO announces strategic partnership with petopia.com to launce the premier online pet commerce site, *Business Wire,* 13/07/1999, www.businesswire.com.

45. Personal communication.

46. Mayer, K. J., Weber, L. L., & Macher, J. T. 2008. Planning for extending and terminating inter-firm relationships: Bringing psychology into the study of contractual governance. Unpublished working paper.

47. Gulati, R., Sytch, M., & Mehrotra, P. 2008. Breaking up is never easy: Planning for exit in a strategic alliance. *California Management Review*, 50(4): 147–163.

CHAPTER 7

MULTIPARTY ALLIANCES AND ALLIANCE PORTFOLIOS

INTRODUCTION

In the earlier chapters our focus has been on two-party relationships, in which an entrepreneurial company and one other company form an alliance. In this chapter, we extend this discussion in two ways. First, we consider the challenges of forming an alliance involving three or more companies. While most alliances have just two parties, a surprising number have more. In one study of the three sectors of telecommunications, information technology, and biotechnology, the number of alliances with more than two companies ranged from 13% in telecommunication to 35% for biotechnology.[1] The move from a two-party to a multiparty arrangement increases the complexity of alliance management. While a two-member or dyadic tie has only one relationship to worry about, four companies forming an alliance produces six dyadic relationships between companies, and adding a fifth company increases this number to ten. Many of the concerns discussed in earlier chapters about finding common goals, writing contracts, communicating, creating trust, and restructuring, to name a few, similarly increase in complexity.

Second, we focus on how companies simultaneously manage multiple alliances. While this topic may seem to be important only for larger companies, many start-ups find themselves involved in more than one alliance. One study of high-technology entrepreneurial companies with alliances reported that on average, each company had eight alliances.[2] As we will discuss, achieving an effective strategic alliance portfolio requires planning. Even a start-up with no alliances should prepare for how to build a portfolio of alliances that is more than just a collection of individual relationships. In addressing these two issues, this chapter explores the challenges of managing these progressively more common but more complex strategic alliance arrangements.

MULTIPARTY ALLIANCES

GENERAL FORMS

Entrepreneurial companies can easily find themselves in an alliance with more than two partners. These arrangements may take a variety of shapes, varying in terms of formality. At one end of the continuum, some start-ups may join informal, information-sharing arrangements that are based primarily on the entrepreneur's social networks. For example, a number of start-ups may be members of a common business incubator. Business incubators are physical facilities that offer shared resources and knowledge to business start-ups and also provide the infrastructure to support these start-ups. Besides sharing physical resources such as office space, companies in a business incubator may exchange information, receive financial support from the incubator, and provide each other with peer support. This information sharing arrangement may help these companies achieve the goal of leaving the incubator and become self-sustaining. A similar arrangement occurs in numerous social networking organizations—often created through trade associations or user groups—designed to help smaller companies share information and collectively benefit from each others' expertise.

A more formal type of multiparty collaboration occurs when companies join together to create a buying cooperative. For example, to survive a recession, Servatii Pastry Shop & Deli Inc., based in Cincinnati, OH, made several adjustments in its business practices. Besides trying to introduce new products that would enhance sales, the owner, Gary Gottenbusch, worked to lower his company's costs, particularly as the price of commodity products rose. Through networking with peers at local industry events, he realized that others also faced the same situation. With ten other people, he founded a purchasing association that reduced members' overall costs by combining the companies' purchase orders to obtain volume discounts for baking commodities like flour and shortening. Through this association, the member companies were able to keep the price of flour well below what nonmember bakeries were paying, and since its beginning, the association has greatly expanded its membership.[3] Such alliances not only save the companies money but also help to preserve the members' independence. They are particularly helpful in situations where the companies may provide similar services but are not direct competitors.

Beyond simple buying relationships, formal multiparty arrangements may emerge when companies join together to explore a new technology. In these alliances, as in two-party arrangements, companies collaborate because one company does not have the resources to create a new technology, and the problem often requires more than just two companies. For example, Sandia National

Laboratories, a U.S. federally funded research laboratory, joined with four drill bit manufacturers to develop and test technologies to reduce the costs of drilling. Standards-setting consortia, such as RosettaNet,[4] are another example. RosettaNet—a not-for-profit supply chain management consortium headquartered in Lawrenceville, NJ—has over five hundred members around the world who establish standards that provide a common language for exchanging supply chain information, such as inventory levels, manufacturing requirements, or payment. This easy communication helps speed up supply chain transactions, provides better information to each party in the transaction, and permits smaller regional companies to interact not only with multinationals but also with other similar companies in other parts of the world. This alliance form helps companies make a footprint in the marketplace when they would not have been able to do so alone, or when they would have had to bear all the expenses single-handedly.

UNIQUE CHALLENGES

Entrepreneurs need to address several unique challenges associated with multiparty alliances in order to form and manage them. In particular, greater complexity is likely to be associated with forming the alliance, with establishing a governance structure to oversee the collaboration, and with addressing alliance evolution and company turnover. These issues, the challenges they present, and recommendations for effectively addressing each are summarized in Table 7.1.

Alliance Formation

The process of creating an alliance with more than two partners affects the types of problems the alliance will focus on, the way potential partners are solicited, and the nature of the negotiations process. Because the arrangement brings together more than two parties, these formation processes are likely to be more complex and take on more importance for subsequent development of the alliance than the process of forming a two-party alliance. The complexity and importance of the formation may well increase as the number of parties involved increases. In forming these arrangements, entrepreneurial companies need to build relationships along three dimensions: (1) convergent interests, (2) strategic relationships, and (3) social relationships.[5] *Convergent interests* develop as companies recognize that they face a common problem or opportunity. The *strategic relationships dimension* refers to companies developing a shared strategic vision for the collaboration, while the third dimension, *social relationships*, relates to the establishment of social ties among the companies.

During the formation, the companies will want to develop strong convergent interests, strong strategic relationships, and strong social relationships. Based upon their prior interactions and the reason for the alliance, the companies may start further along on one dimension than another. Across different alliances, then, some formations will likely have different starting conditions than others. These dissimilar starting points will affect which subsequent issues faced by the companies forming a particular alliance. Research has identified three general formation processes each with a different starting condition and set of issues to address. The

TABLE 7.1 Unique Features of Multiparty Alliances		
Activity	*Challenges*	*Possible Solutions*
Formation	• How to build the relationship along three dimensions: — Convergent interests — Strategic relationships — Social relationships	• Use an emergent, engineered, or embedded formation process to create the multiparty alliance
Governance structure	• Evaluating each party's contribution • Organizing different sized companies • Avoiding free ridership	• Have each partner contribute the same resources • Hire a third party to determine the value of a contribution or a benefit • Set up multitiered memberships which can support larger and smaller companies • Carefully select partners and design the alliance to avoid free ridership • Assign alliance managers to monitor each partner's involvement in the alliance
Alliance member turnover and alliance dissolution	• Some partners may join late • A partner's departure may not lead to the dissolution of the alliance • Dissolution requires all parties to agree to terminate the alliance	• Develop legal agreements that cover the rights of latecomers and early leavers • Develop procedures for managing partner turnover • Establish policies and procedures for dissolution of the alliance

three types are emergent, engineered, and embedded. As illustrated in Figure 7.1, the starting condition along the three dimensions for each formation is indicated by the dotted triangles. Throughout the formation process, the companies will engage in different activities—represented by the arrows in Figure 7.1 and described in more detail in Table 7.2—to advance the overall relationship.

The *emergent formation process* typically occurs among companies that know about each other but may not have worked together previously—for example, they may be direct competitors. They start off with having high convergent interest but low strategic relationships and social relationships. The formation process builds from the convergent interests by searching for a consensus on vision, mission, and structure of the alliance, and defining expectations for continuity. Since this formation often involves direct competitors, the companies spend time defining the purpose and the operations of the alliance. They typically pay attention to reducing the likelihood of conflict that can

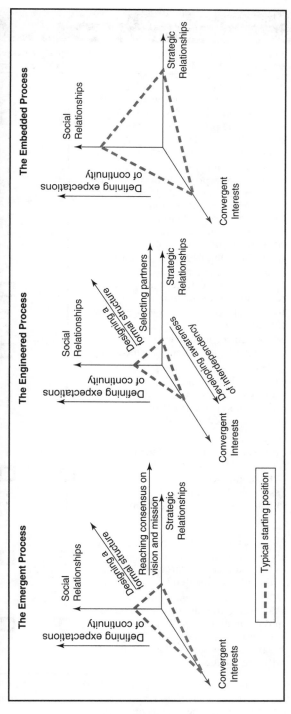

FIGURE 7.1 Dimensions of Three Formation Processes of Multiparty Arrangements

Source: Adapted from "Managing Formation Processes in R&D Consortia" by Ring, Doz, and Olk. Copyright © 2005, by The Regents of the University of California. Reprinted from the *California Management Review*, Vol. 47, No. 4, by permission of The Regents.

TABLE 7.2 Key Issues and Outcomes in R&D Alliance Formation Processes *(Circles signify activities in the process)*

Managerial Activity	Key Issues on the Managerial Agenda	Emergent Process	Engineered Process	Embedded Process
Developing an awareness of environmental interdependence	Are there new entries or increased competition in the markets in which the firms participate? Are markets deregulating/privatizing? Is there a new technological standard that threatens their competitive positions?	◐	◐	◐
Discovering converging interests	How compatible are motives with respect to new product development, need for new resources? How similar are potential members' industries or firm characteristics? Do they have prior or existing ties? Are they strategic or social in nature?	◐		
Triggering collaboration	Is a firm, individual, governmental agency, etc. sees a need for collaboration and orchestrates and guides the evolution of the alliance helping to develop its vision/mission/timeline, etc.?		◐	
Selecting partners	Who is contacted, by what processes, with what logic? When is membership closed?		◐	
Searching for consensus on vision and missions, goals, objectives, etc.	How similar are the potential members' views on the goals of the alliance, its structure, its operations, on information sharing?	◐		
Defining expectations of continuity	How active are the members in the alliance? What are their alternatives? What commitments of additional resources do they make? Is membership for a specific period of time?	◐	◐	◐
Outcomes				
Designing formal structure	What is the size of the alliance? Are there boundaries on membership? Is there a board of directors? Where is the alliance located?	◐	◐	◐
Broadening and deepening collaboration	What changes are made in workers assigned to the alliance, its budgets, and its membership? Are new interorganizational relationships created? How satisfied are managers with the alliance?	◐	◐	◐

Source: Adapted from "Managing Formation Processes in R&D Consortia" by Ring, Doz, and Olk. Copyright © 2005, by The Regents of the University of California. Reprinted from the *California Management Review*, Vol. 47, No. 4, by permission of The Regents.

emerge when working with a competitor and to encouraging collaboration by all members—and avoiding free ridership that might give one company an unfair advantage over another.

An example of emergent formation process is when start-up companies working in an emerging industry find it beneficial to work with some direct competitors in order to establish a larger presence in the marketplace. Customers may require education on the need for the new product or service, particularly if it competes with or replaces a better-known product. By collaborating, the companies can share in the costs of creating the market for their products and then compete once the market becomes established. An emergent formation process may also help smaller companies establish a larger footprint in the market. For example, in 2004 four companies joined together as Dynamic Print Group to promote their collective printing and image media services. The companies all wanted to go after national business, and each company within the consortium added its particular strength to the overall effort. The customer enjoys the benefit of a single contact point, but has the ability to draw from all of the companies' capabilities. As one manager noted, part of the collaborative effort is to "figure out how we are going to produce this piece. Sometimes it takes multiple plants to do this."[6] Another example of an alliance that used an emergent formation process is Maine Built Boats. The boatbuilding industry in Maine primarily consists of small companies developing yachts and sailboats. When these companies had difficulty competing with companies in New Zealand and China, they pooled their efforts and created Maine Built Boats to promote and market boats built in Maine. Membership dues are set according to the size of the company, and the alliance also receives some government funding.[7]

The *engineered formation process* typically occurs when companies with no prior relationship and not much knowledge about one another begin to form an alliance to address a problem that affects them all. They start from a position of having low convergent interests, low strategic relationships, and low social relationships. Because they do not have much prior history, this formation process begins when one company triggers the collaboration. The process emphasizes deciding which potential partners to approach for participation and defining expectations for continuity. An example of the need for this process is a new market entry where companies have not worked together in the past and may not even know of each other's interest in a product, but then find out they have a common interest. In the engineered process, the focus is on finding the common area of overlap rather than on dealing with issues of conflict and free ridership that are part of the emergent process. The formation of the Plastics Recycling Foundation provides a clear example of the engineered formation process. It was started in the 1980s, when Owens-Illinois, a manufacturer of glass bottles, found itself with the technology to recycle plastic bottles made out of polyethylene terephthalate (PET). Knowing that PET recycling was technically feasible, Owens-Illinois set out to explore whether recycling could also be economically feasible. The company's managers quickly realized that recycling did not just involve technology; it also required actions beyond the capability of the company. At that time, recycling of plastic bottles was not common, so two fundamental questions were whether there would be a steady supply of plastic bottles for recycling and what products from the recycled plastic would consumers want. Owens-Illinois' managers set about contacting companies at various stages of the plastic bottle value chain. This chain included companies that provided the material to produce plastic bottles, such as resin manufacturers; the plastic bottle manufacturers; and companies such as beverage companies that use plastic bottles for their products. The resulting consortium focused on developing and promoting the PET recycling technology and included both very large and very small companies—many who had never worked together before—with a range of interest in recycled plastic bottles.

The *embedded formation process* occurs among companies that have a strong history of working together. They often have high convergent interests and have high strategic relationships and social relationships. Thus they are often aware of each others' interests and have an existing set of expectations for the operations of the alliance. The primary issue these companies face when forming the alliance is deciding on the expectations for continuing the relationship. These alliances typically occur in situations where the entrepreneurs already have a strong working relationship and then are presented with a new opportunity. Projects that occur in software development or in the construction industry may reflect this process. When a new opportunity arises, the various parties know very quickly who should be involved, the purpose of the alliance, and, based on what they have done before, how the parties will interact. The questions they face focus on the level of a member company's involvement, including the types of resources committed, and how long the project will last. Compared to the engineered and emergent formation processes, an embedded process is fairly quick and simple.

Governance Structure

Multiparty alliances also face a different set of challenges in developing a governance structure than do two-party alliances. Because so many more companies need to be coordinated than in a two-party alliance, multiparty alliances' governance structures tend to be more formal, with more detailed contracts and formal committees which direct the collaboration. In addition, as the number of alliance companies increases beyond three the alliance is more likely to have a permanent management structure to oversee the alliance's operations and monitor and coordinate the various companies' contributions and commitment. Sometimes a permanent staff oversees the alliance, but in other cases managers from the various partners may rotate through the staff positions so that the workload is shared and every member has a voice in alliance management.

In governing these arrangements, the management structure will probably have to address three potential issues: (1) how to value the contributions of each company; (2) how to organize when companies have different levels of interest in the collaboration; and (3) how to limit free ridership. Valuing contributions may be messy in a multiparty alliance because these alliances often bring together companies with varying interests and resources. Some of the contributions may not be easily compared to others in terms of the value. One approach to avoid this problem is to restrict in-kind contributions and have companies contribute only money. If companies do contribute different resources, valuing contributions requires either negotiations among the members or a third-party evaluation.

A second, and related, issue is how to deal with company differences in ability to contribute. Some smaller companies, for example, may be interested in joining a multiparty alliance, but they do not have the same level of resources as larger partners. In these situations, one approach for addressing the problem—which was used by the Plastics Recycling Foundation and others—is to set up different membership levels. The top tier, often consisting of larger companies, will contribute more resources to the alliance in return for greater input into decision-making or a greater share of the output from the alliance. The lower tier members, often composed of smaller companies, will have some input into decision-making (perhaps through a shared board of director's position) or will gain access to a smaller amount of the output.

A third issue for governance of a multiparty alliance is to address the aforementioned possibility of free ridership. While each company may want the alliance to succeed, some may not be able to, or may not want to, put in a comparable effort. If the expectation is that each company contributes equitably, a company attempting to free ride could undermine the overall collaboration. Companies have addressed free ridership in multiparty alliances in several ways. The first is to spell out the contributions and commitment levels of each partner at the time of joining. For some alliances, this specification is legally mandated in the contract and failure to comply can lead to termination of a company's partnership in the alliance. For others, the subject of contribution level is addressed earlier, in the partner screening and negotiation stages, when organizers make clear the expected level of commitment by each party. Companies that are not willing or able to make such a commitment are not asked to join, and those that do join understand the expectation or norm for involvement. Once the alliance is formed, the alliance managers often assume the responsibility of evaluating the contributions and benefits of members. Because these managers are evaluating the sponsoring companies, they are often given some level of independence from the members' control in order to equitably assess the value of any contribution or benefit.

For some alliances, however, free ridership may not be a significant issue. In an R&D (research and development) alliance where the primary outcome is learning, companies trying to free ride may find that they receive fewer benefits. As some managers have noted, a company only gets out as much as it puts into the alliance. Companies that make a greater investment will receive more benefits.

Alliance Member Turnover and Alliance Dissolution
The last issue unique to multiparty alliances is the likelihood that some companies will join after the formation and some companies will leave before the alliance's eventual dissolution. In a two-party alliance, the alliance forms when

the two parties agree to create it and ends if one company decides to leave or buy out the other partner. For a multiparty alliance, however, it is not uncommon for some companies to join after the formation and for the alliance to continue after a member departs.[8] The alliance Symbian was started in 1998 by four companies (Ericsson, Motorola, Nokia, and Psion) to develop an operating system for mobile devices.[9] Samsung, Siemens, and Sony Ericsson joined a few years later. In 2003 Motorola sold its shares to Nokia and Psion, and then, in 2004, Psion sold its 31.1% stake in Symbian to Nokia. Finally, in 2008, Nokia bought out the remaining partners and created the Symbian Foundation, which is dedicated to promoting the Symbian operating system. In designing multiparty alliances, companies need to pay particular attention to issues of the rights of founding members and those of latecomers, especially whether the founding members have greater ownership over intellectual property or profits developed before other companies join. Similarly, attention has to be devoted to a departing company's contractual rights to intellectual property.

In addition to the legal issues, managers have to be prepared for the organizational and managerial challenges of adding new members or losing existing ones. For some alliances, turnover issues are handled by controlling the time when companies can join. For a departure, timing can be managed by having companies agree to a rolling, multiyear commitment (e.g., three years), so that even if a company decides to leave, it is still an active member for the duration of the commitment. This rolling commitment has the benefit of making sure that any transitions in membership occur over time so the entire alliance does not collapse from sudden departures. With this period, remaining members can decide whether they should keep the alliance operational. If they do, then they have the time to try to find new members to join.

Termination of the alliance is also different for multiparty alliances because it requires a collective decision. As noted, situations may occur in which the loss of several key companies will lead to the collapse of the entire alliance, but in many cases the entire alliance will only end when all the companies decide to terminate. The process and approach for dealing with a multiparty termination are similar to those of a two-party alliance, with companies often negotiating how to separate the remaining assets.

In summary, the presence of more than two companies in an alliance increases the complexity of forming and managing the alliance. The formation process in particular is much more complicated, as companies must find a way to develop an overarching consensus about the activities of the alliance. For governance, the likelihood of free ridership adds to the challenges of communicating and coordinating across many more companies. Finally, a unique challenge associated with multiparty alliances is that some members may leave or join throughout the life of the alliance. Companies and alliance managers have to prepare for such joining and leaving separately from the formation and termination of the alliance itself. Success depends on creating an orderly movement of companies into and out of the alliance.

PORTFOLIO OF ALLIANCES

A very different aspect of multiparty alliances is the situation where a single company has an entire portfolio of different alliances. While entrepreneurial firms' portfolios may not be as extensive as those of larger companies, entrepreneurial firms do sometimes engage in multiple alliances. This participation requires a focus beyond forming and managing an effective single alliance, as the company now must make sure that the set of alliances collectively furthers the company's overall strategy.

An entrepreneurial company enjoys multiple benefits from participating in multiple alliances. First, the company can leverage its internal strengths across a wider array of partners and may not be dependent upon any one partner. This approach is particularly useful for an entrepreneurial company trying to enter multiple new geographical markets, as these alliances help the company reach a much broader market. Second, multiple ties may help to quickly enhance a start-up company's legitimacy and create a new competitive space. An example is Apex Video,[10] a start-up that developed an online help program for retail websites. If a website user needs help placing an order, clicking on a help button activates the program and an interactive help screen pops up. The user sees and hears a person asking questions about the ordering problem. Based on the responses typed in by the user, follow-up video messages appear and help the person through the ordering process. Since these videos are recorded, all of this interaction occurs without a live customer agent providing help unless the customer requests one. Because this business and product were new, the CEO of the company set up a series of alliances with key persons and companies in the retail website community who served as advisors. In exchange for early access to the technology, many of these ties were used to help convince a potential retailer of the benefits of the product and of the reliability and legitimacy of the company. This portfolio of alliances was managed by the CEO, who periodically checked in with each of the portfolio companies to keep them apprised of Apex's progress even if their assistance was not needed at that time.

CHALLENGES

These examples illustrate strategic benefits that entrepreneurial companies might receive from alliance portfolios, but many small and large companies enter into several alliances without a clear understanding of how the alliances might be related to one another, and how their set of alliances collectively benefits the company. In developing more effective use of alliance portfolios, companies have to address three general questions[11]: (1) How do we build the portfolio? (2) How should we configure the portfolio? and (3) How do we manage the portfolio? These issues are summarized in Table 7.3.

TABLE 7.3   Three Questions in Alliance Portfolio Management

Questions	Issues	Recommendations
How do we form a portfolio?	• The company's overall strategy to forming the portfolio: Is there a coherent strategy or are they created in a piecemeal process?	• Portfolios organized around an overall strategy outperform those created serially
How do we configure the portfolio?	• The relationship among the alliances in the portfolio • Determining which alliances are more important than others • The degree to which the alliances in the portfolio constrain or facilitate one another	• Companies should seek to develop portfolios that have — A clear set of relationships among the alliances — Clear priorities about the relative importance of alliances — Positive connections among the alliances
How do we manage the portfolio?	• Developing a management system • Portfolio monitoring	• Create a set of standardized tools and processes to connect the alliances to the company's strategy • Evaluate each alliance in terms of its contribution to the company's strategy

HOW TO BUILD THE PORTFOLIO

In developing the portfolio, a critical question is, "What is the company's overall alliance strategy?"[12] Each alliance should be part of an overall set of relationships that develop from the company's strategy and organization. The managers should know why the company entered into each alliance and how the entire set of alliances furthers the company's overall strategy. Companies can choose from three broad portfolio strategies.[13]

1. A company can attempt to shape the industry through its alliances. In this situation, similar to the Apex Video example, the alliances are focusing on innovation to develop new capabilities or to explore new opportunities that may lead to changing the industry.

2. A company can adapt to already existing industry shifts. Here, the company seeks to develop flexibility or broaden the resource base of the firm, all without making high-level commitments to a strategy. Seeking to introduce a product to multiple markets fits this scenario, as does an options approach, in which a company makes relatively small investments in several, competing alliances in order to find out which has the most chance of success.

3. A company attesmpts to exploit an already existing knowledge or capability in order to stabilize the industry situation.

While these three approaches are distinct, companies can also engage in hybrid approaches which seek to combine features of the different approaches.

Surprisingly, many small companies do not have an overall strategy toward forming a portfolio. Instead, they tend to form alliances sequentially, unguided by any overarching strategy for why the alliances are being formed and how they are connected to each other. While each alliance may be functional and valuable to the company, the overall portfolio may have limited impact on the company. For example, a study of the development of the wireless gaming industry showed that companies pursuing an "architectural strategy" outperformed companies that focused on serial alliance development, where the company forms each alliance without a clear connection to one another.[14] An architectural strategy requires the organizing company to first work out a definition of the roles, interdependencies, and benefits among potential partners in a way that these partners fully understand. The result is an overall coordinated strategy that not only mobilizes the partners but, importantly, gains their commitment to the company's agenda; whether it is to shape, adapt, or stabilize the industry. The study also showed that the benefits of an architectural strategy extend beyond the focal firm's performance as the partners in these alliances also performed better than rivals.

How to Configure the Portfolio

Once the alliance portfolio is built, the next set of issues for an entrepreneurial company relate to managing the composition of the portfolio. Of primary interest is the number of alliances, or direct ties, of the entrepreneurial company.[15] One challenge in developing the configuration is achieving the right balance between too few ties and not enough ties. For some start-ups, the allure of forming many alliances with other companies is strong. As noted in Chapter 2, alliances can help an entrepreneurial company leverage its resources, and the more alliances it has, the more potential opportunities it has. Further, the ability to promote these relationships as a signal of the company's success and to use these ties to gain better name recognition in the marketplace has led some companies to form numerous alliances. To be effective, however, most alliances require attention from both partners. Entrepreneurial companies may not have the resources to oversee many alliances, and the partners, particularly if they are very large companies, may not be fully committed to a relationship. An entrepreneurial company should match the number of alliances in a portfolio with the overall resources it has to manage them, since companies with more alliances tend to dedicate more staff and develop tools to manage the relationships.[16] Too many alliances in a portfolio and not enough internal resources may lead to overall poor performance if relationships are underdeveloped or neglected. In Chapter 8 we will pick up on this theme when we discuss alliance capability and a company's ability to manage the various relationships in its portfolio.

While size provides some measure of the structure of the portfolio, the relatedness among the companies is of greater importance. The alliances within a particular portfolio may vary in the degree to which they are related. Perhaps reflecting the prevalence of the serial approach to portfolio development, according to one study approximately 45% of the alliances in companies' portfolios have no interdependency and no impact on each other.[17] When there is no relationship among alliances, one question for a company to ask is whether to find some way to integrate the alliances or to keep them separate. The reason for keeping alliances separate is generally to avoid any conflict of interest. For example, when a focal company has separate alliances with partners that compete with one another, the company may need to signal to the partners that the information gleaned from one alliance will not be shared with the other alliances. Often this is done by creating a distinct internal "wall" between the managers working on the different alliances to prohibit information sharing, but such a wall can be problematic for entrepreneurial firms. It is harder to signal clear internal boundaries between managers overseeing each alliance when the overall company structure may be fairly informal. Often, for entrepreneurial companies the more successful strategy is to avoid forming separate alliances with companies that compete with one another.

For the remaining 55% of the portfolios in the study, the issue for managers is how these alliances relate to one another.[18] Companies have used several different approaches for categorizing alliances' relatedness. One approach is to rank the alliances by importance, separating out strategically important alliances from those that are tactical or operational. An example of this separation is the creation of various tiers of suppliers by some small firms in the apparel industry.[19] Each small company tends to have primary suppliers which it almost always uses. During peak demand times or when there is a rush order, however, the company turns to less frequently used suppliers. These suppliers may remain in the second-tier position for many years, until the two firms develop a stronger relationship or until one of the first-tier companies loses its primary position. The small apparel company manages its array of ties to suppliers by focusing on those that are more important and devoting more resources to maintaining these relationships, while the secondary relationships receive considerably less attention.

An alternative way to analyze the portfolio is to evaluate the degree to which the alliance concentrates on exploring existing knowledge or activities or is trying to develop new knowledge or activities. Companies can form alliances for either purpose. While there are short-term benefits from exploiting current skills, long-term survival often requires developing new skills. Companies that engage simultaneously in exploratory and exploitative activities tend to gain both short-term and long-term benefits and perform better than those that engage in just one type.[20]

The aforementioned study also found that in approximately 25% of the alliances, one alliance in the portfolio has a negative impact on another alliance.[21] A negative result can occur for a variety of reasons. The company may have partnered with rivals, or may be participating in two or more alliances with each investigating a competing technology, or the investment in one alliance may be restricting the type or amount of resources available to invest in other alliances. If a negative effect develops in the portfolio, the company must examine the source. If there is a conflict between two alliances and one of the alliances is of high strategic importance, the company may want to consider eliminating the less important alliance or seek ways to reduce the impact of the features of less important alliance that affect the other alliance (e.g., try to eliminate any legal agreements that may prevent a firm from investing more in other alliances).

How to Manage the Portfolio

The third challenge associated with alliance portfolios is how to manage the portfolio. Beyond the issues of understanding alliance relatedness and whether any important constraints or synergies should be addressed, managers need to be aware of how the alliances are collectively managed. While we have discussed the need for an overall strategy and for developing synergies among the alliances, two other activities of portfolio management are developing a portfolio management system and portfolio monitoring.

Developing a management system requires creating a set of standardized tools and formalized processes as well as specialized roles and positions that support the overall strategy. The goal is developing consistent and effective practices for the company to set up and coordinate its alliance portfolio. This system may include staff dedicated to overseeing the company's alliances, but may also involve creating tools to help managers form and manage alliances. The tools can include reviews, internal seminars and workshops, benchmarking, manuals, checklists, data warehousing, and intranets. A smaller company may not need all of these formal efforts, but this menu will help to create alliance management knowledge and to store, transfer, and apply the knowledge to new alliances. We will examine these in more detail as part of our discussion of alliance capability in Chapter 8.

Portfolio monitoring concentrates on three activities: regularly evaluating the progress of individual alliances and the overall portfolio and deciding where to allocate resources, coordinating activities across alliances, and adding or subtracting alliances to the portfolio. Monitoring the progress of alliances includes capturing the performance of each individual alliance and of the overall alliance portfolio, and assessing the connection of the portfolio to the overall company's strategy. This issue will be addressed further in Chapter 9. Based upon this information, managers can decide whether an individual alliance requires additional resources if it is going to reach the intended goal. Related, managers may decide to change the coordination of an alliance with the company's internal activities or other alliances. For stronger coordination, the company may consider a number of changes including making the same person(s) responsible for this alliance and the internal activity/alliance, sharing information about the alliance throughout the company, or setting up task forces to coordinate the alliance with the internal activity/alliance. Alternatively, the managers may decide that a particular alliance may be better-off managed separately. For example, a company creating an alliance with a competitor of one of its current partners may keep it separate from the other alliance in order to signal to the two competitors that it will not share information across the alliances. In this situation, the company will set up strong boundaries to limit information sharing.

Finally, in examining its portfolio a company may realize that it needs to change its portfolio composition. An entrepreneurial company will want to have a portfolio that is capable of adapting to new conditions. The company must be willing to terminate alliances that no longer provide significant value or fit with changing environmental considerations, and be willing to form new ones as the strategic direction of the company or the environment shifts over time. Amazon.com's experiences show the changing nature of a company's alliance portfolios. For the company, alliances were initially built on its key publishing and distributor relationships as well as critical marketing relationships.[22] These alliances helped the company establish its presence in the online book retail business. As the company became more successful, it expanded to other products and established a series of alliances with other online retailers. More recently, Amazon.com started to create alliances with brick-and-mortar companies and now has a wide range and type of alliances.

In summary, managing an alliance portfolio involves understanding the connection between the company's overall strategy and the set of alliances it has or is considering entering into, understanding how to build the portfolio, discerning the strategic connection between and among the various alliances in the portfolio, and understanding how to oversee the flow of information among these alliances as well as spreading the learning that occurs from one alliance throughout the organization.

Conclusion

The purpose of this chapter is to move our discussion beyond the more common dyadic or two-party strategic alliances to examine arrangements among several parties. We separated these arrangements into two types: multiparty alliances, in which three or more parties join together to form an alliance; and portfolio alliances, which are the set of alliances developed by the focal company. Forming an alliance that includes more than one other company greatly increases the complexity of the arrangement. As noted in our discussion, including multiple parties changes each aspect of the alliance, from partner selection, negotiations, structuring, and governance to termination. This increase in complexity not only requires a slightly different approach to forming such alliances but it also creates challenges for the managers involved in these relationships. The time and ability to manage these complex relations may test many entrepreneurs, who are likely to be fully occupied with addressing other pressing issues. One would expect an entrepreneurial firm to initiate these complex relationships only when they are necessary or when the potential rewards far offset the added resources they require. More likely, as some of the examples indicate, smaller companies will join such alliances in a supporting role while larger firms with more available resources take the lead.

A second part of our discussion focused on alliance portfolios and how an entrepreneurial company can manage the set of alliances in which it is involved. We addressed several critical issues for an entrepreneurial company in designing its portfolio, including how these alliances benefit the company's overall strategy; identifying the relationship, if any, among the various alliances; and managing the information flow and learning among these relationships. While managing a portfolio of alliances offers many benefits to entrepreneurs for leveraging their limited resources across a broader array of markets or product lines, this advantage may be offset by the added complexity. Compared to most of the earlier topics in this book, understanding the nature and management of multiparty alliances and alliance portfolios is underdeveloped. Becoming better at managing these alliances requires a company to dedicate resources to permit managers the time to reflect upon their experiences and to develop tools and practices that will eventually help the company create better alliance capabilities. We examine this issue in more detail in Chapter 8.

Key Terms

- multiparty alliances
- formation process
- governance structure
- alliance portfolio configuration
- alliance portfolio management

End of Chapter Questions

1. In your view, which of the unique challenges of multiparty alliances— alliance formation, governance structure, alliance evolution, and turnover— is the most difficult for a manager to cope with and why?
2. What are some possible reasons that we have seen an increased interest in alliance portfolios over the past few years?
3. What do you think are the reasons that many companies do not have a clear strategy for their alliance portfolio?
4. What are the risks and benefits for an entrepreneurial firm targeting a gap in a larger company's product offering and attempting to develop an alliance with the larger company? When is such a strategy likely to be effective?
5. What skills and tools does an entrepreneurial firm need to effectively manage its portfolio of alliances?
6. When should a company purposefully keep alliances separate in its portfolio and why?

References

1. De Man, A.-P. 2003. Towards a network economy: Innovation strategies in a world of alliances. Paper presented at the ISPIM Conference, Manchester, June 9th.
2. Olk, P., & Chung, T. 2004. Impact of personal and organizational ties on alliances: Evidence from entrepreneurial companies. Paper presented at the Annual Academy of Management Meetings. New Orleans, LA.

3. "Sweet Returns." *Wall Street Journal* (April 23, 2009).

4. www.RosettaNet.org, accessed April 25, 2009; Boh, W. F., Soh, C., & Yeo, S. 2007. A case study of RosettaNet. *Communications of the ACM*. December, 50(12): 57–62.

5. Ring, P. S. Doz, Y., & Olk, P. 2005. Managing formation processes in R&D consortia, *California Management Review*, 47(4): 137–156.

6. "Alliance of printers widen playing field for small businesses." *Appleton Post-Crescent* (August 24, 2008).

7. www.mainebuiltboats.com, accessed April 25, 2009.

8. Olk, P., & Young, C. 1997. Why members stay in or leave an R&D consortium: Performance and conditions of membership as determinants of continuity. *Strategic Management Journal*, 18: 855–877.

9. Ring, P. S. Doz, Y., & Olk, P. 2005. Op. cit.

10. Not the company's real name.

11. Wassmer, U. In press. Alliance portfolios: A review and research agenda. *Journal of Management*, 31 pages, first published on December 22, 2008 as DOI:10.1177/0149206308328484. Discusses the research gaps related to these three topics and proposes questions for future research.

12. Bamford, J., Gomes-Casseres, B., & Robinson, M. 2003. *Mastering alliance strategy: A comprehensive guide to design, management, and organization.* San Francisco: Jossey-Bass.

13. Hoffman, W. 2007. Strategies for managing a portfolio of alliances. *Strategic Management Journal*, 28: 827–856.

14. Ozcan, P., & Eisenhardt, K. 2009. Origin of alliance portfolios: Entrepreneurs, network strategies and firm performance. *Academy of Management* Journal, 52: 246–279.

15. Examining a company's indirect ties brings one to the level of a network analysis. In this analysis, which is beyond the scope of this book, one examines not only a company's direct ties but also the additional alliances of the partners. Mapping these out produces a network of relationships which can reveal important indirect ties that may influence the activities of a focal company. See, for example, Miles, R., Miles, G., & Snow, C. C. 2005. *Collaborative entrepreneurship: How communities of networked firms use continuous innovation to create economic wealth.* Stanford, CA: Stanford Business Books.

16. Heimeriks, K. H., Klijn, E., & Reuer, J. 2009. Building capabilities for alliance portfolios. *Long Range Planning*, 42: 96–114.

17. Parise, S., & Casher, A. 2003. Alliance portfolios: Designing and managing your network of business-partner relationships. *Academy of Management Executive*, 17: 25–39.

18. Parise, S., & Casher, A. 2003. Op. cit.

19. Uzzi, B. 1997. Social structure and competition in interfirm networks: The paradox of embeddedness. *Administrative Science Quarterly*, 42: 35–67.

20. Lin, Z., Yang, H., & Demirkan, I. 2007. The performance consequences of ambidexterity in strategic alliance formations: Empirical investigation and computational theorizing. *Management Science*, 53: 1645–1658.

21. Parise, S., & Casher, A. 2003. Op. cit.

22. Ibid.

CHAPTER 8

CULTIVATING ALLIANCE MANAGEMENT CAPABILITIES

INTRODUCTION

Earlier chapters have focused on when to use and how to implement an alliance by finding, negotiating with, and then developing a strong relationship with a partner. While these steps are necessary for developing an effective alliance, they do not directly address a broader question: How does a company becomes better at managing alliances? In this chapter we look at the steps an entrepreneurial company can take to develop best practices and become more capable at managing strategic alliances. As alliances continue to proliferate, and as they play a more central role in small companies' strategies, the level of a company's alliance capability—that is, "the mechanisms and routines that are purposefully designed to accumulate, store, integrate, and diffuse relevant organizational knowledge about alliance management"—will likely be related to the company's overall success.[1]

Developing alliance capability is not a simple effort. It took a large, multinational corporation over seven years to make noticeable progress in its alliance capability, even with strong support from the CEO and a full-time staff dedicated to building the company's alliance skills.[2] Small companies, however, do not typically have such resources available and the luxury of a long time horizon. They are likely to start with lower levels of alliance capability and are possibly vulnerable to being taken advantage of by larger, more experienced firms. For example, Sames, an autonomous and relatively small division of a U.S.-owned company, entered into an alliance with a Japanese auto manufacturer to provide customized paint application equipment.[3] The partnership offered Sames the opportunity to double its sales but required an extensive upfront investment in R&D (research and development). Sames jumped at this proposal, made this initial investment, and continued to invest more resources in order to respond to additional requests by the partner, but in doing so neglected other clients' needs. After a few years, the auto manufacturer terminated the relationship and created a new alliance with a different company. Because of the structure of the agreement which Sames signed, the auto manufacturer was only responsible for a minor fraction of the expenses Sames had incurred. Sames never received the expected increase in sales and was forced to declare bankruptcy. Had Sames been more capable in managing alliances it might have avoided entering into an alliance that left it at a disadvantage.

Besides a lack of resources and experience, small companies also have lower capability levels because they tend not to enter into alliances to exchange or acquire new knowledge.[4] While they may use alliances to strengthen or complement existing core competencies, many tend to overlook the significance of knowledge-based competencies. They do not fully recognize that "strategic alliances can help them to acquire those competencies to guarantee long-term survival".[5] Small companies that modify internal operations to capture the new knowledge or resources generated from an alliance tend to outperform companies who do not.[6]

Even though small companies may not have strong capability, they can improve their alliance competencies via several mechanisms. Consider the following example:

> ABC software (disguised name), a start-up company, sought to hire an alliance manager to oversee its sales alliances. The CEO rejected several applicants who had strong sales experience with small companies and instead selected a less experienced manager. When asked why, the CEO said that while the seemingly strong applicants had good sales experience, they were proficient in closing deals and then moving on to the next deal. The alliance manager role required building a long-term relationship with the sales partner and coordinating the alliances' activities with the company's other activities. Although the rejected applicants were effective in creating sales, they were used to acting as "lone wolves" and would probably not be good at coordinating and managing relationships.

The CEO recognized that capability comes in part from having alliance experience—which the more experienced sales managers did not have. He also knew that to improve its alliance capability, the company needed someone who was committed to collecting and sharing information throughout the company. Thus, we explore how entrepreneurial companies can cultivate their alliance capability by first describing different levels of capability. We then focus on three mechanisms—illustrated in Table 8.1—that are associated with enhancing alliance

TABLE 8.1 Mechanisms for Building Entrepreneurial Alliance Capability	
Mechanisms	*Issues*
Experience	How many alliances has the company been involved in?
	How similar are these alliance experiences to one another?
Staffing and structuring the alliance manager position	What are the skills of the alliance manager?
	How is this position structured?
Learning from an alliance and Sharing and accumulating alliance know-how	Is the partner interested in sharing knowledge?
	What type of information is being sent?
	Is the company oriented toward and capable of learning?
	How to get the learning from managers?
	How is this information codified into tools?
	What efforts are made to share knowledge across the organization?
	How much alliance training or mentorship takes place?

capability.[7] The first is just having more alliance experience. A company tends to practice "learning by doing," and setting up and managing more alliances gives it a greater opportunity to develop a set of best practices. Second, a company enhances its alliance capability by dedicating an individual to a formal position—which we will refer to as the *alliance manager role*—or creating a formal unit within the company to manage its alliances. Having such a position helps the company collect the best practices from each alliance and then disseminate them throughout the company. Third, the processes used for how a company learns and accumulates its alliance knowledge will also lead to greater alliance capability.

LEVELS OF ALLIANCE CAPABILITY DEVELOPMENT

Over the last several years it has become apparent that some companies are better and more sophisticated at managing alliances. As noted, the differences in skill levels are associated with better alliance performance as well as overall company performance. An investigation into the range of variations across companies has differentiated three levels of alliance capability.[8] As listed in Table 8.2, these levels are informal, advanced, and world-class. Many small companies are at an *informal* level, or even take an ad hoc approach to managing alliances.[9] As we described in Chapter 7, many companies form their alliances in a piecemeal manner; most learn from their collection of alliances in a similar way. These

TABLE 8.2 Description of the Three Levels of Alliance Capabilities	
Levels	*Capabilities*
Informal	Alliances are managed in a piecemeal manner
	No set of best practices developed
	A few key managers with alliance experience are the resident experts
Advanced	A set of best practices developed
	A community of practice established to share information
	Alliances are likely connected to one another
World class	A strong infrastructure designed to oversee alliance practices
	Staff are dedicated
	Tools are developed to guide alliance managers
	Formal training is offered

companies typically do not collect a set of best practices for how to manage alliances or develop tools that will help managers engaging in an alliance. Rather, a few individuals who have experience become the resident experts in alliance management. When an alliance problem arises, managers often turn to these individuals for guidance.

As companies become more experienced and learn how to use alliances better, they may start to develop more methodical internal processes. These companies have *advanced* capabilities, and they will develop standard alliance processes, a community of practice around alliance management, and greater ability to manage different types of alliances (e.g., customer–supplier alliance, R&D alliance).[10] Further, the alliances will begin to be linked together. Finally, in a company at the third level—*world-class* capability—widespread resources exist across the organization for how to manage alliances.[11] Such companies will likely have a developed infrastructure to oversee its alliance practices. This infrastructure may include:

- Staff—which includes not only managers to oversee the company's alliances but also specialists to help out with critical activities (e.g., negotiations, trainers)
- Tools—for example, clearly stated corporate alliance policies, approved deal-making methodologies, case histories of prior efforts, and sample contracts
- Organization—clearly defined alliance roles, alliance training, communities of practice
- Systems—for example, a website dedicated to the partners, an alliance database

While few entrepreneurial companies may be able to develop a world-class capability, most can improve their capability beyond the informal level. With an aim toward helping them accelerate their way down the learning curve of strategic alliance management, we now turn to discussing how entrepreneurial companies can improve their alliance capability.

BUILDING ALLIANCE CAPABILITY

GAIN MORE EXPERIENCE

The first step in this process is to gain firsthand experience with managing different alliances. Joining one alliance leads to some learning as the company engages in learning by doing. Managers who have formed and managed an alliance should have developed some knowledge about effective approaches. Joining additional alliances should lead to an even greater level of learning. However, small companies need not overextend themselves by joining too many alliances. It has been estimated that a company tends to learn more from each of its first several alliances, but after around six, each alliance contributes proportionally less to the company's internal knowledge.[12] Further, a small company should pay attention to the type of alliances it is joining. Companies tend to learn more quickly by joining similar types of alliances (e.g., multiple manufacturing alliances).[13] By focusing on alliances which are alike, companies can become more adept at managing this particular type and at developing their skill at managing an alliance portfolio. If their strategies later call for different types of alliances, these companies can build on their current capabilities and more easily learn from these new alliances.

STAFFING AND STRUCTURING THE MANAGERIAL POSITION

The second step in this process is assigning key individuals in the company to manage the alliance and the company's overall alliances. We focus on two aspects of overseeing the alliances: the skills of the manager and the structure of the position.

Managerial Skills for Alliances

Research on alliances has shown that companies utilizing formal alliance functional units outperform those companies that do not. These functions are associated with developing better alliance capability for the company. Since most entrepreneurial companies do not have the resources to create a separate strategic alliance unit, they are more likely to turn the responsibility for overseeing an alliance over to one manager. Thus, an important consideration for capability development is determining who will represent the company in the alliance. More than a few alliances have faltered because of poor management skills. One manager reported that while a potential alliance looked good on paper, he decided against forming it because he didn't want to work with a particular manager in the other company. From the early interactions between the two individuals, the manager anticipated that his counterpart would create a host of problems, such as not supplying reliable or timely information, haggling over minor issues, and not considering the interests of both companies, and he concluded that the company would be better off not allying with this potential partner and instead found another partner to form an alliance.

The preceding chapters have identified a variety of managerial activities that go into forming an alliance: Identify an opportunity and create an investment rationale, search for and select a partner, negotiate an agreement and design the governance, develop the relationship with the partner, assess performance and make decisions about when to terminate or restructure the alliance, and coordinate this alliance with others in the company. These activities require a manager to have a range of abilities to design a successful alliance. What specific skills make for an effective alliance manager and how do they differ from entrepreneurial skills? While no definitive list exists of skills for either the alliance manager[14] or an entrepreneur,[15] commonly cited competencies are presented in Table 8.3. According to recent discussions, entrepreneurs need to have the right mindset for thinking about the opportunity, a framework for how to take advantage of the opportunity, and the leadership skills for mobilizing resources and

TABLE 8.3 Comparing Skills of an Entrepreneur and an Alliance Manager	
Entrepreneur	*Alliance Manager*
Entrepreneurial mindset	**Alliance mindset**
• Recognizing opportunity	• Tolerance for ambiguity
• Alertness to changing environmental conditions	• Ability to take and appreciate multiple perspectives on an issue
• Passion for Work	**Alliance framework**
• Tenacity	• Fit of alliance with company's overall strategy
Entrepreneurial framework	• Representation of the company's interests in the alliance
• Setting growth goals	
• Recording possible opportunities for the company	• Recoginition of partner's goals
• Timing of the launch	• Understanding of the alliance formation and development process
Entrepreneurial leadership	**Alliance leadership skills**
• Information sharing	• Reputation for being credible
• Challenging the dominant logic—vision	• Respected and trusted
• Self-efficacy	• An extensive network of connections to:
• Reputation	— Other managers inside the company, the alliance and the partner
• Social skills	— Other managers in the industry
Specific competencies	• Strong interpersonal skills including communication, negotiation, and persuasion
• Industry skill	
• Technical skill	**Specific competencies**
	• Line management or functional skills related to the alliance's focus
	• General business knowledge

people, as well as possessing the relevant industry or technical skills for the company. Some of the specific abilities listed include recognizing and having the tenacity and passion to pursue an opportunity, understanding when to launch a business and how fast to grow it, being able to communicate with and convince others inside and outside the company of the opportunity, and having the vision and self-confidence to challenge the dominant logic in the industry.

Mapping the proficiencies an alliance manager needs across the same categories reveals several similarities. Like entrepreneurs, alliance managers should have a good reputation, have proficient social skills and connections within and outside of the company, know how to build an organization, and have strong technical and industry skills for the position. The differences appear in the areas of the mindset and the framework. While an entrepreneur focuses on identifying and taking advantage of an opportunity, an alliance manager builds a relationship with another company, has to be able to represent the company's goals and if necessary adjust them to accommodate the partner's goals, may not challenge a dominant logic but work with and appreciate a different logic, and must be able to develop trust with those outside the company. Although many entrepreneurs may have these skills or may be able to develop them, some essential attributes of an entrepreneur, such as tenacity, a strong vision, and the willingness to challenge a dominant view, may conflict with being a good alliance manager.

The entrepreneur will have to assess whether he or she is really the best person to oversee alliances for the company. If not, the company will need to consider whether to train the entrepreneur in these competencies or to bring in a second manager who already has well-developed alliance skills. One way a small company can identify potential managers with such skills is to screen candidates by first using them as contractors. Slingshot Technology, an Indian start-up software firm, initially staffed its positions with contractors.[16] Then, as the company grew, those who were the best fit for the company were brought on board as employees.

Structuring the Alliance Position

Besides finding the right individuals to oversee the alliance, how the position is structured will also affect the company's ability to enhance its alliance capabilities. We highlight in Table 8.4 three features of the role: the connection of the position to top management, the formalization of the position, and how integrated it is with the rest of the company's activities.

Connection to top management.   One characteristic of the alliance manager's role is the degree to which the manager is connected to the company's overall strategy. If the alliance manager is the entrepreneur, then probably there will not be much of a problem because the same person is overseeing both the alliance and the company. If the alliance manager is someone else, however, the potential for coordination difficulties arises. An example of how management of the alliance can become an issue occurred when a start-up company, which had expertise in working with high temperature superconductivity (HTS), formed an alliance with a large defense contractor. The alliance developed out of a personal

TABLE 8.4 Features of the Alliance Manager Role Affecting Alliance Capability

Features	Capabilities
Connection to top management	Involvement of the alliance manager role in the company's decision-making
	Ability of the alliance manager to make decisions on behalf of the company
Formalization	Full- or part-time position
	Dependence of the alliance relationship on the particular alliance manager
Integration with other company activities	Coordination with any other alliance managers in the company
	Information sharing about the alliance throughout the company

relationship between two scientists in each company and had initial commitment by each company's top managers. The goal was to develop a prototype for a product based on HTS. The alliance started off successfully but ran into some trouble when the founder/CEO of the start-up company decided to create a similar but separate alliance with a direct competitor of the defense contractor. The defense contractor viewed the start-up company as uncommitted to their alliance and also worried that any information given to the start-up company would end up being known by the competitor. The large company kept the alliance active but was much less committed to it. As this example illustrates, the responsibilities of the manager include being able to represent the company's interests in the alliance. If the manager does not have the authority to commit the company to the alliance, the manager will need support from the company's top managers to do so.

Formalization. A related feature of the role is the degree to which it is formalized. For many smaller companies, the alliance manager may also have additional responsibilities. For example, Peter Brown (a disguised name) not only oversaw two of his company's marketing alliances but was also the director of new product development. While he was interested in enhancing the company's alliance skills, his primary attention was dedicated to making sure its internal activities were running smoothly.

A related issue is that in some small companies, only one person has oversight for a company's alliance. If the relationship with the other company is more at the individual level than between the companies—for example where one person is the sole face of the company to the alliance—the alliance may falter if that person leaves the company. Among the problems that may develop is that the psychological contract, the quality of the relationship between the firms, and the established decision-making rules may all be disrupted. To keep the alliance going, the company will have to spend time and energy rebuilding the relationship. An entrepreneurial company in particular will have to weigh the expense of dedicating more than one person to managing the alliance against the cost of rebuilding the alliance should the primary contact leave the company.

Integration with other activities. The ability of the manager to help develop the company's alliance capability will be affected by how integrated the person is with the rest of the company's activities. This includes not only coordination with managers who are involved in other alliances but also with complementary activities elsewhere in the company. For the company to institutionalize any knowledge that comes from an alliance, it will need to share this information beyond the focal manager.

Companies have taken several approaches to managing this process. As the example of Peter Brown illustrates, one approach is to make the alliance the responsibility of a manager who is already overseeing other company activities. While this aids in integration, however, it has the risk of the alliance not receiving enough attention. A second is to routinely keep other managers informed of the alliance's activities. For some companies this means including others in any alliance-related communications (e.g., conference calls, memos, meetings), developing an intranet devoted to the alliance that can be accessed by anyone in the company, or debriefing all others in the company after any significant alliance event (e.g., negotiations, contract signing, restructuring, termination). For a particularly important or complex alliance, there may not be one person who is capable of overseeing the breadth of alliance activities. The company may opt to form a task force with representatives from across the company to oversee the alliance, with a few managers taking the lead on a particular topic about which they have some expertise (e.g., partner screening and selection, negotiation, and design of the alliance) and then letting others lead on different issues.

A more formal approach toward sharing information about and integrating the activities of the alliance with others in the company is to rotate managers through the alliance manager role. Companies find that this helps spread knowledge about the alliance around the company as the previous manager is now in a new position but has knowledge about the alliance. Rotation also helps to ensure that the relationship does not become too dependent upon any one person in the role. If this person leaves early, there are likely others still in the company who can step into the role. In this situation the alliance relationship has already experienced one turnover in the alliance manager position and is likely to survive a second. Another benefit of moving new managers into the alliance manager role is that it is one way for those without much alliance experience to enhance their partnering skills.

PROCESSES TO LEARN AND ACCUMULATE ALLIANCE KNOW-HOW

The third source of alliance capability comes from developing processes to learn from the alliance and then accumulating and sharing alliance know-how. We separate our discussion by first examining learning from a single alliance. Our interest is in two types of learning. The first is the functional knowledge related to the tasks of the alliance. That is, the company may learn more about the joint activities the company and the partner are engaged in, such as marketing, new product development, or manufacturing. The second type is about how to manage the alliance. This is the knowledge that comes from forming and managing an alliance. When this experience is combined with the learning from other alliance experiences, it leads to our second topic of how a company accumulates and shares this knowledge around the company.

Learning

As we have noted, how a company learns from an alliance is an often overlooked aspect of alliance management,[17] and entrepreneurial companies in particular rarely approach alliances as a "learning race" and usually do not emphasize learning from an alliance.[18] This inattention is unfortunate since it can have important consequences for a company over time, as is illustrated by the experiences of a small Indian company that had an alliance with Intel. The company did not seek to learn from the alliance, and one of the managers noted, "We did not do justice to the potential to acquire knowledge through that association before it ended. We should have managed the process better. It was a missed opportunity."[19] As one study concluded about the relationship between small businesses and learning from alliances, "[F]irms are not taking advantage of opportunities to develop skills and competencies through their alliances . . . it is important to make learning a specific objective for alliances and to ensure that steps are taken to ensure that organisations are receptive to opportunities to learn from their partners."[20]

Understanding how to become more effective at learning is helped by considering the key elements in the process.[21] As Figure 8.1 illustrates, the learning process depends on a sender of the information or knowledge, the knowledge or information that is being shared, and the company itself. For the sake of simplicity, in describing the alliance learning process model we discuss the partner as the sender of the information. If the alliance involves creating a separate structure then the alliance may also be the sender.

Both partner characteristics and knowledge being shared affect a company's overall potential for learning from an alliance. Two relevant partner characteristics to learning are the intent of the partner to share and the quality of the relationship.

A partner's intent may vary from actively trying to prevent a company from accessing its knowledge, to being indifferent to the sharing of information, to actively promoting the transfer of the knowledge. Although some small companies are not even aware of the danger of information loss when setting up an alliance,[22] for many small companies a major concern about entering an alliance with a larger company is that it will lose its knowledge and its competitive advantage to the other company.[23] As a manager in one study of small business alliances reported: "These competencies are too important to us. . . . we have spent many years building our strength in these sectors. . . . frankly we have

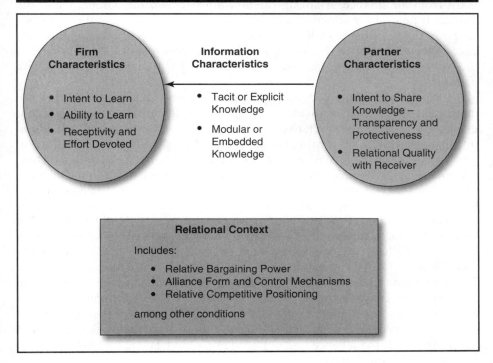

FIGURE 8.1   Model of Alliance Learning Process

world class competences. . . . I am loathe to consider letting anyone near our technology. We only use alliances [in these areas] if we have to."[24]

Alternatively, some partners will have a high level of transparency and actively try to share knowledge with the company. This transparency occurs most often in vertical alliances where the company and the partner need to share their expertise with each other. It may also occur in an R&D alliance, where the alliance is creating knowledge to be shared with each of the partners. As an example, consider the alliance between ENER, a small Swedish company which produced and distributed heat, electricity, and steam, and AROM, a large Norwegian power company.[25] AROM wanted to learn more about ENER's plant design while ENER sought to know more about operations in a different country and about documentation management. The alliance focused on each company giving seminars and organizing capability-improving projects for the other company. The success of these activities has increased the potential for stronger relationships between the two companies. The more intently the partner protects its knowledge or information—for example, through nondisclosure agreements or restrictions on access to information—the more difficult it will be for the company to learn from the partner.

Similarly, the quality of the relationship will also likely affect the ability to learn from an alliance. A strong relationship between the company and the partner is helpful for effective sharing of knowledge. As discussed in previous chapters, this relationship relies on good communication practices and the presence of trust. The better the communication and the stronger the trust between the two companies, the greater the probability they will share information with each other.

Turning to the knowledge or information being shared, some types are more easily learned in an alliance than others. Specifically, knowledge which is explicit or modularized is relatively easy to transfer. Explicit knowledge is that information which can be articulated, explained, or shared with another party. This type of knowledge may appear in written reports, manuals, or demonstration videos and is comparatively simple to obtain from a partner in the alliance. Modularized knowledge, meanwhile, can be separated into discrete components each of which can then be taken from a company and transferred to another company. An example is provided in the experience of HMD Clinical,[26] a Glasgow-based company that wanted to extend its existing knowledge by exploring whether its Web-based technology could be used with radio frequency identification (RFID) technology. It sought an alliance with an established RFID company to develop a product prototype and ended up allying with Sun Microsystems. Because this set of activities was narrowly designed and was a modular set of knowledge, even when the alliance was terminated early for external reasons, HMD Clinical had learned enough from the partnership about the prototype. If the alliance had not been as focused, HMD Clinical might not have learned as much from it.

Alternatively, information or knowledge that is tacit or embedded is harder to transfer. Tacit knowledge often involves understanding complex processes, which a party in an alliance acquires only through active engagement and participating in joint activities, such as the aforementioned capability-improving projects between AROM and ENER. Examples of tacit knowledge might be the process of developing new drugs or designing complex equipment. Similarly, embedded knowledge is ingrained in the company. The more embedded in the company the knowledge is, the harder it will be to transfer it to another. This knowledge is considered "sticky"[27] and is not easy to share with those outside. An example might be a company's synergistic communication practices between departments (such as R&D and marketing), which simply emerge from the way the company's culture works ("this is the way we do things here") and may or may not be possible in another company's culture.

If after assessing the knowledge, a company finds itself in an alliance where the knowledge is tacit or embedded, it can expect that learning levels will be lower or that learning will be more difficult. If it is going to learn, it is likely that the company will have to become very engaged in the alliance. For example, a company may decide to colocate some of its employees with the partners' so that the company employees gain access to any tacit or embedded knowledge. Less intensive efforts will not likely lead to too much learning.

The final element in this process is most under the control of company managers. This consists of the company's intent to learn, ability to learn, and receptivity and effort devoted to learning.

Intent to learn. Companies may vary in the depth of their interest in learning from a partner, depending on the goals of the company in forming the alliance. As we noted, too often entrepreneurial companies do not enter into alliances to learn. But making the intent to learn a goal for entering the alliance will facilitate the learning process.

A company's intent to learn may be influenced by its view of external knowledge. Some companies may view external knowledge as irrelevant to their situation or may disparage the quality of the knowledge because it was developed elsewhere.[28] This "not-invented-here" mindset generally slows down a company's learning because it makes the company unreceptive to new ideas. For example, one study of new ventures located in incubators found that entrepreneurial teams varied in their ability to innovate.[29] Those teams that were more receptive to outside information and did not tend to automatically favor internally generated ideas produced more patents and had an overall higher level of innovation capability.

Ability to learn. A second factor is a company's overall ability to learn from the alliance. To be able to receive the knowledge from a partner and use it, the company must have "absorptive capacity,"[30] which allows the company to value and use the knowledge from an alliance. Without this capacity, a company will not benefit from possessing the knowledge. RSL, a small, family-owned manufacturing company, found that it was initially not taking advantage of the knowledge it had access to in a strategic alliance. Consequently, it had to make several internal changes in order to assimilate knowledge from its collaboration.[31] The changes started with appointing a manager to oversee the transfer, and included creating committees to collect and analyze external information, holding regular meetings to discuss opportunities, and designing an "idea capturing form," which allowed all employees to pass along new ideas to the committees. These changes took several years to initiate but led to the development of new products and to an increase in sales.

Besides having access to the knowledge they will learn, companies have to be ready for the transfer. The timing of the transfer may affect the company's ability to use the knowledge. For example, when a partner is developing a technology for a company, the company must be kept aware of the progress of the development. One of the causes of failure in transferring technology developed by a university researcher to an industry company is the company's inability to immediately use the research results.[32]

Receptivity and effort devoted to learning. The third characteristic of the company is the energy put forward to learn from the alliance. As noted, whether the knowledge is tacit or embedded, successfully transferring it to a company requires considerable effort. Such a transfer has been described as a contact sport in which the only way to transfer the knowledge successfully is to become actively engaged in the alliance. This engagement typically requires great inter-action between individuals in each firm, and often the most effective course of action is to transfer the individuals involved. Rotating personnel through the alliance increases the chances that the knowledge will be transferred, but it is expensive and not all entrepreneurial companies can dedicate a full-time person or two to an alliance. Alternative technology transfer mechanisms—for example, site visits, meetings, telephone calls, videos, written reports—will have to be used as a company trades off between the costs of a particular mechanism and its effectiveness in transferring the knowledge. One variable to consider is whether the transfer gets the information to the right individuals. In a study of these mechanisms in collaborations between university and industry, research has found that having the technical experts communicate with one another—whether through one-on-one meetings, site visits, or e-mail or tele-phone communication—was more effective for knowledge transfer than rely-ing on team meetings (e.g., formal committees or task forces) designed for joint decision-making.[33]

In summary, for any individual alliance, entrepreneurs should focus on the learning potential. The degree of learning will be affected by the willingness and ability of the partner to share information, by the type of information that is being shared, and by the interest and aptitude of the company in absorbing the information. If the initial assessment reveals that the partner or the type of knowledge will make learning difficult, the company will either have to make a large commitment to the alliance to learn or accept that it may not learn too much from the alliance.

Sharing and Accumulating Knowledge

The process of sharing and accumulating knowledge requires the company to move beyond what it has learned from a particular alliance experience. This process involves four activities (summarized in Table 8.5): articulating, codifying, sharing, and internalizing alliance management know-how and skills.[34]

Articulating knowledge. The first activity in this process involves managers ar-ticulating their knowledge. Since the managers overseeing the alliance are the most likely holders of any lessons learned from the alliance, the more these man-agers can convey this knowledge, the better the learning from an alliance. Since some of the information may be relatively tacit, not all of it will be able to be written down.

Many smaller companies, particularly those that are just getting started with alliances, may not have a critical mass of alliance managers and may benefit from bringing in an outsider to discuss alliance management. This person may be a consultant, a manager at another company with alliance experience, or someone from a professional association who helps the company develop alliances. The company may also consider sending managers to attend training seminars that can provide additional ideas on possible best practices.

TABLE 8.5   Activities for Accumulating Alliance Know-How

Activities	*Recommendations*
Draw from managers experiences	Have managers with alliance experience record as much information as they can about alliance best practices
	Rely upon external training sessions, consultants, and third party providers for additional information
Codify this knowledge into guidelines	Create standardized checklists for how to approach different activities (e.g., partner selection, contract writing) for managers to use at different stages of forming an alliance
Share more tacit knowledge throughout the company	Experienced alliance managers—either inside or external to the company—train company managers on effective alliance management practices
	Create communities of practice among these managers to share information and insights into current alliance issues
Mentoring relationships	Experienced alliance managers set up mentoring relationships with less experienced managers to help them internalize the know-how

Codifying knowledge.   The next activity is to take what knowledge can be written down and use it to create a set of tools to help alliance managers. Often this leads to company guidelines for how managers should approach alliances. These may be templates or checklists for managers to follow through particular alliance activities. Some typical alliance activities and possible checklists or guidelines for each are given in the following:[35]

- Strategic analysis—to ensure that an alliance is the best option for the company, instead of a merger or a simple contract, and that the alliance fits with the company's overall strategy. Some checklists may focus on mapping out the relationship between the two companies' value chains or on making the decision whether the company needs to set up an alliance or make an acquisition.

- Alliance preparation—to make sure that the company has the right people and resources in place for the alliance. Checklists may include evaluating the company's culture for collaboration and the skills of the manager responsible for the alliance.

- Partner selection—to help the manager select the best alliance partner. The checklists here may be comprised of forms on partner screening and on mapping out the different types of fit between the company and a potential partner.

- Alliance design—to assist the manager in developing the formal structure of the alliance. These tools may consist of negotiation guidelines, contract templates, and guidelines for selecting the appropriate alliance structure.

- Alliance management—to aid managers in overcoming any conflicts or problems that arise after alliance formation. Possible checklists for this activity are problem tracking or conflict recognition templates, relational development worksheets, alliance contact lists, and guidelines for improving alliance communication.

- Evaluation—to assess the ongoing performance of the alliance and intervene if problems arise. Specific forms that managers may use for evaluation include relationship evaluation form, yearly status report, and worksheets for termination planning.

Examples of the specific information that might go into each of these can be found in the various discussions of the respective topics throughout this book. An important part of developing these tools is to update them regularly. A useful approach is to assign any manager using one of the tools with the responsibility for adding new material or updating the tools to incorporate any new insights gained from that alliance.

Sharing knowledge. The third step is to engage in knowledge-sharing activities throughout the company. This step is particularly important for companies that do not have much alliance experience[36] and may become part of a training program in alliance management. An organization with more experience and resources may be able to conduct the training internally, as experienced managers share their lessons learned with other managers within the company. This knowledge-sharing activity may take the form of a community of practice in which individuals meet on a regular basis to discuss current issues and to share their experiences. This step is also important for transferring that information which is too tacit or embedded to be converted into a guidelines or a checklist.

As noted, some larger firms may have an entire unit within the company; entrepreneurial companies may have only a single individual in the business development or marketing department. Regardless of the size of the alliance management staff, the presence of these specialized positions in a company is associated with greater alliance performance for the company.[37] Several reasons explain this greater performance. First, the person(s) in the position become the repository of the company's best practices and can spread the knowledge around faster than in a less formal approach. These individuals may also be better connected within the company than the alliance manager and can help with requests for additional resources for an alliance, such as input or coordination with other units in the company. Second, these individuals are likely to go beyond just sharing information developed from other alliance experiences and put together some of the tools and training seminars discussed earlier. Finally, having a dedicated staff to oversee the company's alliances communicates to other companies the importance of alliances. Designated staff sends a signal to prospective partners that alliances are important to the company and that it will likely engage in good partnering practices, such as information sharing, being concerned for the partner's interests, and having the interest in and the ability to solve conflicts.

Internalize knowledge. The final step to accumulate and share knowledge is to help managers internalize it by designing alliance apprentice programs. This helps to transfer even more tacit knowledge than could be shared via other activities. Here, the more experienced alliance managers mentor less experienced managers to not only develop the skills of the managers but also to create more practiced alliance managers in the company, which raises the company's overall alliance capability level.

Conclusion

Many entrepreneurial companies rely upon alliances to achieve their overall strategy. The focus of earlier chapters has been to help these companies properly design and manage an alliance or portfolio of alliances. This chapter builds from these chapters by addressing how a company develops its alliance capability and becomes better at managing alliances. Alliance capability has been linked to improved alliance and company performance. Unfortunately, most entrepreneurial companies are at a low or informal capability level which will likely make it harder for them to achieve their strategic goals. Part of our message is that as much as is possible, entrepreneurial companies should make alliance capability development a priority and find ways to dedicate resources to become more effective at alliance management.

To help these companies improve their skills, we focused on three drivers of alliance capability. First, we noted that experience—and the resulting learning by doing—may provide managers with some knowledge they can use to enhance their ability. Second, alliance capability will be improved by having dedicated staff to oversee the alliance. Central to our discussion is that the skills needed to manage an alliance may not match perfectly with those of an entrepreneur. Some good entrepreneurs may not possess the appropriate alliance management competencies and should be willing to either get training or put another person in charge of alliances. Further, we noted that the more connected the alliance manager role is to top management and to the company's other activities as well as the more the role is formalized, the more the role will improve alliance capability. Finally, learning and knowledge sharing and accumulation are influential in creating alliance capability. Too often entrepreneurial companies do not approach alliances as opportunities to learn. Small companies may believe they do not have the energy to devote to learning from alliances, but neglecting learning can lead to lost opportunities and diminished competitive advantage. Learning leads to knowledge which can be developed into a set of best practices to guide future alliance activity. This process involves the steps of articulating the knowledge managers have developed, codifying this into tools and guidelines to use in forming and managing subsequent alliances, sharing this knowledge through communities of practices and training sessions, and internalizing this know-how through mentoring inexperienced managers by more experienced ones.

Enhancing alliance capability will lead to entrepreneurial companies becoming more adept at forming and managing their alliances. Better alliances will likely lead to better overall strategic goal attainment and result in enhanced company performance. In determining if the company is developing more effective alliances, company managers have to address the issue of Chapter 9: How to evaluate strategic alliance performance.

Key Terms

- alliance capability
- alliance experience
- alliance manager skills
- alliance learning
- strategic alliance unit

End of Chapter Questions

1. Why do many small companies not have good alliance capabilities? Which of these reasons is the most difficult one for smaller companies to overcome and why?
2. Why is learning from an alliance an important company outcome?
3. What skills should a manager have to be effective in managing an alliance?
4. If a particular manager does not currently have these skills, how might the manager or the company acquire them?
5. Why is the desire to learn not enough for a company to learn from an alliance?
6. Which checklists or tools do you think will be more helpful for a small company embarking on an alliance?

References

1. Dyer, J. Kale, P., & Singh, H. 2001. How to make strategic alliances work. *MIT Sloan Management* Review, 42(4): 37–44.
2. Kale, P., & Singh, H. 2009. Managing strategic alliances: What do we know now, and where do we go from here? *Academy of Management Perspectives*, 23(4): 45–62.
3. Gulati, R., Sytch, M., & Meyrotra, P. 2008. Breaking up is never easy: Planning for exit in a strategic alliance. *California Management Review*, 50(4): 147–163.
4. Palakshappa, N., & Gordon, M. E. 2007. Collaboration business relationships: Helping firms to acquire skills and economies to prosper. *Journal of Small Business and Enterprise Development*, 14: 264–279.
5. Page 690 from Van Gils, A., & Zwart, P. 2004. Knowledge acquisition and learning in Dutch and Belgian SMEs: The role of strategic alliances. *European Management Journal*, 22: 685–692.
6. Wiklund, J., & Shepherd, D. A. 2009. The effectiveness of alliances and acquisition: The role of resource combination activities. *Entrepreneurship: Theory & Practice*, 33: 193–212.
7. Kale, P., & Singh, H. 2009. Op. cit.
8. Bamford, J., & Ernst, D. 2003. Growth of alliance capabilities. In J. Bamford, B. Gomes-Casseres., & M. Robinson (Eds.), *Mastering Alliance Strategy: A Comprehensive Guide to Design, Management and Organization*: 321–333. San Francisco, CA: Jossey-Bass.

9. Bamford, J., & Ernst, D. 2003. Op. cit.
10. Bamford, J., & Ernst, D. 2003. Op. cit.
11. Bamford, J. , & Ernst, D. 2003. Op. cit.
12. Draulans, J., deMan, A.-P., & Volberda, H. 2003. Building alliance capability: Management techniques for superior alliance performance. *Long Range Planning*, 36: 151–166.
13. Draulans, J., deMan, A.-P. , Volberda, H. 2003. Op cit.
14. For discussions of alliance management skills, see Spekman, R. E., Isabella, L. A., MacAvoy, T. C., & Forbes, III, T. 1996. Creating strategic alliances which endure. *Long Range Planning,* 29: 346–357; MacAvoy, T. C. 1997. Chosing an alliance manager. *Research Technology Management*, 40(5): 12–14.
15. For discussions of an entrepreneur's skills, see Baron, R. A., & Markman, G. D. 2000. Beyond social capital: How social skills can enhance entrepreneur's success. *Academy of Management* Executive, 14: 106–116; Baum, J. R., & Locke, E. A. 2004. The relationship of entrepreneurial traits, skill, and motivation to subsequent venture growth. *Journal of Applied Psychology*, 89: 587–598; Baum, J. R., Locke, E. A., & Smith, K. G. 2001. A multidimensional model of venture growth. *Academy of Management Journal*, 44: 292–303; Ireland, R. D., Hitt, M. A., & Sirmon, D. G. 2003. A model of strategic entrepreneurship: The construct and its dimensions. *Journal of Management*, 29: 963–989; Markman, G. D., Balkin, D. B., & Baron, R. A. 2002. Inventors and new venture formation: The effects of general self-efficacy and regretful thinking. *Entrepreneurship Theory and Practice*, 26: 149–165.
16. Applegate, L., & Collins, E. 2004. *Slingshot Technologies*. Harvard Business School Teaching Case.
17. Hamel, G. 1991. Competition for competence and inter-partner learning within international strategic alliances [Special Issue]. *Strategic Management Journal*, 12: 83–104.
18. Palakshappa, N., & Gordon, M. E. 2007. Op. cit.
19. Page 16 from Prashantham, S., & Birkinshaw, J. 2009. Dancing with gorillas: How small companies can partner effectively with MNCs. *California Management Review*, 51: 6–23.
20. Page 275 from Palakshappa, N., & Gordon, M. E. 2007. Op. cit.
21. See for example, Inkpen, A. C., & Tsang, E. W. K. 2007. Learning and strategic alliances. *The Academy of Management Annals*, 1: 479–511.
22. Alvarez, S., & Barney, J. 2001. How entrepreneurial firms can benefit from alliances with large partners. *Academy of Management Executive*, 15: 139–148.
23. Van Gils, A., & Zwart, P. 2004. Op. cit.
24. Page 157 from Narula, R. 2004. R&D collaboration by SMEs: New opportunities and limitations in the face of globalization. *Technovation*, 24: 153–161.
25. Hyder, A., & Abraha, D. 2004. Product and skills development in small- and medium-sized high-tech firms through international strategic alliances. *Singapore Management Review,* 26(2): 1–24.
26. Prashantham, S., & Birkinshaw, J. 2009. Op. cit.
27. Szulanski, G. 1996. Exploring internal stickiness: Impediments to the transfer of best practice within the firm. *Strategic Management Journal*, 17(Special Issue): 27–43; Inkpen, A. 2005. Learning through alliances: General Motors and NUMMI. *California Management Review,* 47(4): 114–136.
28. Lichtenthaler, U., & Ernst, H. 2006. Attitudes to externally organizing knowledge management tasks: A review, reconsideration and extension of the NIH syndrome. *R&D Management*, 36: 367–386.

29. Chen, M.-H., & Wang, M.-C. 2008. Social networks and a new venture's innovative capability: The role of trust within entrepreneurial teams. *R&D Management*, 38: 253–264.

30. George, G., Zahra, S., Wheatley, K., & Khan, R. 2001. The effects of alliance portfolio characteristics and absorptive capacity on performance: A study of biotechnology firms. *Journal of High Technology Management Research*, 12: 205–226.

31. Jones, O., & Craven, M. 2001. Expanding capabilities in a mature manufacturing firm: Absorptive capacity and the TCS. *International Small Business Journal*, 19(3): 39–55.

32. Bernados Barbolla, A. M., & Casar Corredera, J. R. 2009. Critical factors for success in university–industry research projects. *Technology Analysis & Strategic Management*, 21: 599–616.

33. Sherwood, A. L., & Corvin, J. 2008. Knowledge acquisition in university–industry alliances: An empirical investigation from a learning theory perspective. *The Journal of Product Innovation Management*, 25: 162–179.

34. Kale, P., & Singh, H. 2009. Op. cit.

35. This material draws from Bell, J. 2003. *Walking the tight rope: Balancing between cooperation and competition*. Inaugural speech. University.of Nijmegen; Kale, P., & Singh, H. 2009. Op. cit.

36. Draulans, J., deMan, A.-P., & Volberda, H. 2003. Op. cit.

37. Dyer, J., Kale, P., & Singh, H. 2001. Op. cit.

CHAPTER

PERFORMANCE EVALUATION OF ENTREPRENEURIAL ALLIANCES

"The company measures performance of the alliance using sales, but it takes over 18 months to make a sale. How useful of a measure is that?"

—A MANAGER COMMENTING ON ANOTHER COMPANY'S ALLIANCE

INTRODUCTION

The previous chapters have provided recommendations for when and how an entrepreneurial company should create and manage an alliance. In this chapter we address how to determine whether all of these efforts have been worthwhile. Given the importance of alliances for both large and small companies and the amount of time and energy required to develop and manage them, managers will want to know whether an alliance performs well or enhances the company's performance. For such an important issue one might expect companies to have developed a straightforward approach for evaluating performance. But in reality, evaluating alliance performance is difficult and complex and something for which most managers do not have a well thought-out solution. For example, interviews we conducted with entrepreneurs report that entrepreneurs typically do not spend much time thinking about which performance measures to use, whether to use a single measure or multiple measures of performance, and if they decide to use multiple measures, how these measures are related. Not surprisingly, then, most managers end up using inappropriate measures.[1]

In this chapter, we explore entrepreneurial alliance performance evaluation. We begin by noting several challenges that make it difficult to evaluate alliance performance. Important to this discussion is that performance has multiple dimensions and that some measures capture only one or a few of the dimensions. We then turn to a discussion of more commonly used measures and describe the relative advantages and disadvantages of each. We note that these measures tend to differ in terms of whether they capture detailed information on the alliance's situation and whether they permit easy comparison with evaluations from other alliances. As entrepreneurial companies build their alliance portfolios, managers will need to decide which alliances are performing better than others and which practices should be shared across alliances. To make these decisions, managers will need performance measures for each alliance that are comparable to the measures used in other alliances. We conclude the chapter by proposing a five-step process for creating a set of measures. Central to our discussion is that we argue that no single measure or set of measures is appropriate for every alliance, and that a manager should not automatically adopt a set of measures used for one alliance to evaluate another. Rather, managers should use measures which are not only appropriate for the situation but also permit comparison with other alliances. Taking the time to develop such a set of measures will provide more useful information over most current approaches to determining the effectiveness of the alliance.

ERRORS IN STRATEGIC ALLIANCE PERFORMANCE MEASUREMENT

The difficulty with evaluating performance of a strategic alliance stems from two underlying issues. The first is the general challenge of evaluating organizational performance. While progress has been made in recent years on how to evaluate performance, there is still no universally accepted measure or set of measures. The second is the challenge stemming from the hybrid structure of an alliance which includes activities not only inside the company but also inside the partner's, making it difficult to gather the relevant information. These issues cause many managers to make one of several common errors in selecting performance measures. These are summarized in Table 9.1.

TABLE 9.1 Common Errors in Selecting Measures for Evaluating Strategic Alliance Performance	
• Errors related to general performance measurement	• Using incomplete measures • Using inappropriate measures • Using difficult-to-collect measures • Using measures which require expensive-to-collect information
• Errors related to strategic alliances	• Using measures requiring unobtainable information • Measuring at only one level of analysis

ERRORS RELATED TO GENERAL PERFORMANCE MEASUREMENT

The first set of errors stems from the general difficulties that arise in evaluating any type of organization's performance. This includes: using incomplete measures, using inappropriate measures, using measures that require information that is difficult to collect, and using measures that require information that is expensive to collect.

Using Incomplete Measures

While it is appealing to consider performance to be a simple concept which can be captured by a single measure, performance is generally considered to have multiple dimensions.[2] Table 9.2 identifies some of the dimensions that can be used to characterize different alliance performance measures, including time orientation (past, current, or future), level of analysis (alliance, company, or collective) and functional focus on the measure (financial, strategic, or operational). Since there are no measures which capture all of these dimensions, using just one performance measure will likely provide information on only part of the overall performance.[3] For example, financial performance measures such as return on investment (ROI), return on equity (ROE), and return on assets (ROA) are commonly used, but they focus on past activities, typically on the alliance or company levels, and on financial activities. In fact, they have been labeled "trailing indicators"[4] because they provide good indications of past activities (i.e., whether the firm was profitable in the past), but may not indicate future financial performance or how the alliance is performing on strategic or operational activities. Thus, a common problem by managers is using measures that provide information on only some dimensions of performance.

Using Inappropriate Measures

A second problem is that managers will sometimes use measures that are inappropriate for the setting. The quote at the beginning of the chapter comes from an entrepreneurial company's efforts to sell a complex software package to large companies through an alliance. The company discovered that selling to large companies typically required multiple visits to a prospective client over months or even years before closing a sale. Still, the entrepreneurial company used sales to measure the alliance's performance since increasing sales was the company's long-term goal. However, sales provided the company with no information on how the alliance was doing in the interim, including the activities of the alliance's sales team. Better measures for this situation might have been the leads generated or knowledge about potential customers obtained by the sales team.

Using Difficult-to-Collect Measures

A related problem is that alliance managers may be asked by important stakeholders (e.g., investors, other managers in the company) to use measures which are challenging to calculate. Managers in some firms report that they are requested to calculate profit evaluations (e.g., ROI) of each of the company's alliances so the alliance can be compared with other activities—either with another alliance or an

TABLE 9.2 Different Approaches to and Commonly Used Measures of Alliance Performance

Approach	Measure	Level of Analysis	Time Orientation	Type of Information Represented	Permits Easy and Reliable Comparison	Other Advantages	Other Disadvantages
One size fits all	Financial returns	Company or alliance	Past	Financial	Yes	Understood by most managers	May not be valid for all alliance types
	Stability/termination	Alliance	Past	Operational	Yes	Simple to collect	Ambiguous interpretation; information provided only after an event
Situationally appropriate	Balanced scorecard variables	Company or Alliance or Collective	Past Current Future	Financial operational strategic	No	Provides fine-grained assessment	Often difficult to collect
	Milestones	Company or alliance or collective	Past Current	Financial operational strategic	Only if the same milestones	Provides information on alliance progress	
In-between	Satisfaction	Company or alliance or collective	Current	Financial operational strategic	Yes	Simple to collect	
	Strategic goal attainment	Company or alliance or collective	Current	Financial operational strategic	Only if the same goals		Difficult to compare to other investments; goals may change

internal operation. Besides the problem with profit measures not capturing other dimensions of performance, for alliances that are engaged in activities like research and development or on standards setting, the profit measures are hard to calculate. These managers acknowledge that for many of their alliances, the ROI figures are really only guesses.

Using Measures that Require Expensive-to-Collect Information

Similarly, sometimes managers are asked to use measures that require extensive time and resources to collect. For example, a small company reported that its investors wanted to know how committed a long-term supplier was to the company's cost reduction program. Collecting this information required several days of phone calling. While this was good information to have, the results were not surprising to the company managers and the time and energy it took to collect it was considered extensive. Such requests may overburden an entrepreneurial firm with limited resources or may lead to only marginally better information than using less expensive information.

ERRORS DUE TO STRATEGIC ALLIANCE FEATURES

The hybrid nature of alliances provides additional challenges for evaluating performance. These include using measures which require unobtainable information and measuring at only one level of analysis.

Using Measures Requiring Unobtainable Information

When a company attempts to evaluate the performance of the alliance, some information may not be available, particularly information that comes from a partner. For example, E-com (a disguised name) is a small e-commerce company. It entered into an alliance with ProMan (a disguised name) to develop an online shopping website for ProMan's products. When the website was finished, E-com was interested in promoting its website development capability. It thought a measure of how much time and money the alliance had saved ProMan in developing the website would be an effective indicator of the alliance's success. ProMan, however, was not willing to release this information.

Measuring at Only One Level of Analysis

A second issue stemming from the hybrid structure of alliances involves the different levels at which performance can be measured. The three more common ones are the alliance level; the company level; and the collective or common level, which examines the joint benefits to the company and the partner. At the alliance level, performance can be measured by what the alliance itself creates in terms of products and services; which we discussed in Chapter 5 as value creation.[5] At the company level, the performance may be calculated in terms of how the company uses the products, services, or information generated by the alliance. This is referred to as the *value capture* and reflects whether the company is receiving the benefits from the alliance's activities. Finally, a company may seek to evaluate the alliance in terms of the common benefits that accrue to the company and its partners.

In evaluating an alliance, managers may focus on only one level and miss evaluating performance on other levels. This is the problem sometimes made by companies using international alliances. In this classic scenario, a small foreign company sets up an alliance with a local, domestic company to produce and sell its product in the local market.[6] Because of the distance between the two countries, a lack of resources, or the desire to just focus on improving sales, the foreign company may commit few personnel to the alliance and evaluate performance only in terms of the sales generated by the alliance. Over time, the alliance might produce sales and the foreign partner's evaluation, based on sales, would suggest that this alliance was effective. However, this measure overlooks partner level benefits, particularly learning by the partner if the partner is engaging in a learning race. Because the local partner is more active in managing the day-to-day operations of the alliance, it learns how to make and sell the product in the local market. The foreign partner, because of its limited involvement, does not learn about selling in the local market. At some point, the local partner may realize that it has learned enough from the foreign partner that it doesn't need the alliance and terminates it. It then starts to sell its own version of the foreign company's product. The foreign partner, meanwhile, not only has to find a new local partner to sell its product but it has created a competitor in the market. In this situation, the foreign partner measured performance only at the alliance level, in terms of total product sales, without considering whether it was learning about how to sell in the local market—the benefit of the alliance at the company level. If it had, the company would have seen that the benefits were more than just sales and would have not likely let its partner learn so much about the company's products.

ALTERNATIVE APPROACHES TO ALLIANCE PERFORMANCE MEASUREMENT

The problems discussed previously indicated that managers have to pay careful attention to which measures they use for indicating alliance performance. To aid in determining which of several commonly employed measures managers should use, we now turn to a discussion of the relative qualities of each. The select measures fall into three general approaches which we label "one-size-fits-all," "situationally-appropriate," and "in-between."[7] The one-size-fits-all approach emphasizes using a single measure for any condition and permits easy comparison of one alliance with another. The situationally appropriate approach, on the other hand, uses measures which are relevant to a particular alliance's circumstances. The measures are selected for their ability to capture the specific activities of that alliance, with less concern over whether the measures permit easy comparison to other alliances. Because of the limitations of these two approaches, the third, in-between approach has developed.

Table 9.2 compares the three approaches and six more commonly used measures of entrepreneurial alliance performance. As mentioned earlier, each measure is described in terms of its level of analysis, time orientation, and type of information represented. Besides these dimensions, the table notes whether the performance measure permits easy and reliable comparison to other alliances or investments and any other advantages or disadvantages each measure may have.

ONE-SIZE-FITS-ALL APPROACH

This category includes measures that are used regardless of the nature of the particular alliance. Two of the more popular one-size-fits-all measures are financial performance and stability/termination.

Financial Performance

Financial performance measures of alliances—such as net income, ROA, and ROI—draw attention to the economic impact of the alliance on the company.[8] These measures have the advantage of being generally well understood by managers in both the alliance and the focal company. Most managers understand how these are calculated and how to interpret them. Because they are single measures, they permit easy comparison to the performance of other alliances. Importantly, as measures that can be calculated at any point in time, they allow a manager to track changes in the alliance's financial performance with reasonable accuracy.

Financial measures, despite their ubiquity, have shortcomings. First, as trailing indicators they reflect past behavior and do not provide reliable information about expected future performance.[9] Second, they only focus on one dimension of performance and are not very useful for some types of alliances, such as a new product venture where financial returns are not expected for some time.

STABILITY/TERMINATION

A second one-size-fits-all measure is whether the alliance continues to exist or had to be renegotiated.[10] As we have noted in earlier chapters, many entrepreneurs—such as the founder of Apex Video discussed in Chapter 7—report that their alliances with larger firms were sometimes started to give the small company greater name recognition or legitimacy, as they attempt to overcome their liability of newness. What mattered most to these entrepreneurs was simply that the alliance existed and the partner's name could be used to promote the entrepreneurial company either in conversation with other companies or on its website. Performance is indicated by whether the alliance exists or is stable (which is believed to indicate good performance) or whether it has been disbanded or renegotiated (which indicates poor performance).

The stability/termination measure has a few advantages. First, it is easy to collect. Not only managers in the alliance, of course, but also outsiders can quickly determine whether the alliance exists. Second, the calculation of performance is also relatively simple. Terminating or restructuring an alliance is clear, and generally unambiguous events lead to a simple coding of the alliance's performance. Third, because these are single measures, performance evaluations are easy to compare across alliances. Finally, a stability/termination measure provides some indication of the strength of the relationship developing between the partners. Managers who have used the stability/termination measure argue that the companies have achieved some degree of operational success because the partners are still in the alliance or have not restructured it.[11]

Stability/termination measure as an indication of performance, however, has several limitations. First, it provides no information about the specific benefits to either the company or the partner. While it is assumed, for example, that a small company may have increased legitimacy due to its alliance with a larger company, the stability/termination measure does not capture it.

A second limitation of stability/termination as a performance measure is that the interpretation may be inaccurate. Generally it is assumed that an existing alliance signifies acceptable or superior performance, whereas a terminated alliance corresponds to poor performance. This may not always be the case. Some alliances, as noted in Chapter 6 on discussing restructuring, may continue in name only because the time and effort required to terminate the alliance are greater than the costs of keeping it operating; the managers involved do not want to admit they made a mistake, or because notoriety may result from termination.[12] While on paper these alliances may be recorded as continuing and be viewed as a success, in practice there are not. Aegis Analytical, a small process manufacturing software firm, faced this issue in deciding how to manage two distribution alliances—with very large companies—that had not produced a sale.[13] Among the options were trying to stimulate both alliances to create more sales, terminating either alliance early, or letting each contract quietly expire. Early termination of either alliance by Aegis was not an attractive option, however, because it would have likely damaged the company's reputation as a partner in future alliances. The company's choices were between attempting to reinvigorate the alliances and stopping active investment and letting each alliance quietly expire at the end of the current contract.

Alternatively, some alliances are designed to be terminated, or are terminated because of a change in circumstances. A project-oriented alliance that has a limited expected duration and has achieved its goals will likely be terminated. Even though it attained its goals and is ended because it is no longer needed, the termination measure score may suggest that the alliance was unsuccessful. Similarly, an alliance that functioned well but is no longer relevant because of a shift in a firm's strategy (e.g., it has more attractive options to pursue) will also likely be coded on this measure as a poor performer.

A final limitation is that stability/termination only provides a change in performance *after* an event.[14] While the alliance continues or is stable, the assumed performance is good. Only after a termination or renegotiation does the measure signal performance was poor. Thus this measure provides information about how the alliance performed in the past, rather than providing an indication of current or future performance.

SITUATIONALLY APPROPRIATE APPROACH

The second approach to alliance performance measurement is opposite to the one-size-fits-all approach in that it makes an explicit attempt to find measures that best suit the nature of the particular alliance being assessed. Two methods in this category are the balanced scorecard approach and the milestone attainment measures.

Balanced Scorecard

Over the last fifteen years, managers have become interested in developing measures that capture more of a particular alliance's unique situation. One—the balanced scorecard (BSC)—is adapted from the general BSC approach.[15] In the general approach, managers evaluate a company on four dimensions—financial performance, customer satisfaction, internal business processes, and innovation and learning—using five to six measures for each dimension. In applying the BSC to strategic alliances, managers have revised these dimensions. For example, Eli Lilly modified the BSC to examine three dimensions of the relationship between itself and a partner: strategic fit, operational fit, and cultural fit. The company measures these three dimensions using fourteen specific items such as team coordination, leadership, roles, organizational values, and conflict management.[16] These measures are then placed on a "spider-web" diagram, and the scores of the company are compared to scores of the partner. This comparison gives managers a visual representation of how the alliance is performing across each of these aspects. The company also seeks feedback from the partner in the alliance and adds this information to the spider-web chart. Figure 9.1 shows a hypothetical spider web in which the company and the partner each evaluated the performance of the alliance on eight dimensions—trust, communication, commitment, goal alignment, ROI, common values, skills/competence, and operational compatibility—on a scale of 1 = low to 5 = high and then plotted the results on the spider web. This graphical representation permits the focal company to see the specific dimensions on which the company and the partner believe that the alliance is performing well (e.g., commitment), on which it is performing poorly (e.g., skill enhancement), and on which dimensions they disagree about the alliance's performance (e.g., goal alignment). A related approach recommends that managers evaluate an alliance on four performance dimensions: financial, strategic, operational, and relationship.[17]

The balanced scorecard approach encourages managers to construct measures specifically for the alliance. An advantage of the BSC is that it collects very detailed information about the alliance that is appropriate for the context. Further, it provides information across multiple dimensions of performance, including not only financial, operational, and strategic information but also information about the alliance's past, present, and likely future activities.

While the BSC approach is growing in popularity, it has a few disadvantages when compared to other measures. First, because many more measures are used to evaluate performance, it requires more time and effort to calculate than the one-size-fits-all measure. Second, with so many different measures

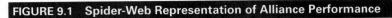

FIGURE 9.1 Spider-Web Representation of Alliance Performance

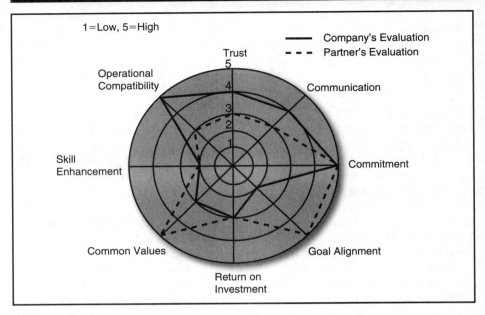

representing diverse dimensions, it is harder to compare one alliance's performance with another. A shortcoming to the general BSC approach is that there is no clear way to combine the different measures into an overall evaluation of performance.[18] Trying to compare two alliances across all of the different dimensions is challenging. For example, if the company with the alliance in Figure 9.1 had a second alliance with a different performance profile, consider the difficulties for managers trying to provide an overall comparison. Mapping these onto the same spider web chart—as indicated in Figure 9.2—would reveal differences on specific dimensions but it is not clear if one alliance performs better than the other overall.

ATTAINING MILESTONES

A second set of measures in the situationally appropriate approach is evaluating the alliance's progress against milestones. Here, managers lay out interim expectations for the alliance and then periodically evaluate the degree to which these expectations are being met. Examples of milestone measures include:

- The first sale by an alliance between a start-up manufacturing company and a sales company.
- Successful development of a prototype by a small engineering consulting firm and a software company of an online version of the engineering firm's consulting tools.

FIGURE 9.2 Spider-Web Representation of a Second Alliance Performance

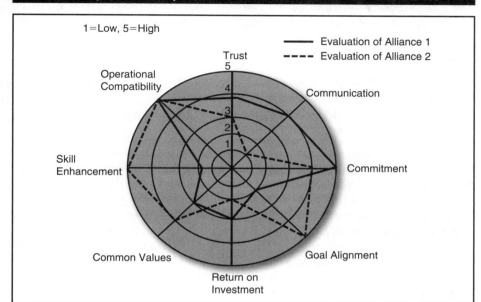

- Achieving a measureable level of trust between two competitors in an economies-of-scale alliance.
- Development of a new drug by a biotechnology firm and a pharmaceutical company.

Milestones provide interim performance information that permits the firm to decide whether mid-course correction is needed. Because the milestones are specific to the alliance, the measures typically provide information appropriate for that alliance. They can also be easily adapted to capture different dimensions of performance and they provide interim evaluations of the alliance's activities. However, since different alliances rarely have the same milestones, milestone measures usually do not permit easy comparison across alliances. In addition, milestone measures typically increase the time and resources spent on monitoring the alliance's progress.[19]

IN-BETWEEN APPROACH

Managers have recognized the limitations of using the one-size-fits-all and the situationally appropriate approaches, and many have turned to a third approach. The managers have sought to combine some degree of information about the specific alliance but also to permit a more general comparison across different alliances. We label this an in-between approach and focus on two of the more commonly used measures: satisfaction and achieving strategic goals.

Satisfaction

The focal company's satisfaction with an alliance represents a common approach to evaluating performance. A measure about satisfaction can be worded in various ways. Some examples include:

- Overall, how satisfied are we with the alliance? (1 = not at all, 7 = extremely)
- To what extent has the alliance met our expectations for its activities? (1 = not at all, 7 = completely)
- To what extent would we change the manner in which the alliance conducts its activities? (1 = not at all, 7 = completely)

Satisfaction measures are fairly easy and economical to collect.[20] Also, because satisfaction measures provide a single indicator of performance, satisfaction scores can be compared across a focal company's multiple alliances.

One limitation to using satisfaction to evaluate performance is that any biases of the manager will affect the evaluation. The evaluation by a particular manager—who perhaps has higher expectations for the alliance—may not be shared by other managers. Further, managers may base their evaluation on different activities of the alliance. Some managers may be satisfied because the alliance is operating well, others may be unsatisfied because although the alliance is operating well, it is not achieving the intended strategy.

Achieving Strategic Goal(s)

A second in-between measure that is often related to satisfaction is evaluating the alliance against the focal company's strategic reason(s) for participating.[21] The evaluation may be in terms of a single general strategic goal or several specific goals. For example, "Overall, to what degree have we achieved our goals for entering the alliance" (1 = not at all, 7 = very much) measures performance toward a general goal, while:

- To what extent has the alliance helped us gain access to a new market?
- To what extent has the alliance helped us develop new technologies?
- To what extent has the alliance helped us block competitors?
- To what extent has the alliance helped us develop new skills?

Each measures a specific goal achievement. A global goal achievement measure—or several specific ones—helps capture some information about the alliance by evaluating the reasons the company entered the alliance.

Since goal achievement is typically measured on a scale (e.g., 1 = low to 7 = high), it is relatively easy for a manager to evaluate. Also, since there is usually a single measure of goal attainment, comparing two alliances on this measure is easy. The comparison may not be meaningful, however, if the alliances have different goals. A start-up company's goal of using a marketing alliance to introduce an existing product to a new market will probably be easier to reach than the goal of using an R&D (research and development) alliance to develop a brand-new product. Because it has a simpler goal, the marketing alliance may be perceived as more successful than the R&D alliance. Finally, strategic goal comparisons generally do not reveal whether the alliance was the best choice for the activity. These measures of goal attainment do not provide any information on whether the resources devoted would have been better used elsewhere.[22]

SUMMARY

Managers have used different indicators of performance[23] and as we have described, each indicator has both strengths and limitations. Unfortunately, our discussions with managers reveal that they often do not think too much about the advantages or limitations of the selected measures. Further, they generally do not explore how various measures, if they use them, may be related to one another or how different measures might be combined into a single, overall indicator of performance. We next address how managers should develop measures that are both relevant for the alliance's situation as well as permitting comparisons to other alliances.

STEPS TO EVALUATING ALLIANCE PERFORMANCE

Since no single measure is suitable for evaluating all entrepreneurial alliances, managers need to be selective about which measures to use. In making this decision, we propose that managers should proceed through a five-step process that starts with identifying appropriate measures and ends with creating measures which permit a simple comparison of alliance's performance relative to other options. The five steps are summarized in Figure 9.3.

STEP 1: IDENTIFY PERFORMANCE MEASURES RELEVANT FOR THE ALLIANCE CONTEXT

The first step for an entrepreneurial alliance manager is to identify measures that capture the nature and purpose of the alliance. As noted earlier, while there are a number of contextual factors to consider, common ones include the type of information desired by the focal company, the level of analysis, the nature of the task being conducted, the lifecycle stage of the alliance, the company's alliance capability, and the degree of change within the environment. Table 9.3 summarizes some of the different conditions and measures that will likely capture the relevant information.

Type of Information

Earlier we noted that because companies may enter into an alliance for various reasons, they may require different types of information, and we distinguished between strategic, financial, or operational information. Managers should identify which type of information is most relevant for the nature and the purpose of the alliance. The first type—strategic—should be included in most evaluations since companies usually design alliances to help achieve strategic goals. Therefore most performance evaluation efforts will probably incorporate measures

FIGURE 9.3 Steps in Evaluating Alliance Performance

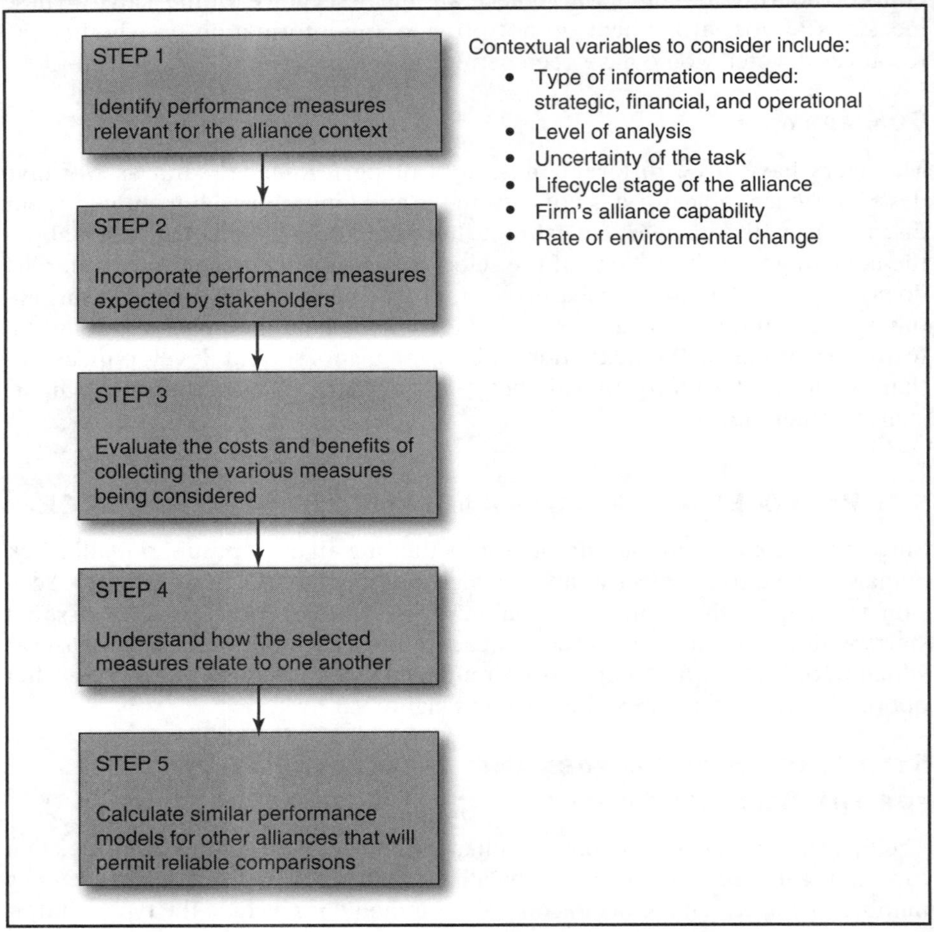

STEP 1

Identify performance measures relevant for the alliance context

STEP 2

Incorporate performance measures expected by stakeholders

STEP 3

Evaluate the costs and benefits of collecting the various measures being considered

STEP 4

Understand how the selected measures relate to one another

STEP 5

Calculate similar performance models for other alliances that will permit reliable comparisons

Contextual variables to consider include:

- Type of information needed: strategic, financial, and operational
- Level of analysis
- Uncertainty of the task
- Lifecycle stage of the alliance
- Firm's alliance capability
- Rate of environmental change

that capture strategic information, including the balanced scorecard, strategic goal assessment, satisfaction, or milestone measures.

The second type of information—financial—may also be relevant for many alliances, especially since entrepreneurial ventures may ally with a larger firm because they want to enhance financial performance. A common approach for entrepreneurial manufacturing companies and for biotechnology firms is to partner with larger firms who will handle product distribution and marketing. The increased sales should help the small company's financial performance, and a measure of the financial benefits (e.g., return on sales) may provide one indication of alliance effectiveness. Likewise, an entrepreneurial company focusing on supplying services may find that an alliance provides a source of additional

TABLE 9.3	Different Contextual Conditions and Relevant Measures	
Contextual Condition	*General Issues*	*Recommended Measures*
Type of information	Which type of information to collect: strategic, financial, or operational?	Strategic information—balanced scorecard measures, strategic goal assessment, or milestone attainment Financial information—standard financial measures Operational information—milestone attainment, stability, balanced scorecard, or satisfaction
Level of analysis	Which level of analysis to collect information on: alliance, company, or collective?	Most measures can be adapted to different levels. Likely ones are balanced scorecard measures, strategic goal assessment or milestone attainment
Nature of the task	Is the nature of the alliance's task very routine and predictable or is it uncertain?	Routine or predictable tasks—outcome measures such as financial performance or goal attainment Uncertain tasks—milestone attainment, balanced scorecard, or satisfaction
Lifecycle stage	What is the developmental stage of the alliance?	Early-stage alliances—milestone attainment, satisfaction, or stability Later-stage alliances—strategic goal attainment, financial returns, or balanced scorecard measures
Firm's alliance capability	What is the firm's capability with managing alliances?	Higher capability level—milestone attainment Lower capability level—outcome measures like goal attainment
Degree of environmental change	How frequently does the alliance's environment change?	Stable environment—outcome measures like financial measures or strategic goal achievement Unstable environments—interim measures like milestone attainment, satisfaction, balanced scorecard measures, or stability

revenue. For example, an entrepreneurial online seller of travel products formed an alliance with a high-end luggage manufacturer to operate the luggage firm's website. The luggage firm did not want to sell its bags on websites that sold competitors' products, and it did not have the internal capabilities to develop its own website. It turned to the entrepreneurial venture, which had the expertise to design and operate the website. For the entrepreneurial firm, the benefits to the relationship were building a stronger tie with the luggage company and bringing in needed revenue during a slow economic period. In this situation, evaluation of the alliance included not only longer-term strategic interests but also financial ones. While standard financial performance measures may be used alone, as we have discussed in this chapter, financial evaluations are better used as part of a balanced scorecard approach or used with other measures such as milestone, strategic goals, or overall satisfaction assessment.

Finally, operational data will reflect how well the alliance is functioning. Operational data provide useful information in the early stages of an alliance's development, when the focus is on building the relationship and the alliance has not yet generated measureable outcomes. When managers are interested in evaluating the alliance's operational development, milestone assessment, stability, a balanced scorecard or, possibly, satisfaction measures would provide this information.

Level of analysis

In looking for relevant measures, managers should also consider the level at which they want to analyze performance. As discussed, the more common levels of analysis include: the alliance, the company, and the collective. In selecting performance measures, managers should be careful in weighing the different levels. There are dangers in ignoring levels but it is likely that each level will not be equal. Rather, managers should evaluate the relative importance of performance at the different levels. As noted in Table 9.2, many measures may be applied to different levels. Measures which are useful for adapting to these different levels include balanced scorecard, strategic goals, satisfaction, and milestones.

Nature of the task

The measures chosen may also depend on the level of uncertainty of the alliance's tasks. For alliance activities that are fairly routine or familiar, such as selling an existing product, the measures can focus on outcomes such as sales or financial returns. For activities with a less certain outcome, the measures should focus on milestones and ongoing operations of the alliance rather than the outcome. For example, companies in an R&D alliance are unlikely to know at the time of formation what the alliance may produce, or when, or even if there will be results. Rather than trying to evaluate the alliance on what it produces or on the expected outcome, a better approach would be to use milestone attainment or a balanced scorecard metric for measuring operational activities.

Lifecycle of the Alliance

The appropriate performance measure may also vary depending on the lifecycle stage of the alliance. A fairly new alliance will need measures that are connected to meeting interim goals or to the development of the relationship between the partners, such as the development of trust. Measures such as satisfaction, stability, and milestone attainment will be useful. More established alliances should be producing an outcome, and will need measures such as strategic goal attainment, financial returns, or the balanced scorecard.

Alliance Capability

The choice of performance measures also depends on the company's alliance capability. If the company has developed a higher level of capability, as discussed in Chapter 8, it may have established measures in place.[24] Also, a more capable company may better understand how early alliance activities lead to outcomes. The more capable firm will be better able than a less capable firm to evaluate whether the alliance is on its way toward the overall goal. Companies with stronger capabilities in using alliances can concentrate their performance attention on alliance development activities and use milestone measures, while less capable firms will probably need to focus more on outcome measures.

Rate of Change in the Environment
The dynamics of the market or the industry environment will also affect the choice of performance measures. If the environment is changing substantially, the firm will probably have to use milestones, stability, general satisfaction, or some of the balanced scorecard measures that indicate interim progress. In a stable environment, the firm can use measures that focus more on the expected outcomes, such as financial measures or strategic goal achievement.

The first step in this process, then, is to begin to consider the broad context of the alliance and determine which types of measures would be most likely to capture the information needed to provide an accurate evaluation of the alliance's performance.

STEP 2: INCORPORATE PREFERRED MEASURES EXPECTED BY STAKEHOLDERS

After settling on a list of measures that are appropriate for the situation, the next step is to add performance measures that major stakeholders would like the entrepreneurial alliance managers to use. Examples of other parties with a vested interest in the effectiveness of the alliance might include a business partner or venture capital investors who may not be interested in the attainment of milestones but rather in financial return. For these investors, a financial performance measure might be included. Similarly, two alliance partners may have complementary interests—for example, an entrepreneurial venture with an interest in software development and a partner with an interest in sales. The performance evaluation might include measures that each partner wants as a way to ensure that the alliance benefits both. In each of these situations, the entrepreneurial alliance manager will need to incorporate performance measures that may not seem relevant but which reflect a stakeholder's interests. Although each of the measures we have discussed may be used, measures that are internally generated or that have a degree of comparability, such as goal attainment, financial performance, or milestones, are more likely to be the ones stakeholders request.

STEP 3: EVALUATE THE COSTS AND BENEFITS OF COLLECTING THE VARIOUS MEASURES BEING CONSIDERED

The third stage in this process is to evaluate the amount of time and resources available for collecting these measures. An advantage of the situationally appropriate approaches—such as the balanced scorecard and milestone attainment—is that they provide a fine-grained evaluation of the alliance's activities on multiple dimensions. However as noted, collecting this information takes time and other resources. Measures such as stability/termination and satisfaction provide less (or ambiguous) information but are much easier to collect. Alliance managers must consider whether they have the resources for a more detailed data collection process and whether the additional information is worth the extra effort it requires. One factor affecting this decision is whether the alliance actually warrants more detailed data collection. Some alliances, such as a simple feasibility study for a new product, may not merit intensive data collection efforts while more complicated alliances will. A second issue is determining how often to collect the data. Weekly sales reports may provide a detailed assessment of the progress of a sales alliance, but if the partners only meet quarterly, such frequent data collection may not be necessary.

Factoring in all of these considerations will give alliance managers a defined set of performance measures.

STEP 4: UNDERSTAND HOW THE SELECTED MEASURES RELATE TO ONE ANOTHER

Perhaps the most challenging but critical step in the process is determining how these various measures are related. We noted earlier that measures that capture the performance of a single alliance often do not permit simple comparisons of multiple alliances, while measures that provide easy comparisons (e.g., satisfaction, financial returns) often overlook important elements of a specific alliance. If a company has only one alliance, the situationally appropriate approaches will be useful. For managers with multiple alliances, however, the goal is to develop valid measures that are also comparable. This will require reducing the set of measures developed in Step 3 to a single measure. One way to achieve this is to explore the relationship among different measures. Some indicators may reflect a single, underlying idea. For example, it may be that a manager's level of satisfaction is consistent with the more detailed balanced scorecard assessment. Here, the measures could be used interchangeably, perhaps choosing satisfaction for a quick assessment of the alliance in comparison to other alliances, and a balanced scorecard approach when more detailed support for the assessment is needed. But both are not needed in an evaluation.

Alternatively, some performance measures may not be identical. For example, a financial measure may be useful for evaluating a ROI while goal attainment would be helpful if the goal includes learning (as discussed in Chapter 8). The two measures may not be related but the firm may have an interest in both learning and profitability. The challenge is how to compare the alliance's performance—either over time or with other alliances or investments. Since these measures are not identical, managers will need to figure out how to combine them to create a single measure which can be compared to the performance of other alliances.

One approach would be to convert each performance measure to a similar scale. In the example of learning and profits, the measures the company might use for learning (e.g., increased understanding about a new technology) and of profits (e.g., ROI) can be converted to a numerical scale of how the alliance is performing relative to expectations (1 = very much below, 7 = very much above). If managers believe that the alliance is generating good knowledge about the technology but is producing less-than-expected profits, they might evaluate the alliance as a 6 (on the scale of 1 to 7) for learning and a 3 for profits. If they consider the benefits of learning to be less important than the profits, they might weigh learning as only 0.3 but the profits as 0.7. Using these weights, the managers could then determine the overall performance of the alliances by multiplying each performance score by the weight. In this example, the calculation would be 6*0.3 + 3*0.7 = 3.9. The alliance could then be compared to other alliances evaluated in the same way to determine whether this alliance is a worthwhile investment.

A more complex approach would be to look for a causal relationship between the measures. That is, instead of treating the various measures as separate, unrelated measures that are just added together, managers can examine whether performance on one measure influences performance on another measure. To take a simple example, a company may know that achieving early milestones increases the probability of subsequent good financial performance. If the company has enough data from either its own or other companies' experiences, it might be able to quantify this likelihood. That is, it can develop an equation that specifies the numeric impact of attaining early milestones on the financial outcome. Using more sophisticated statistical techniques (e.g., structural equation modeling) the managers may develop an overall model of the relationship among the performance measures that can be used to create a single performance measure. This would permit the managers to combine the information from different measures to create a single indicator of alliance performance.

In either of these two approaches—simple addition of measures or more complex modeling—the alliance manager's overall goal is to map out how the various measures can be reliably and validly combined into a composite measure. This process may be complicated, but it can result in a measure that not only captures the nuances of the alliance's situation but also permits comparison with the firm's other alliances.

STEP 5: CALCULATE SIMILAR PERFORMANCE MODELS FOR OTHER ALLIANCES THAT WILL PERMIT RELIABLE COMPARISONS

The final step in the evaluation process is to do similar analyses for a company's other alliances or investment opportunities. While the specific measures used will likely be different than those used for the current alliance, company managers should be able to develop a single measure of each alliance's performance. Having these overall measures of alliance performance for the various alliances, a manager can then begin to make informed decisions about continued investment in any one alliance. That is, whether to continue with the alliance as is, to bring the alliance activities in house, to stop investing in the alliance activities all together, or to modify its involvement in the alliance in order to improve performance. This will also be critical in determining which practices have the most impact on alliance performance as a company develops its alliance capability. But only after developing such comparable and reliable measures can a manager make such an informed decision.

Conclusion

Evaluating the performance of a strategic alliance is difficult. No single measure is appropriate for every situation, and measures will vary in their degree of fit with any one alliance's situation. Since there is no ideal measure, alliance managers have to select among different measures to identify one measure or a combination of possible measures.

Traditionally, entrepreneurial alliance managers have selected simple, flawed measures in the hope that these measures will capture most of the underlying performance, or on occasion, they have developed more complex measures for one alliance and then made crude, if any, comparisons across alliances. This chapter sets out a five-step process for developing a set of measures that not only provides a more complete understanding of the alliance's performance but also creates comparable measures of performance. This stepwise evaluation process requires much more effort than some entrepreneurs have been willing to expend, but it results in worthwhile benefits. A more informed appraisal of the performance of a strategic alliance will help the company evaluate whether the alliance is effective and how it compares to other alliances as the company seeks to achieve its overall strategy.

Key Terms

- performance
- financial
- termination
- balanced scorecard
- satisfactions
- strategic goals
- milestones

End of Chapter Questions

1. Why is alliance performance so difficult to evaluate?
2. What attributes of strategic alliances make it more difficult to evaluate their performance than for other company activities?
3. What are the disadvantages of using simple measures that permit comparability?
4. Why is the situationally appropriate approach to assessment (e.g., the balanced scorecard approach) not always useful for assessing strategic alliances?
5. What are the limitations to using in-between measures—such as goal attainment, satisfaction, or milestones—for evaluating a strategic alliance?

6. What are critical dimensions for comparing possible performance measures?
7. For a resource-strapped start-sup, which specific measures are likely to be useful for evaluating an alliance?

References

1. Bamford, J., & Ernst, D. 2002. Tracking the real pay-offs from alliances. *Mergers & Acquisitions: The Dealmaker's Journal.* 37(12): 33–37.
2. Cameron, K., & Whetten, D. 1983. Organizational effectiveness: One model or several. In K. Cameron & D. Whetten (Eds.) *Organizational effectiveness: A comparison of multiple models*: 1–24. San Diego: Academic Press.
3. For discussions of the multidimensional nature of strategic alliance performance and of relationships among different performance metrics, see, Ariño, A. 2003. Measures of collaborative venture performance: An analysis of construct validity. *Journal of International Business Studies*, 34: 66–79; Geringer, J. M., & Herbert, L. 1991. Measuring performance of international joint ventures. *Journal of International Business Studies,* 22: 249–263; Glaister, K. W., & Buckley, P. J. 1998. Measures of performance in UK international alliances. *Organization Studies* 19: 89–118; Harrigan, K. 1986. *Managing for Joint Venture Success*. Lexington, MA: Lexington Books; Hatfield, L., Pearce, J. A., Sleeth, R., & Pitts, M. 1998. Toward validation of partner goal achievement as a measure of joint venture performance. *Journal of Managerial Issues,* 10: 355–372; Lunnan, R., & Haugland, S. 2008. Predicting and measuring alliance performance: A multidimensional analysis. *Strategic Management Journal*, 29: 545–556; Parkhe, A. 1991. Interfirm diversity, organizational learning, and longevity in global strategic alliances, *Journal of International Business Studies*, 22: 579–601.
4. Kaplan, R., & Norton, D. 1992. The balance scorecard—measures that drive performance. *Harvard Business Review*, January–February: 71–79.
5. Doz, Y., & Hamel, G. 1998. *Alliance advantage: The art of creating value through partnering*. Boston: Harvard Business School Press.
6. Hamel, G. 1991. Competition for competence and inter-partner learning within international strategic alliances [Special Issue]. *Strategic Management Journal*, 12: 83–104.
7. Olk, P. 2006. Modeling and measuring the performance of alliances. In O. Shenkar & J. Reuer (Eds.). *Handbook of Strategic Alliances*: 397–412. Thousand Oaks, CA: Sage Publications; See also Gray, B. 2000. Assessing inter-organizational collaboration: multiple conceptions and multiple methods. In D. Faulkner., & M. de Rond (Eds.). *Cooperative strategies: Economic business and organizational issues*: 243–260. Oxford: Oxford University Press.
8. Afuha, A. 2000. How much do your co-opetitors capabilities matter in the face of technological change? *Strategic Management Journal,* 21: 387–404; Combs, J., & Ketchen, D. 1999. Explaining interfirm cooperation and performance: Toward a reconciliation of predictions from the resource-based view and organizational economics. *Strategic Management Journal* 20: 867–888; Reuer, J. 2001. From hybrids to hierarchies: Shareholder wealth effects of joint venture partner buyouts. *Strategic Management Journal* 22: 27–44; Reuer, J., & Leiblein, M. 2000. Downside risk implications of multinationality and international joint ventures. *Academy of Management Journal*, 43: 203–214. Rowley, T., Behrens, D., & Krackhardt, D. 2000. Redundant governance structures: An analysis of structural and relational

embeddedness in the steel and semiconductor industries. *Strategic Management Journal,* 21: 369–386.

9. Kaplan, R., & Norton, D. 1992. Op. cit; Kaplan, R., & Norton, D. 1993. Putting the balanced scorecard to work. *Harvard Business Review*, September–October: 134–143.

10. Blodgett, L. 1991. Partner contributions as predictors of equity share in international joint ventures. *Journal of International Business Studies*, 22: 63–78. Das, T. K., & Teng, B.-S. 2000. Instabilities of strategic alliance: An internal tensions perspective, *Organization Science*, 11: 77–101; Reuer, J., & Koza, M. 2000. International joint venture instability and corporate strategy. In D. Faulker, D., & M. de Rond (Eds.) *Cooperative strategies: economic, business, and organizational issues*: 261–280. Oxford: Oxford University Press.

11. Cropper, S. 1996. Collaboration in practice: Key issues. In C. Huxham (Ed.), *Creating collaborative advantage*: 80–100. London: Sage Publication; Olk, P. 2002. Measuring strategic alliance performance. In F. Contractor & P. Lorange (Eds.), *Cooperative strategies and alliances*: 119–143. London: Elsevier Press; Yan, A., & Zeng, M. 1999. International joint venture instability: A critique of previous research a reconceptualization and directions for future research. *Journal of International Business Studies,* 30: 397–414.

12. Inkpen, A., & Ross, G. 2001. Why do some strategic alliances persist beyond their useful life? *California Management Review*, 44: 132–148.

13. Olk, P., & Winn, J. 2005. Aegis analytical corporation's strategic alliances. *Case Research Journal*, 25(1): 10–23.

14. Gualati, R. 1998. Alliances and networks. *Strategic Management Journal*, 19(4): 293–317.

15. Kaplan, R., & Norton, D. 1996. *The Balanced Scorecard*. Boston: Harvard Business School Press.

16. Futrell, D., Slugay, M., & Stephens, C. Becoming a premier partner: Measuring, managing, changing partnering capabilities at Eli Lilly and Company.*Journal of Commercial Biotechnology,* 8: 5–13.

17. Bamford, J., & Ernst, D. 2002. Op. cit.

18. Meyer, M. 2002. *Rethinking performance measurement: Beyond the balanced scorecard*. Cambridge, UK: Cambridge University Press.

19. Ariño, A. 2003. Op. cit.

20. Barkema, H. G., Shenkar, O., Vermeulen, F., & Bell, J. 1997. Working abroad, working with others: How firms learn to operate international joint ventures. *Academy of Management Journal*, 40: 426–442; Dussauge, P., Garrett, B., & Mitchell, W. 2000. Learning from competing partners: Outcomes and durations of scale and link alliances in Europe, North America and Asia. *Strategic Management Journal*, 21: 99–126; Makino, S., & Delios, A. 1997. Local knowledge transfer and performance: Implications for alliance formation in Asia. *Journal of International Business Studies*, 27: 905–927; Steensma, K., & Lyles, M.. 2000. Explaining IJV survival in a transitional economy through social exchange and knowledge-based perspectives. *Strategic Management Journal*, 21: 831–852.

21. Saxton, T. 1997. The effects of partner and relationship characteristics on alliance outcomes, *Academy of Management Journal*, 40: 443–462. Yan, A., & Gray, B. 1994. Bargaining power, management control, and performance in United States–China joint ventures: A comparative case study. *Academy of Management Journal*, 37: 1478–1517.

22. Olk, P. 2002. Op. cit.
23. Ariño, A. 2003. Op cit.; Cullen, J., Johnson, J., & Sakano, T. 1995. Japanese and local partner commitments to IJVs: Psychological consequences of outcomes and investments in the IJV relationship. *Journal of International Business Studies*, 26: 91–116; Futrell, D., Slugay, M., & Stephens, C. 2001. Becoming a premier partner: Measuring, managing, changing partnering capabilities at Eli Lilly and Company. *Journal of Commercial Biotechnology,* 8: 5–13; Lunnan, R., & Haugland, S. 2008. Predicting and measuring alliance performance: A multidimensional analysis. *Strategic Management Journal*, 29: 545–556; Mjoen, H., & Tallman, S. 1997. Control and performance in international joint ventures. *Organization Science,* 8: 257–274; Parkhe, A. 1993. Strategic alliance structuring: A game theoretic and transaction cost examination of interfirm cooperation. *Academy of Management Journal,* 36: 794–829.
24. Ireland, R. D., Hitt, M. A., & Vaidyanath, D. 2002. Alliance management as a source of competitive advantage, *Journal of Management*, 156: 1–35. Kale, P., Dyer, J., & Singh, H. 2002. Alliance capability, stock market response and long-term alliance success: The role of the alliance function, *Strategic Management Journal*, 23: 747–7

INDEX